MAKING

MAKING STORIES

How ten Australian novels were written

Kate Grenville and Sue Woolfe

ALLEN & UNWIN

© K. Grenville & S. Woolfe, 1993
© Extracts, individual authors

This book is copyright under the Berne Convention.
No reproduction without permission.

Publication of this title was assisted by the Australia Council,
the Federal Government's arts funding and advisory body.

First published in 1993
Allen & Unwin Australia Pty Ltd
9 Atchison Street, St Leonards, NSW 2065 Australia

National Library of Australia
Cataloguing-in-Publication entry:

Grenville, Kate, 1950–
    Making stories: how ten Australian novels were written.

Bibliography.
ISBN 1 86373 316 7.

1. English language—Style. 2. Fiction—Authorship.
3. Fiction—Technique. 4. Australian fiction—20th
century—History and criticism. I. Woolfe, Sue.
II. Title

808.042

Set in Courier and Garamond
by Graphicraft Typesetters Ltd, Hong Kong.
Printed by Australian Print Group, Maryborough, Victoria.

10 9 8 7 6 5 4 3 2 1

For Isobel (K.G.)

For Alice Graham (S.W.)

Contents

Acknowledgments ix
How this book came about xi
How we transcribed manuscripts xv

Jessica Anderson—*The Commandant* 1

Peter Carey—*Oscar and Lucinda* 33

Helen Garner—*The Children's Bach* 59

Kate Grenville—*Lilian's Story* 94

David Ireland—*A Woman of the Future* 124

Elizabeth Jolley—*Mr Scobie's Riddle* 154

Thomas Keneally—*The Chant of Jimmie Blacksmith* 184

Finola Moorhead—*Remember the Tarantella* 206

Patrick White—*Memoirs of Many in One* 232

Sue Woolfe—*Painted Woman* 252

Appendix: Teachers' notes 283
Bibliography 293

Acknowledgments

We are indebted to the following publishers: Penguin Books Australia for permission to reproduce extracts from Jessica Anderson, *The Commandant*, 1981; David Ireland, *A Woman of the Future*, 1982; Elizabeth Jolley, *Mr Scobie's Riddle*, 1983; Thomas Keneally, *The Chant of Jimmie Blacksmith*, 1973; University of Queensland Press for permission to reproduce extracts from Peter Carey, *Oscar and Lucinda*, 1988; McPhee Gribble for permission to reproduce extracts from Helen Garner, *The Children's Bach*, 1984; Allen & Unwin for permission to reproduce extracts from Kate Grenville, *Lilian's Story*, 1986; Primavera Press for permission to reproduce extracts from Finola Moorhead, *Remember the Tarantella*, 1987; Jonathan Cape for permission to reproduce extracts from Patrick White, *Memoirs of Many in One*, 1986; and Hudson Publishing for permission to reproduce extracts from Sue Woolfe, *Painted Woman*, 1989.

We also wish to thank the Mitchell Library, State Library of New South Wales, for permission to reproduce facsimiles and extracts from the manuscripts of Jessica Anderson, Kate Grenville, David Ireland, Elizabeth Jolley, Thomas Keneally, and Patrick White, and the Fryer Library, University of Queensland, for permission to reproduce the facsimile and extracts from Peter Carey's manuscripts.

How this book came about

In a book that explores how particular works of fiction came about, it seems reasonable to explain how *Making Stories* evolved.

At the beginning, our attention centred on how writers revised—revision, we believe, is at the centre of a work of art. We wanted to show revision happening on the page. Writing is an invisible art: once a phrase or a line or a novel feels right, it seems inevitable. When Keats first wrote his most famous line, it read:

'A thing of beauty is a constant joy.'

We will never know how long it took him, and how many drafts, before he decided on:

'A thing of beauty is a joy for ever.'

We were interested in X-raying revision so that, as far as possible, its usual invisibility could be examined. We wanted to erode the idea that the writer is someone unlike other people, someone to whom the Muse has simply dictated a masterpiece.

As soon as we began to work on the book, however, our assumptions were tested. We thought most writers probably revised in a conscious, coherent fashion, and when we first invited a group of writers to participate, we set up a model of revision that reflected this assumption:

> The aim of the book [we wrote to them] is to give some insight into the invisible work that goes on behind the creation of a piece of writing, in particular the evolution of one draft into another.

For our first list of potential contributors we cast our net very wide, knowing that some, for various reasons, would decline. Some of the responses we received to that first letter made us realise that we had to rethink our model of how a novel is revised. For example, one writer explained that she didn't work in anything as coherent as 'drafts'.

At this stage, we had begun to read early versions and jottings, and they showed us that another shift in our thinking was needed—that we should be looking not only at the revising process, but at the entire evolution of a work, from its gestation onwards. We realised that we were investigating what happens inside the entire making of a story, as far as its creator can apprehend the process. It wasn't possible to distinguish between 'revising' and 'writing the book'. When we next wrote to potential contributors, we talked about 'versions' of a story rather than 'drafts', and tried to accommodate the unpredictable ways a novel might come to be written:

> The aim of the book [we explained in our new letters] is to give some insight into the wide variety of ways a work evolves: the contractions, expansions, shiftings, replottings, the sharpenings of focus.

Our choices about whom we should invite to contribute were based on personal preferences, but we early agreed that we each had to feel a passionate curiosity about a work before we included it. And we often allowed that curiosity to prevail: Why had *Mr Scobie's Riddle* taken twenty years to write? How did Peter Carey control the enormous fabrication of *Oscar and Lucinda*? How could any writer's first draft be entirely made up of mathematical diagrams, as Finola Moorhead's *Remember the Tarantella* had been? When a writer embarks on a historical novel like Jessica Anderson's *The Commandant*, how does she convey the tactile reality of another time? How is it that Thomas Keneally can write so many acclaimed books so fast? What techniques does Helen Garner use to capture contemporary life so accurately? Was it true that *A Woman of the Future* by David Ireland began as a series of disparate jottings he made while he worked in a factory, and how did he make them into a novel?

It was a difficult decision to include ourselves, but we decided, on the balance of things, that since we were asking people to make public the processes that are usually private and that many writers are reluctant to explore, we should also be willing to do this.

Our choice of the particular work by each writer was guided to some extent by practical considerations: which manuscripts had physically survived, and, in the case of manuscripts not in libraries, which ones the writers decided to show us. We chose manuscripts in

How this book came about

various stages of completeness. Some writers are represented by their earliest, most fragmentary notes. Some are shown at the point where much of the material is written, but is undergoing major transformations. Some are shown at a late stage of finetuning.

As we looked at those early manuscripts and jottings, we constantly discovered that behind the published novels was a mass of material so good it must have been very hard for the authors to abandon it. Observing their process of artistic selection and control made us re-read the published works in a new way—it was as if we were learning to read them all over again, with a greater sense of awe.

We usually read in libraries, and always in the absence of the authors. Although the library material was meticulously organised and indexed, it was not always possible to deduce the order in which the work had proceeded. Occasionally it was difficult even to read the words, and despite our best efforts, we may have made errors in transcribing.

Because of these difficulties, we were often forced to make conjectures about what had been written earlier and what was written later, about which section shaped another, and so on. We were conscious that we could have misrepresented writers' methods by our conjectures, or by selecting particular material, so we sent each writer his or her section for approval. This included the interviews, which we invited the writers to change if they wished. After all, we had asked them to recall, on the spur of the moment, activities of mind that had engaged them some time ago—usually, some books ago. Moreover, we reasoned, we were not involved in exposé but exploration, and occasionally, though not always, the two differ. Second thoughts are sometimes more focused and pertinent than first ones.

In our interviews, we asked each writer a combination of specific questions arising out of the particular nature of his or her work, and more general questions so that some comparison of method or attitudes might be prompted. Often we had to abandon our preconceptions during the interview. We discussed the questions with each other before each interview took place, except in the interviews with Finola Moorhead and with each other. For that reason we have identified our separate selves simply as 'interviewer'.

We were tempted to show the work of editors in shaping the final novel, because their contribution can be very significant. We decided in the end, however, to emphasise the work in its early stages, before it was looked at by a professional editor.

The Patrick White manuscript of *Memoirs of Many in One* is an exception to the method we employed with all the other writers. His

Making Stories

section consists simply of an extract from the manuscript, and a few notes.

Many of the manuscripts we finally chose were held in the Mitchell Library, in Sydney. We were very fortunate in this circumstance, because Paul Brunton, Curator of Manuscripts, and his staff were always generous with their time and expertise. John Murphy in particular was a patient and knowledgeable guide through the complexities of manuscripts. Our debt to them, and to the library, is immense.

We are also grateful to Margaret O'Hagan, who helped us find our way around the enormous *Oscar and Lucinda* archives in the University of Queensland's Fryer Library.

There are other people who came to our assistance. Professor Elizabeth Webby helped us for our interview with Thomas Keneally at Sydney University; Rosanne Fitzgibbons and Barbara Ker Wilson from University of Queensland Press facilitated our background research on Peter Carey; and Dr Maureen Aitken, Principal of the Women's College, University of Queensland, provided us with the Olga Masters Place to Write during our research.

Most of all, we are indebted to the writers who contributed to *Making Stories*. They gave us their time, their enthusiasm for the project, and above all they were willing to explore the way their imaginations work—and to reveal all the uncertainties and doubts of the creative endeavour. We had intended to demystify the process, but in the end this did not seem possible. It was another assumption we had to abandon. We remembered Werner Heisenberg's words on a very different subject: 'Since the measuring device has been constructed by the observer, we have to remember that what we observe is not nature in itself, but nature exposed to our method of questioning.'

Sue Woolfe and Kate Grenville
Sydney, May 1992

How we transcribed manuscripts

In some of the manuscripts we found nuances we were not able to transcribe, or which would have led to a very awkward transcription. Helen Garner's notebook, for example, contained previously typed and handwritten fragments taped in, and fragments that had been written directly onto the pages. As well, there were margin notes and textual changes made at later stages on all of these fragments. We decided for ease of reading to adopt a uniform style of transcribing all manuscripts in *Making Stories*, while recognising that this carries with it some inaccuracies.

In general, with all writers, we corrected the spelling of ordinary words and obvious typing errors, but tried to reflect as far as practicable the jerks and jumps and physical look of the manuscripts as they were written.

We used the following conventions to transcribe the alterations on manuscripts:

/ / indicates material inserted by the author after the initial writing.
A line through a word indicates material crossed out by the author.
Margin notes are so named, and are placed just before the text they annotate.
[ ] indicates our own interpolations into the interview or manuscript.

Jessica Anderson
The Commandant

I believe imagination is the primary necessity. It's not a process of reasoning, but letting one set of words fire off another, and another, and another...like improvising a dance.

Jessica Anderson

Part Two   Eyes: Clunie, Henry.
        Chapter Nine

The Govr. Phillip has been. Letters from Col. Allen,
Leland, Cesander, Edmund Foyce, Agricultural Co. (a
refusal) None covering Clunie's arrival. News of Bulbridge,
Fagan.

P.L. comes to Clunie's cottage. Lunchtime. He has returned
discharging the Isabella. Brings Clunie mail. Tells
him of his coming departure. His grief. Knowing how
he stands. His loyalty. Clunie reflects that none of his
moodiness has been vented on him only. His exploration.
"I che Lazarus." He is on the treadmill. "I can't flog
him again so soon," says Logan in apology. Who is
Boylan? No horses. Covering letter not arriving is
no more mysterious than that. P.L. goes. & Clunie
opens letter of his wife. Banjanjo. His brother's joke.
Clunie is annoyed. As he walks out, he composes his
reply in his head.   Bulbridge. Fagan

Logan takes letter to Henry, who quickly puts it in drawer.
Tells him of his departure. Henry's now almost
completely prank. Logan's 1st worry. Says he will
not allow opinion to alter his attitude to the
prisoner. Henry still withholds his opinion of
Govr. Darling's betrayal, feeling its
effect on moody P.L. (silver notebook)
    Bulbridge. Fagan

Jessica Anderson—The Commandant

In *The Commandant*, the reader suspects from the earliest pages that some momentous fate awaits Captain Logan, the Commandant of the Moreton Bay penal settlement. The official version of the terrible events that happened in Moreton Bay in the 1830s was that Captain Logan was murdered by Aborigines while on an exploring expedition. Anderson's novel probes other possibilities. Although Captain Logan is the main character in the book, the story is seen mainly through the eyes of his sister-in-law Frances, who is different from him in every way: she is powerless, sensitive, and naive. Her perspective helps to give us a keen sense of what it was like to live in the colony at that time.

In Jessica Anderson's file at the Mitchell Library, we found a dense archive of historical material she had collected before and during the writing of *The Commandant*—school exercise books filled with names, dates and historical events. Scattered among this raw research were pages of handwritten narrative surprisingly similar to the published version. The juxtapositions of narrative and research were also surprising because to us they did not seem connected to each other—they suggested leaps of imagination we could only guess at.

We chose four extracts, each progressively more like the published version. The first is raw research, the second the earliest attempt at a beginning, the third another beginning, and the fourth is fairly close to the beginning of the published book. In the extract from the published book, traces of all those 'false starts' can be glimpsed.

Our interview with Jessica Anderson took place at her home in Sydney in December 1991.

INT: How did you begin writing *The Commandant*?

JA: I can recall how it actually started. I was interested in doing something on Mrs Eliza Fraser. I was just poking around in the library, and I got out the Moreton Bay file and came across a letter describing Logan's death—how when he was ambushed, he ran with long strides to his horse. [See letter, page 14.] Something about that image—that was the subject I wanted. I instantly put all the Fraser material away, and started off from there. I started by reading convict history, including Moreton Bay, then went to English history of the eighteenth and nineteenth centuries, especially the history and correspondence of the Colonial Office of the time. After that I wandered off in all directions; I believe most of the

Making Stories

wandering helped. Last of all, I got down to the details of life on the settlement on Moreton Bay, no detail too trivial.

INT: But it was Logan who interested you more than anything else?

JA: It was Logan as a character that interested me at the start, but I had to create other people around him. His sister-in-law, Frances, who is the main carrier of the story, I made up. The historical characters are fairly truthfully created from research. Henry Cowper and James Murray, the surgeons, are pretty much, I believe, like they were. But Frances is my witness and commentator.

INT: What was it that attracted you to Logan?

JA: I think the story, you know, that I heard as a child. About the murder. Logan's murder was still one of the local legends. And the legend said that he was murdered by escaped convicts. Or that the blacks, as they were called then, had a hand in it, but that it was instigated and planned by the convicts. A revenge killing. Convicts certainly contributed to that legend. I don't know, of course. It mightn't have been. But convicts were great liars. They were as bad as novelists. Nobody knows the truth. I presented a probability.

That was the plot, the story. And it fitted into one of the themes I liked. Authority—who has it, how well or badly they use it—who accepts it and who resists it. Especially who resists it, and how.

But first of all, I think, I was drawn to the place. I knew that territory so well—how the grass grew, the sky, the trees. It was the place I grew up in. Even the first streets of the settlements, the tracks, I could imagine them under the buildings and bitumen.

Even so, I made mistakes. When I was about three chapters into the book, I realised I was seeing it all by electric light. So I had to go back and visualise it lit by lamps or candles or burning torches. Or wicks dipped in fat—anything they could get—improvise. I wanted to see it in my mind's eye as it must have been then. The nights as dark as they are in the bush, those absolutely black nights, or with the moon lighting the landscape, alone.

INT: How comfortable were you with the period?

JA: Very. Very. Does that sound boastful?

INT: How long had you been researching it?

JA: It took me two years—not quite, because towards the end I was trying out beginnings. I should say I read solidly for eighteen months.

I was reading around about the subject too. When you find an interesting path, it's hard not to go down it, isn't it? I was luxurious about it. I had a grant. I had a grant for a year. It lasted me three years.

INT: You mentioned at the beginning that you had been interested in Eliza Fraser. Did the interest in the period come first, or the ease with it?

JA: The interest. The ease came with the research. About Eliza Fraser—I wanted to find out if she had brought a lot of massive furniture with her. It's extraordinary how much travellers brought on those sailing ships. And shipwreck was not uncommon. I think I had an image of drawers and Sheraton chairs bobbing about on the waves. A shred of this interest survived into *The Commandant*, when Captain Clunie writes to his wife in England suggesting she doesn't bring furniture.

INT: Even after your eighteen months of research, did you find that you needed to do spot research on this detail and that as you wrote?

JA: Not much after I started. I took notes, as you know, and I used those. Though now and then I had to go back to books, or the Mitchell Library. There must be mistakes, but I'm pretty sure they're all trivial. My brother, who's a natural antiquarian, went through the published book very carefully. And he said: Jess, I don't believe they used the stocks in Australia then. But it turned out that they did. I was so pleased. They used them in Sydney, as I had them used, but not at Moreton Bay. Nor did they hang at Moreton Bay in Logan's time. It was poor Captain Clunie who had to order the first hangings.

INT: What about dialogue for the period? Was that a problem?

JA: Dialogue is a problem. I tried a more modern dialogue, but in a realist setting, it didn't work. And the language of contemporary correspondence was just too antiquated. So I re-read the novelists of that time—approximately that time—Mrs Gaskell's *Cranford*, Maria Edgeworth, Thackeray. And Dickens. (Imagine forgetting Dickens!) I believe that any writer trying to reconstruct the language of the English who colonised Australia would go to Dickens. He did all the social classes we had here. It must be the closest thing to an audio-tape we have. In fact, I recall comparing Provis's long speech in *Great Expectations* with convict depositions.

Dickens was more ornamental; otherwise they were very much alike. So I used those sources, and others, and devised a style for each character, and I tried to be true to that.

INT: Did that take a lot of trial and error?

JA: Not after I got used to it, after I decided that Logan would speak in one way, and Henry Cowper would talk in another, and their servants in another, and the convict Lazarus in another. And the women all in their different ways.

INT: How far were you into it when you made those decisions?

JA: Oh, I didn't go far until I was at ease. Did you find many corrections in my dialogue?

INT: No. No. Not at all.

JA: If I hadn't been at ease, there would have been lots of corrections. I must have tried it out and thought, you know, that it was okay. Some critic said it was poncy. And maybe it was. And maybe it had to be poncy.

INT: But it was a convincing nineteenth-century world...

JA: Well, the governors and the commandants—Darling, Logan, Clunie—can be seen as the politicians of their time. There was a power structure, and if we understand ours, up to a point we can understand theirs. There was the same kind of plotting and manoeuvring and scrambling for place. After the Napoleonic wars ended, most English officers were simply unemployed men. They could live frugally in a village on half-pay, or go to the colonies. Men with families and no private income couldn't manage on half-pay, so they went to the various colonies. Australia was the least popular. They came for the money. I almost called the novel *Post And Pay*. When Clunie thinks about getting Logan's job, he scribbles out his little financial calculations, just as you and I might do.

And Logan—I speculated on whether Logan was a gambler. He had a gambler's face and a gambler's character. I wondered if he owed money here in Sydney. Darling made an honour-and-glory speech about him after his murder, but I couldn't find a plaque to him in St James's Church. I think there may have been a subterranean disgrace there. May have been. I gave my speculations to Clunie, but didn't present them as fact. I found myself feeling sorry for Logan. He was trapped from childhood into the army. He was a soldier—and a good soldier—and sometimes we need soldiers. But he was only a soldier. That's all he knew. Clunie's punishments were not much less severe than Logan's yet he didn't incur anything like the same hatred. Maybe he had more tact, or maybe only another kind of face. Or perhaps the prisoners saw Logan's murder as sacrificial—I think they did, in fact—and after the sacrifice had been celebrated, they settled down.

INT: Given your original interest in him, did you ever consider telling the story from his point of view?

JA: I thought of it. But I'm too unlike him. It was better to carry the story through characters I can identify with, as I could with Frances and Letty and Louisa. And with James Murray and Henry Cowper to a lesser degree.

INT: Did it take a lot of trial and error to find Frances as a character?

JA: No, Frances came in early. The radical virgin, as Logan called her. I knew I had to make her Letty's sister, or he wouldn't have tolerated her. Letty really did have a sister, but she married and went to the Indies. So I invented some more sisters in Ireland and brought one of them out. That was Frances.

INT: Did you consciously seek a character to, as you say, 'identify with', or did the character come to you?

JA: Well, I came to myself. I had to have someone who could see and comment on the action. But not just one person, and not just one point of view. So I had Frances, Louisa and Letty. Particularly Frances, though the other points of view are both well within my own range. My daughter said it was quite easy to see who I was. But she saw me as Louisa.

INT: Was there ever a moment when you were tempted to use Louisa as the central consciousness?

JA: No, never. I don't think she would have been a good chief witness. Do you think she would have been? Now that you mention it, she could have been good. I think it would have been a kind of black comedy. But to work it out as a drama, I had to have someone closer to Logan. And subordinate to him. Louisa wouldn't have been an opponent. She wouldn't have been indignant enough. She would have consoled herself by painting butterflies.

INT: We talked with Helen Garner when she'd just finished *Cosmo Cosmolino*, and one of her characters had come in and threatened to take over the book. She had to, in her phrase, 'hose him down'. You don't have that experience?

JA: Yes I have. In my first book [*An Ordinary Lunacy*] there's a woman named Daisy, who people said ran away with the book. And she probably did, too. But since then, like Helen, I hose them down. For the sake of structure.

INT: Is Frances really, in fact, a twentieth-century character?

JA: There were people like Frances, radicals and reformers, in Sydney. There was nobody like her at Moreton Bay. But I couldn't have done it without her. I needed an opponent for Logan.

INT: You said somewhere that Clunie was an aspect of yourself.

JA: I should have said *even* Clunie, I can identify *even* with Clunie. I think I was commenting on how we are likely to use aspects of ourselves even in the most unlikely characters. Logan was the exception. That's why we never see through his eyes. We never get into his head. His thoughts are never given.

INT: The slippage between your own life and the characters' lives is hard to describe. Many people who don't write feel that it either happened to you or it didn't.

JA: But all writers understand it. I often say that fiction springs from observation, memory and imagination. There's always a touch of memory there, even though you may not recognise it at the time. I believe imagination is the primary necessity. It's not a process of reasoning, but letting one set of words fire off another, and another, and another. Well, memory is the same, isn't it? Perhaps the two are indistinguishable, and we shouldn't try to explain it, but treat it as a natural process.

INT: It almost feels like a coming-together of things which till then have been quite artificially split.

JA: Yes. Like improvising a dance. Listening to the music and doing the steps over and over until you have it complete.

INT: Peter Carey used a phrase, 'finding a corner of your own experience' to be able to get into a character.

JA: Yes. Or a touch. A shade. Sometimes you write an episode, and it isn't till years later that you realise that that episode, or that character, originated in something you yourself did or saw, but thought you had forgotten. And sometimes it's much more conscious. But to be entirely conscious would be paralysing. You would be caught in the process.

INT: What about finding the tone? Is this a process that happens suddenly, with a single phrase or sentence being 'right'?

JA: I call it tone of voice. When I strike the right tone of voice for the book, then I know I can keep on, discard the false starts. That beginning set in Dublin was the wrong tone [see Extract 2]. And the part in Sydney struck the tone but was set in the wrong place [see Extract 3]. I notice that I transferred some of Mrs Darling's characteristics to Letty. The gliding walk, and the determination to be sensible and charming no matter what.

INT: How do you know when you've got the right tone?

JA: You hear it. You open a book, it's one tone. You open another —it's another. Perhaps style is a better word, but tone is more like it to me. Style embraces too much.

INT: You're very sure, are you, when you've found the tone?

JA: No. Sometimes I delude myself, and keep on writing, knowing it's against the grain but stubbornly refusing to admit it. But if I'm lucky, and strike the right tone, I can throw out that false start.

INT: Do you read it aloud?

JA: Never. I hear it in my head.

INT: Can you tell us the process of beginning—is that about tone?

JA: In *The Commandant* it was about economy too. To start in Dublin was to stretch my lines too far. Then I tried Sydney because I could put in the political background there. But while I was doing that part, it became clear that Moreton Bay, the place itself, was so important, and such a presence in the book, that I had to start there, and keep it as a core, an anchor [see Extract 4]. It was claustrophobic, actually, keeping it all on the settlement. I was so relieved when the search party rode out to look for Logan. I have Henry Cowper reflecting that getting away from the settlement was always an enormous relief to Logan. It was my relief I gave to Logan.

INT: At that point in the novel, the point of view shifts a little. In the earlier part, although Frances isn't always in the scenes, it's her sensibility that's the framework.

JA: Well, the detached narrative voice is there all the time, behind the other voices. But at that stage it takes over, and Frances's sensibility becomes irrelevant, which does broaden it out.

Making Stories

INT: Was that a relief too?

JA: Yes, to come to action, to write about people moving through a landscape.

INT: And to broaden the point of view, which up to then was Frances's.

JA: Mostly hers. Yes, she was a bit of a pain at times. But I sympathised with her shock, and her idealism which was quite often mistaken. The greatest impediment to her understanding was her sexual ignorance, as Captain Clunie sees.

INT: But somehow she is us.

JA: Politically, a modern conscience. Perhaps not quite so standardised as today.

INT: You've said that endings are much easier, that they're inevitable.

JA: I believe that if a book is sound, the ending ought to be the easiest part because it is derived out of action in the body of the book. If there's an error in the body, the end will need falsification. And nothing is harder than that, to wilfully impose an ending. If an ending is hard, I would return and find out where I had gone wrong in the body of the book.

INT: Do you generally start at the beginning and work through, or do you sometimes write the last part first?

JA: Never. The last part is what has to come to me. That's the nicest part.

INT: You don't want to know the end in advance?

JA: Well, if you know what's going to happen, you can't allow for the things that occur because your characters have altered as you write them. They've developed, and that engenders possibilities, and if you plan ahead, you can't allow for that. I would *like* to plan a whole book, and just write into the plan. It would avoid that awful suspense when you don't quite know what's going to happen. You have your rough idea, but as you write, things sometimes take you by surprise, as you know, and they often lead to changes. Sometimes you will write things that surprise you as they appear, and those are the things that you never change. You know those few, unexpected things will stand. They're truthful—they have the truth of the book. They aren't actually truthful in any objective sense.

INT: Yet *The Commandant* is a very carefully structured book...

JA: With an inevitable flaw. I start off each chapter, or most of them, in the present, then I have to feed in information about things immediately past, to fill the time gap, as it were, and it gives that yoyo effect. I tried to avoid it, but there was so much information to give, that I had to yield. That was the most difficult part.

INT: Did that take a lot of revising?

JA: Yes. That was hard technically.

INT: The reader wouldn't know it.

JA: I'm pleased you wouldn't. I couldn't find another way to make the plot coherent.

INT: Do you ever plan it all out in advance?

JA: Never. I have an ideal shape in my head, but I try not to examine it too much, because that would harden the possibilities. About two-thirds of the way through, though, I can plan the rest of it in a notebook or on cards. Then I don't have to change that plan, or not much. I can just put in the details. The last chapter, or the last two—well, they're like a race against my exhaustion. But I'm so relieved and happy too. I'm like Logan riding out of the settlement, and I think that shows in my writing.

INT: In your notes [see Extract 2], you mention the theory that when the creative state is arrived at, everything that one sees or hears contributes to it.

JA: That's Henry James's theory. I think it's partly true, but not entirely. He said 'everything'. But he just strolled around reflecting, or went to stimulating dinner parties, whereas we cook and clean and buy vegetables, and usually serve our families in various ways. Still, there is truth in the theory.

INT: But as you cook and buy vegetables, are you still in the novel?

JA: Part of me is, and part of me is competently cooking and buying vegetables. Not as competently as usual, though. I'm a bit distracted.

Making Stories

INT: If the novel becomes an obsession, how do you feel about finishing?

JA: When it's over? Oh, what a relief. It's over. I've done it. Oh, I hate writing, don't you? I'm so relieved.

INT: No sense of loss?

JA: Not in the slightest. I'm very tired, but so relieved.

INT: When the end of the novel comes, do you have a sense that whatever has been driving you through it has been resolved?

JA: I'm free. Don't you feel that?

INT: You don't feel an urge to go on and on, having one more go at it?

JA: I do very little correcting on the proofs. But I make changes on all the drafts—not single words so much as whole pages. If I'm desperate, and I often am, I'll do a lot of retyping, or rewriting, to get that kind of impetus, hoping that at some point it will just come right.

INT: So you type the whole thing out again?

JA: The whole novel? No, no, no. Usually I go back to the beginning of a chapter or a section. Sometimes it's a part where a lot of information has to be fed in, and it's lost its naturalness.

INT: We ask everybody if they have doubts about whether the writing is working, whether the book is working, whether it's a good idea. Do you have doubts?

JA: Usually during the early parts. But with *The Commandant* I had no doubts, because the historical framework was so firm that I had fewer choices. I was full of doubt with my first novel until I had thrown most of it away, and could see a shape emerging. I've often thrown away thirty or forty pages, but the only thing I've thrown out entirely was a novella strongly based on personal experience. It was very bad. It was even maudlin. Though it was true. So evidently I have to invent in order to tell the truth. Objective truth is so misleading. No, really, I believe the truth can be better told imaginatively. I honestly do.

INT: When you're sitting down to a day's writing, what do you do?

JA: I make tea. Walk around. Stare out the window. Some days I eat too much...get up and make a snackie.

INT: Peter Carey writes quite a lot of notes in his manuscripts saying: 'This is a story about.' At some point in his day's work he reminds himself what he's actually doing. Do you have any process like that?

JA: No, but I can see it would be useful. Perhaps I ought to have something like that. Well, I do have it. I have it at the start, but it doesn't suit me to keep defining it.

INT: When you're writing, do you feel you're inventing, or do you feel you're uncovering something you already know?

JA: I feel as I go along as if I'm forming a section of the whole thing. The whole is there already, but I keep it at a distance, and don't look at it too much. The actual writing is a method of arriving at that whole idea or form. Is that an answer?

INT: Does the idea change?

JA: Not the ideal idea, if you know what I mean, not the first conception of it, not the first grasp of it. But the working-out of it changes, because it is all new...I'm not sure that I'm not telling some lies here.

INT: Everyone says that.

JA: When you're asked questions, you sometimes start to write, don't you?

INT: To tell a good story.

JA: Confusing to a reader who'd never done any writing.

INT: So in some way, every day it's new?

JA: Yes. Yes. It has to be new.

INT: When you leave your writing the day before, do you have in your mind an idea of how you'll start in the morning?

JA: I try not to think of it till just before I start.

INT: You mentioned before that process of retyping to get a run-up.

JA: Yes.

INT: Is that your way of getting into the day's work?

JA: Sometimes. The best start of all is when I'm up to a part where I feel really at ease. Then I'm always eager when I get up. For instance, in the Louisa parts, I would always think: Oh, good, I have Louisa today.

Making Stories

INT: You mentioned the novel's shape being important to you. Can you tell us more about that?

JA: Well, that is form. And form is part of what you're saying. If you make part of a novel slow and weighty, that has its effect. If you make it light and brief, it would have another effect. Form is silent eloquence. As a reader, a satisfying form is something I look for.

INT: At what stage would you be thinking about the shape of the novel?

JA: Oh, the form is in the material. You put too much in one place, so you do something—divide it and move it to other places, or move it all to another place. With practice, you do that instinctively, because the form demands it. You feel—I suppose—like a painter who says: 'There's too much blue there.'

INT: And you do a lot of that moving around?

JA: Oh yes, a lot. There's often too much blue there.

INT: Does the writing ever come automatically for you, as if it's falling out of the sky?

INT: Yes, but not for long. Never for a whole page. I've had dialogue at times that feels as if I'm taking it down. But never for long.

INT: Is there any part of your process we haven't talked about?

JA: Writers depend on the subconscious. As a process it's very hard, perhaps impossible, to describe. It's a conscious foray into the subconscious. No, that's wrong. But there must be a balance between those two states, or writing would be only a mechanical exercise.

Extract 1 from Jessica Anderson's research notes

A copy of this letter is among Jessica Anderson's research notes for *The Commandant*. The letter was written shortly after Logan's death, and is addressed to his superior officer in Sydney.

            Moreton Bay, 8th November, 1830.

Sir—I have the honour to communicate to you the
painful and distressing intelligence of the death of

Captain Logan, who was surprised and killed by the blacks, while on a journey of discovery...

[The writer explains that a search party was sent out to follow Logan, reported missing]

Not finding Captain Logan at the above station as was expected, [the party] arrived at the camp, where Captain Logan's horse was lost on the former journey. The first thing seen on reaching the ground was the saddle laying beside a tree, with the stirrup-leather cut asunder, evidently by a stone tomahawk, and the stirrup-irons gone. The saddle was about thirty yards from the remains of a fire, and it appeared to have been taken there by the Blacks, for the purpose of cutting it on a fallen tree. A space had been eaten round where the horse had been tethered—and there were marks where Captain Logan had taken the horse to water. It also appeared that he had roasted some chestnuts at this fire: the remains of the roasted chestnuts lay about the stump of a tree that had been burning, and it was at this place the Blacks must have surprised him, for his foot-marks were very distinct, with long strides, where he had rushed from the fire to his horse.

The party then went over the creek, and about seven or ten yards from the bank, the body of poor Captain Logan was found. The back of his head appeared to have been much beaten about by waddies. The blacks made him a grave about two feet deep, and buried him with his face downwards...

> I have the honour to be, &c.,
> (Signed) George Edwards,
> Lieut. 5th Regiment.

To: Lieut. Colonel Allen,
Commanding 57th Regiment, Sydney.

(Reproduced courtesy of Mitchell Library, State Library of New South Wales.)

Making Stories

A second letter was written many years after Logan's death by his widow.

Unto the Honorable the Legislative Assembly of the
  Colony of Moreton Bay.
    The Memorial of Letitia Anne Logan,

Humbly Sheweth;—
  That your memorialist is widow of the late Captain Patrick Logan, of the 57th Regiment of Foot, who was murdered by the natives of Moreton Bay, New South Wales, on the 18th October, 1830, when in the performance of a public and important duty, namely, forming a chart, by order of the Government, of the tract of land he had discovered on the 21st August, 1826, and thoroughly explored during the succeeding four years.
  Captain Logan being desirous of completing his chart of the immense tract of land which he had discovered ...left the settlement for the purpose of making some final observations, and, as before stated, was barbarously murdered by the natives. Your memorialist and her infant children were thus bereaved of their protector and means of support,—Captain Logan's patrimony having been expended in the purchase of his commissions.
  Your memorialist has the pride and satisfaction to think that, as an officer in the military service, her husband's character stood high. He was present at six general actions in the Peninsula, in which his regiment served with distinction, besides having also served in America....As her husband lost his life in the performance of a public and important duty, which has added so materially to the geographical knowledge and subsequent wealth of the Colony, (she ventures to hope) that she may now receive whatever compensation your Honorable House may feel disposed to grant.
  And your memorialist will ever pray, &c.
    (Signed) Letitia Anne Logan.

(Reproduced courtesy of Mitchell Library, State Library of New South Wales.)

Extracts from 'A CURIOUS OLD RECORD', published in the newspaper, *The Queenslander*, in 1901.

MORETON BAY PENAL ESTABLISHMENT
UNDER CAPTAIN LOGAN

By W.H. Traill

...The period of his control has been described as a reign of terror. He has been represented as a ruthless tyrant...His recourse to the lash was said to have been constant and pitiless. To the convicts he made the establishment a hell...

But the evidence respecting Logan's alleged severity is almost entirely indirect, traditional and circumstantial...When the penal establishment was broken up and removed in 1830, the books and records were presumably packed up and transferred to Sydney. It is supposed that they were destroyed in that memorable holocaust of an immense heap of official records relating to the convict regime, which was executed by order of the late Sir John Robertson during one of his terms of office as Premier of New South Wales.

But there was inadvertently left behind in Brisbane one book, a shabby, calf-bound, foolscap volume, which, after lying long neglected amidst the raffle and odds and ends on the shelves of the old offices, passed into the possession of a gentleman capable of appreciating the value of such a unique record, who preserved it in his library.

...Analysis of the scale of punishments during the period covered by the long-lost-sight-of record now become available, must be regarded as distinctly adverse to the idea that Captain Logan was ferocious in his temperament...At the period when all this occurred, corporal punishment to that extent when administered to felons under sentence, would almost certainly be regarded as no more than reasonably sharp correction of intractibility of breaches of discipline.

...In pursuance of his habit of exploring the country, Logan went on an expedition up the valley of the Brisbane River, above Limestone (the present Ipswich) attended by one 'free' servant and half-a-dozen convicts...search parties were despatched, and first the saddle, then the carcass of Logan's horse were found, and near by, the disturbed soil indicated more. Under this, in a shallow trench, barely covered with earth, was Logan's body, face downward, the head and face shockingly battered... The deed was ascribed to the natives. But natives do not so bury their victims...

(Reproduced courtesy Mitchell Library, State Library of New South Wales.)

Extract 2 from an early manuscript

Jessica Anderson sent us the first beginning of *The Commandant* (she refers to it in the interview as 'that beginning set in Dublin'), with the following letter:

> I'm sure that the first paragraph was a first try at entering *The Commandant*, but then I added bits to it, and the last paragraph became the first.
> It must have been done very early because, as you will see, Frances has not begun to take on the character of the girl in the novel. In fact, it is more like the author herself, especially the restless walking about at night and looking out of windows when trying to enter into a theme.
> It's in a notebook of fragments I wanted to keep, so I must have copied it out from another scrap—probably illegible, possibly destroyed. There is a margin note: Connection—that theory that when the creative state is arrived at, everything one sees or hears contributes to it. And another: idea for beginning of *The Commandant*—recall by Frances.

> Memory awaits its season. Events lie in its ~~darkness~~, dark reaches, unforced, but oh, it is tropical territory down there, and once they start up, there is no stopping the growth, even if one hacked; so that I have been out of bed these last few warm nights, walking about the house ~~flat~~ with no purpose, parting the curtains and looking down into Baggot Street, seeing the mist of rain, and the smudged dandelions of gaslight set on their tall stems, and in the mornings, the same soft days, but still warm.

It would not be considered warm there

Humid warmth is uncommon in Dublin. Perhaps that is it. It? I mean the spring, the mystery, what made it all start up.

I once thought that I should never forget ~~a single detail of~~ those events. Indeed I proclaimed that belief. 'Not if I live to be a hundred shall I forget a single detail.' But such was my exaggerated /vehement/ way of speaking at that time. I forgot many details. Indeed the ~~main body~~ events themselves, the main body of them, had grown in less than 2 years dim and mundane. I was young, and my wise, healthy, and voracious body fed on what would nourish it and rejected the rest.

And yet, in a way, when I swore that I would never forget, I was right.

Extract 3 from an early manuscript

This is another beginning, the one that Anderson calls 'the part in Sydney'.

CHAPTER ONE

'I have just written to Letty Logan,' said Mrs Darling to her husband. 'How is your fever, my love?'
~~Lieut Gen~~ /General/ ~~General Darling~~ He was unhooking his uniform coat. 'I am going back to bed.' His voice was thick, muffled by a head cold. He had risen from bed to confer with Colonel Dumeresque and Mr Alexander Macleay. One ~~of~~ was his wife's brother, the other ~~his~~ the colonial secretary. ~~The meeting had been short~~. He could ~~easily~~ have summoned them to his bedside, but he was a man, someone had once said, who mistook formality ~~to~~ for dignity. 'Pray ring for Simpson,' he said to his wife. 'What have you written to Mrs Logan?'
She pulled the bell cord. 'Oh, this and that.'
'Quite. But what?'
She spoke with surprise /~~& a shred of coldness~~/ at his persistence. 'I asked if she is to come to Sydney with Captain Logan. For Mr Hall's trial, you know.' 'Anything

19

about Clunie taking Logan's place?'
'Certainly not. It is your business to send such information.'
'Anything that implies it.'
'Only that we ~~would will~~ shall regret their absence from the colony when Captain Logan goes with his regiment to India.'
'Tear it up.'
'My dear Ralph—'
'There is no certainty that the fifty-seventh is for India. Not for some months, in any case.'
'Then why have you sent Captain Clunie—'
'Tear it up. Tear it up.'
Simpson arriving at that moment, Mrs Darling left the folded letter on her writing table and hurried from the room, ~~walking~~ walking with the gliding step she had been taught as a /young/ girl. It was no longer in fashion, but when she had tried to correct it she had found, being little and fat, /~~though pretty,~~/ that she tended to bob and bounce, so she had returned to ~~the~~ a modified glide. Walking in this fashion through the corridors of Government House, she came to the office of her brother, Colonel Dumeresque.

[Inserts handwritten on the other side of the manuscript page]

As she ext she set her young and pleasant ~~pretty~~ face to smile, just in

her private policy

'Henry, Ralph forbids me to imply to Mrs Logan— ~~even to~~ imply ~~Her pretty face was did not was smiling, to make clear that this was no complaint, for the /mere/ idea of disloyalty to her husband must never~~.

'There's a cat that hasn't jumped. That's my opinion.'
'A cat, Henry?'
Her amusement nettled him. '~~Well,~~ I mean, /you/ never know what could come out at that trial.'

Her pretty face was smiling in accord with her private policy that /even/ the thinnest edge of ~~the~~ disloyalty ~~to her husband~~ to her husband must not be employed. Nevertheless, since this was her brother, she did say—even to imply—that Capt. Clunie is to replace her husband in the Commandant M/ B. Why?

[End of inserts]

Henry...'
But she was looking through the door of the inner office, where the two clerks could be seen at work. The colonel shut the door and set a chair for her beside his own. 'Henry, Ralph forbids me to imply to Mrs Logan—even to imply—that Captain Clunie is to replace her husband in the command at Moreton Bay. Why?
'Don't know, Liz.'
'You must know.'
He was silent.
Your opinion then,' ~~She said impatiently~~. She said impatiently.
~~There's a cat that hasn't jumped.'~~
'Never know what ~~will~~ might comes out at that trial. That's my opinion.
'But Captain Logan is not to be tried. Mr Smith Hall is to be tried for a libel on Captain Logan.'
'Never know what /might/ comes out at a libel trial. Defence says this. Defence says that. And if some of it sticks, you know, even if it's not true, you never know what may have to happen.'
'You mean that Captain Clunie, under guise of relieving Lieutenant Bainbridge, is being sent to Moreton Bay as a provision? A provision against something coming out, as you put it, that would lead to Poor Captain Logan's removal from ~~the~~ his place?'
'Didn't say that, /you know/. Said you never knew.'
/~~But first best to see how the cat jumps~~/
They had been speaking all the time in low voices, but now Eliza Darling's voice dropped lower still,—~~though it increased in vehemence~~ though it increased in vehemence.
'Nonsense, Henry. I'll not believe it. A place is not so easily lost. Only think what poor Ralph suffered when that unfortunate man Sudds died. The intemperance,—~~and~~ the slander...'
She would have said more, but faltered before the look he turned on her, so full of private knowledge, of secret

Making Stories

meaning. He took a piece of paper, beckoned her to lean forward, and wrote, 'Sudds ~~business~~ rumpus not over yet. Questions at home. House of Commons.'
She leaned back in her chair and expelled a long breath, half indignant, half incredulous. He beckoned her forward again, this time to watch him write HUME. He underlined the name three times, then tore the paper into shreds and flung himself back— ~~complacently~~ /~~triumphantly~~/ triumphantly back in his chair.
But his sister snatched up ~~the~~ his pen and wrote rapidly, 'I am not ~~distressed~~ worried for Ralph. The thing is absurd.'
'And I did not come here to speak of it,' she said as she put down the pen.
'No, but, now, listen Liz—' He was tearing up her message as he spoke. 'Logan. If anything comes out there, well, fuel to flame, you know.'
'Flame!' she ~~said dismissively~~ could not help laughing. He shrugged. The day's correspondence, unsealed and laid flat, awaited him on the desk. ~~She put an elbow~~ He riffled it with a thumb. She put an elbow on the desk, her chin in ~~a hand~~ on the back of her hand. 'I am distressed for Letty,' she said in a complaining voice. 'What will the Logans think, pray, when Captain Clunie arrives?'
'That he's come to relieve Bainbrigge. Which he has, you know.'
'They will wonder why a captain ~~comes~~ is sent to relieve a lieutenant.'
'They will think ~~Captain~~ Logan's regiment is posted to India.'
'If that were certain, he would have word from his commanding officer. For any other /purpose/ he would have word—' she turned enquiring eyes upon her brother— 'from Mr Macleay.'
He did not look at her, but cocked an eyebrow at his letters.
'What has Mr Macleay written, Henry?'
'Not supposed to say, you know.'
'Well, as long as he <u>has</u> written...'
'Well, no, he hasn't, in fact. /We/ thought, Ralph thought, we all thought, better leave it, you know. Wait and see.'

22

Jessica Anderson—The Commandant

'See what?' How the cat jumps?' How the famous cat jumps. How the cat of yours jumps.
'Well...a precaution.'
'A precaution, indeed! Perhaps someone ought to take the precaution of telling Letty's sister to stay here.'
'That tall girl with who's had—' the colonel tapped his left cheek.
'Yes. Although Though those her scars hardly show. She embarks on the Isabella this morning. She goes to join the Logan household. She might just as well have wait here until your the famous cat /of yours/ jumps. Although perhaps not. She /has/ made some rather indiscreet friendships here. She travels with Mrs Bulwer.'
Her brother, as if absent-minded, lifted the first letter. 'Bulwer?' he murmured, reading it. 'Bulwer?'
'The fortieth.'
'Ah, yes.'

(Reproduced courtesy Mitchell Library, State Library of New South Wales.)

Extract 4 from an early manuscript

A third beginning, set in Moreton Bay, which is the setting for the final version of the novel.

CHAPTER ONE

'Dunwich is only a depot,' said Mrs Bulwer. 'Don't judge us by a depot. Wait, my dear Miss O'Bierne—Frances, I am going to call you Frances—wait till we get to the settlement. Which with this wind behind us—' She drew a hand from her muff and held it into the wind—'will be some five hours more. It is quite a pretty little place, I assure you. And <u>not</u> as unhealthy as is supposed at home. Healthier than most of the India stations, certainly. True, we have the intermittent fever, and ophthalmia and dysentery. But the last two are not /so/ prevalent with <u>us</u>. And of course, we have nothing as dreadful as the cholera. Do you know how bad it was at home last winter? Why, of course you do, you were there.'

Frances said, well, she had been in Ireland.

'Quite. But Ireland is as bad as England for the cholera. Did Letty write you that since May we have had two surgeons on the settlement? Both young,' she said, on a note of persuasion, and with a bold look at Frances, 'and both such dear clever <u>good</u> men.'

Frances sunk her chin in her collar and opened her eyes wide. 'Mr Henry Cowper is good?'

'Oh, why, certainly he is.' Mrs Bulwer's note of persuasion deepened into bluster. 'I can't think with whom you have been associating in Sydney if they told you he is <u>not</u>.'

'But I saw him myself, ma'am, on this very voyage—'

'He has his weaknesses and oddities, certainly, but at heart he is the best of men. And as for Mr Murray— ~~he~~ Mr Murray is the new surgeon— ~~he~~ Mr Murray is all that is amiable and gentlemanly. He is single—' she flashed Frances another of her bold looks—'and ~~he so~~ so dines quite often with your dear sister and the commandant. You will not be dull, I assure you. And the commandant's cottage is charming. Letty has such taste. Well,—I ~~shan't tell you~~ I ~~shall~~ say no more, you will soon see it all for yourself, and meet your adorable little nephew and niece as well. So come, my dear, let us have a smile. It's a shame to see a young creature so dejected.'

'It is the architecture of my face,' said Frances.

'Architecture?'

'Yes. It makes me look dejected, when I am only thoughtful.'

'It does not do to be too thoughtful.'

'~~No~~ But—too thoughtful for what?'

'Why, that's a question I hardly know how to answer.' Mrs Bulwer's voice was slower. Without looking away from Frances' face, she had withdrawn behind a mask of abstraction. Their whole conversation had been like this, each of her galloping advances having been followed by these abrupt retreats, pauses for fresh appraisal. 'If you're going to ask questions like <u>that</u>,' she said slowly, 'you would do better to talk to Louisa Harbin.'

'I've hardly seen Mrs Harbin since—'

'~~Not that Louisa is a blue stocking.~~'

'Since we left Sydney Heads. She was so sick.'

'We were all sick. I myself suffer dreadfully from the

sea. You don't resemble Letty, do you? Or Cassandra? You are in quite a different style.'

'Letty and Cass take after papa. I resemble mama. Or did, when she was alive.'

Mrs Bulwer responded only with a brief but most reflective murmur. 'H'mm.' Frances, uncomfortable under her close scrutiny, put a hand to her left cheek, where the smallpox had left an area of roughness, and raised herself slightly in her seat so that she could see out over the water. They had disembarked at Dunwich from the 'Isabella', and were now on the deck of the Regent Bird, going up Moreton Bay. ~~Mrs Bulwer was still staring at her~~

'What island is that?' asked Frances ~~in her most animated voice.~~

~~But~~ Mrs Bulwer did not even look. 'Green Island. I understand there are two more of you.'

'Yes. It's not very green.'

'Both girls?'

'Yes. Hermoine and Lydia.'

'Your poor father,' said Mrs Bulwer with sudden frank gloom.

'Well, ma'am, he <u>is</u> poor, you see.'

'I meant, of course, unfortunate.'

'I know. But it's being poor that makes him unfortunate.'

'You look much more like Cassandra when you laugh. Oh, we <u>do</u> miss Cassandra. She was so uniformly agreeable, so animated and tactful. Well, never mind. /The Indies are <u>not</u> healthy, but/ she will be /as/ happy as a bird with her lieutenant. And you will take her place. You will have Letty to guide you now. And the dear commandant.'

Murmuring ~~an~~ an excuse, Frances got up, gathered her shawl tightly ~~round~~ about her, and went to the side. Mrs Bulwer's warning voice followed her, 'It does not do to be opinionated.' Frances pretended not to hear. On the bay were amazing stretches of turquoise and violet, and the sky was empty of everything except a dandelion of sun, mildly blazing, and a meek white crescent of moon. Mrs Bulwer had raised her muff to her chin and was watching Frances without approval. From beneath the frill on the back of Frances' bonnet a strand of dark hair dropped and was caught and ~~extended by~~ extended by the wind. The sun, the boom of sails, and the race of water,

25

would have held her there at the side, in a dream or trance, as had happened so often on the ~~way~~ voyage out, had not Mrs Bulwer, small and black and compact in her side vision, waited. And waiting, too, the more insistent because only inwardly visible, was the commandant. He would come to meet the 'Regent Bird': ~~How vividly~~ She saw him vividly in her mind's eye,—~~He was~~ descending the slope to the river.—A tall gingery man, very straight-backed, ~~dressed in his scarlet and gold~~, dressed in his scarlet and gold, he was walking with a high-stepping but curbed stiffness and setting his feet upon the ground so fastidiously as to make it seem almost a gesture of distaste. As ~~the~~ his image become fixed in her mind, ~~and~~ as detail accrued, /such as/ the restless carriage of his head,—~~and the pointless downward flick of one hand~~, the background she had provided—settlement, slope and river, all constructed ~~by~~ from hearsay and her imagination—faded away around him and was replaced by the unkempt incline in front of her father's house; for it was there that she had first seen him in reality, walking like that, and in spite of later views, ~~where they had met~~, face to face, it ~~is~~ was to that first setting that her imagination always ~~drew back returned~~ returned. In those later meetings he had spoken to her, catechizing her on her lessons, but her own squirming shyness, and her simultaneous shame about it, had ~~perhaps~~ all but obliterated from ~~the~~ those—~~occasion~~ occasions everything but itself, whereas at the window of her father's house, safe between the adult softnesses of Bridie and Margaret, she had had nothing else to do but gape.
'Here comes Miss Letty's captain.'
'/Just/ look at him legging it!'
Bridie and Margaret had managed to convey mockery, admiration, and resentment, all at the same time; but in Sydney the Hall girls had simply said, 'Oh, Logan,' and had refrained from looking at her, or each other. Another strand of hair fell from her bonnet and streamed into the wind. She gathered it all together, wound it on two fingers, and tucked it beneath her bonnet. ~~Then~~ She turned to face Mrs Bulwer. Feeling this to be an occasion for courage, she was sad to be betrayed by her shy voice. 'How will—they—come up the bay?'

Mrs Bulwer's look of cold interrogation made her shyer still.

'I mean—the convicts.'

'Oh, the prisoners? Why how else but in a boat. And /pray/ be assured ~~that~~ they will be made as comfortable as is consistent with their ~~position~~ condition. As indeed they were on the voyage from Sydney. The Isabella has more room between decks than one might think. Lieutenant Bulwer assures me it is quite commodious. If only the Isabella could cross the bar I am sure the journey would be a great deal less tedious for everyone. Do sit down, my dear, you will blow away. Did Letty write you about the "Letetia Bingham"? The commandant had her built on the settlement. I believe there's nothing that man can not do, if he puts his mind to it. He named ~~it~~ her /of course/ after Letty.'

Against such purposeful animation Frances could persist no further. It left her only with the trifling independence of continuing to stand, and of asserting that Letty's name was Laetitia Anne. 'So ~~I think it~~ he must have ~~been~~ named /it/ after the little girl.'

'Indeed? Oh, but I am certain.'

So was Frances /certain/, but her bonnet now blew off, and saved her from ~~further assertion~~ insistence. ~~As~~ as she flung up her hands and turned to catch it, /but/ it changed direction and hurtled over her head,— ~~and~~ Her shawl slipped down her back and dropped to the deck, and the wind took it up and slapped it against her ankles, making her trip as she raced after her bonnet. Falling, she heard Mrs Bulwer say with disgust, 'Good Gracious!' She plucked up her shawl, jumped to her feet, and as she turned wildly to look for her bonnet, she saw that Captain Clunie, who had evidently just come on deck, had picked it up and was offering it to her with a bow. He was about thirty-five, big and staid, and during a seven day voyage on which neither of them had been ~~sea~~ sick, she had discovered him to be almost entirely silent. Frances was seventeen. She was not silly, but was sometimes absurd. ~~She~~ His silences had had the unexpected effect of making her gush. Shamed by this, she had vowed each time never to do it again, yet at each meeting had done it again, and indeed, was doing it now. 'Oh, thank you, Captain! You have saved my very life!' He gave his little

27

Making Stories

blink, his little bow. Mrs Bulwer fluttered up and set herself at Frances' side. Her clothes had /so/ many loose surfaces—shawls, veils, ribbons, capes, fringes /that/ In the wind ~~she seemed to ripple with~~ rippled ~~with black flame~~ all over. She confronted Captain Clunie with her muff ~~held up~~ raised vertically on one hand. 'Captain Clunie, do tell us your dear wife is soon to join you on the settlement.' ~~whether his wife~~ His wife was visiting her parents in England, he said, and whether she joined him or not,—~~he said,~~ must depend on the length of his stay. He excused himself with another bow, then turned and set himself to pace the small deck. Mrs Bulwer set her chin in the end of her muff.
'H'mm.'
Louisa Harbin came up from below, dragging her feet.

[Inserts handwritten on a separate page]

She was very tall, thin
She was very tall, very thin, slightly stooped, & was clutching about her a dark /blue/ hooded mantle trimmed with fur worn down thin at the breast & inside cuffs.

(Reproduced courtesy of Mitchell Library, State Library of New South Wales.)

Extract 5 from the published version

The Commandant, pages 1–11

CHAPTER ONE

'But Dunwich is only a depot. Don't judge us by a depot. Wait my dear Miss O'Beirne, wait till we get to the settlement. Which this wind –' Mrs Bulwer drew a hand from her muff and held it into the wind – 'will be some five hours more. It's quite a pretty little place, I assure you. And healthy besides. None of us has gone to our graveyard. Not one. And only one soldier. Quite a contrast with the India stations. At least with Madras. I am sure the rumour that the fifty-seventh is to go to Madras is quite unfounded. Agra. It will be Agra. Agra is delightful. Very little fever at Agra. On the settlement we do have the fever, but not the India sort, not the sort to carry one off. And we have the ophthalmia and the dysentery, though neither is so prevalent with *us*. But of course we have nothing so dreadful as the cholera. The cholera! Do you know how bad it was at home last year? Why, of course you do, you were there.'

Frances said, well, she had been in Ireland.

'Well, Ireland. Ireland is as bad as England for the cholera. Did Letty write you that we have two surgeons on the settlement now? Both young,' she said, on a note of persuasion, and with a sudden bold look at Frances, 'and both such dear clever *good* men.'

Frances sank her chin in her collar and opened her eyes wide. 'Mr Henry Cowper is good?'

'Why, certainly he is.' Mrs Bulwer's note of persuasion deepened into bluster. 'I can't think with whom you associated in Sydney if they told you he is not.'

'But I saw him myself, ma'am, on this very voyage –'

'And so you may have. But you have not yet seen him conducting divine service.'

'*He* conducts –'

'He does. We were sent a chaplain, but he and the commandant – We all have our failings, and our good commandant is sometimes short of temper. Mr James Murray is the other surgeon, the new one. He is single –' she flashed Frances another of her bold looks – 'and dines quite often with your sister and the commandant. Oh, you will not be dull, I assure you. And the commandant's cottage is charming. Letty has such taste. Well, I will say no more. You will soon see it all for yourself, and meet your little niece and nephew besides. So come, my dear, let us have a smile. Such a young creature, yet so-o dejected!'

'It's the architecture of my face,' said Frances.

'*Arch*-itecture?'

'Yes. It makes me look dejected when I am only thoughtful.'

'It does not do to be too thoughtful.'

'But – does not do for what?'

'Why, that's a question I hardly know how to answer.' Mrs Bulwer's voice was slower. Without looking away from Frances's face, she withdrew into preoccupation. 'If you're going to ask clever questions, you had better talk to Mrs Harbin.'

'I've hardly seen Mrs Harbin since we left Sydney Heads. She was so sick.'

'We were *all* sick. You don't resemble Letty, do you? Or Cassandra? You are in quite a different style.'

'Letty and Cass take after papa. I resemble mama. Or did, when she was alive.'

Mrs Bulwer responded only with a brief but most reflective murmur.

'H'mmm.' Frances, made uneasy by her continued scrutiny, put a hand to her left cheek, where smallpox had left an area of roughness, and raised herself slightly in her seat to look out over the water. They had disembarked at Dunwich from the *Isabella*, and were now on the deck of the *Regent Bird*, going up Moreton Bay. 'What island is that?' asked Frances.

But Mrs Bulwer didn't even look. 'Green Island. I understand there are two more of you.'

'Yes. It's not very green.'

'Both girls?'

'Yes. Hermione and Lydia.'

'Your poor father,' said Mrs Bulwer, with sudden frank gloom.

'Well, ma'am, he is poor, you see.'

'I meant, of course, unfortunate.'

'I know. But it's being poor that makes him unfortunate.'

'You look much more like Cassandra when you laugh. Oh, we do miss Cassandra. Always so agreeable, so patient and tactful. But never mind, she will be as happy as a bird with her lieutenant, *even* in the Indies. And you will take her place. You will have Letty to help you now. And the commandant.'

Frances murmured an excuse and got up, gathering her shawl tightly around her, and went to the side. Mrs Bulwer's warning voice followed her. 'It does not do to be opinionated.' She pretended not to hear. On the bay were amazing stretches of turquoise and violet, and the sky was empty of everything except a dandelion of sun, mildly blazing, and a meek white crescent of moon. From beneath the frill on the back of her bonnet a strand of dark hair dropped and was caught and extended by the wind. The sun, the boom of sails and the race of water, would have held her there at the side, in a dream or trance, as had happened so often on the voyage out, had not Mrs Bulwer, small and black and compact in her side vision, waited. And with a sense of facing something lately evaded, Frances admitted that also waiting, the more insistent because only inwardly visible, was the commandant. Deliberately, she set herself to visualise him, in five hours or so, descending the river bank to meet the *Regent Bird*.

She saw a tall, straight-backed, cold-faced, gingery man, who walked with a kind of curbed stiffness, and who moved his head restlessly, or as if fretted by his high neck band. And as detail accrued – the scarlet and gold of his uniform, the gloss and weight of the braid – the background her imagination had provided, slope and river and blurred sky, faded away and left him as she had first seen him in reality. Walking like that, he had descended the unkempt incline before her father's house in Sligo, while she, nine years old, had peeped from a window with Bridie and Meg. Later she had met him face to face, but it was only as a dim tallness that she could see him bending from the waist to catechise her on her lessons. Her own squirming shyness, and her simultaneous shame of it, had perhaps obliterated from those later meetings nearly everything but itself, whereas at the window, safe between the adult softnesses of Bridie and Meg, she had been free simply to gape.

'Here comes Miss Letty's captain.'

'Look at him legging it!'

Bridie and Meg had managed to convey mockery, dislike, and admiration, all at the same time; but in Sydney the Hall girls had said, 'Oh, Logan,' and had refrained from looking at her, or at each other. Another strand of hair fell from her bonnet into the wind. She gathered it all together, wound it on two fingers, and poked it beneath her bonnet as she turned to face Mrs Bulwer.

'How will – they – come up the bay?'

Feeling the occasion to be one for courage, she was sad to be betrayed by her shy voice. And now, forced to persist against Mrs Bulwer's look of cool interrogation, she sounded shyer still.

'I mean – the convicts?'

'Oh, the *pris*-oners? Why, how else but in a boat? And be assured they will be made as comfortable as is consistent with their condition. As indeed they were on the voyage from Sydney. There is more room between decks on the *Isabella* than one might think. If only she could cross the bar I am sure the journey would be less tedious for everyone. Or if there was a way by land. Of course there *is* a way. The runaways find it. But such a wild rough terrible way it must be, it doesn't bear thinking of. Do sit down, my dear, you will blow away. Did Letty write you about the *Laetitia Bingham*? The commandant had her built on the settlement. I believe there's nothing that man can *not* do, if he puts his mind to it. He named her, of course, after Letty.'

Against such purposeful animation Frances could persist no further, but was left only with the trifling independence of continuing to stand, and of asserting that Letty's second name was Anne, not Bingham. 'So he must have named the boat after their little girl.'

'Indeed? Oh, but I am certain.'

So was Frances certain, but her bonnet now blew off and saved her from insistence. As she twirled on a heel and threw up her hands to catch it, she let go her shawl, which slipped down her back and dropped to the deck. By the time she had retrieved it she saw that Captain Clunie, who had evidently just come up on deck, had picked up her bonnet and was offering it to her with a bow. He was about thirty-five, big and staid, and during a seven-day voyage on which neither had been sick, she had found him almost entirely silent. Frances was seventeen; she was not stupid, but was often absurd. His silences had had the unexpected effect of making her gush. Shamed by this, she had vowed each time never to do it again, yet at each meeting had done it again, and indeed, was doing it now.

'Oh, *thank* you, Captain. You have saved my very life!'

He gave his little blink, his little bow. Mrs Bulwer fluttered up and set herself at Frances's side. Her clothes had so many loose surfaces – shawls, veils, ribbons, capes, fringes – that in the wind she seemed to ripple all over with sharp little black flames. She confronted Captain Clunie with her muff raised vertically on one hand. 'Captain, do tell us your wife is soon to join you on the settlement?'

His wife, he replied, was visiting her parents in Oxfordshire. She would soon sail for the colony, but whether she came to the settlement or not would depend on the length of his stay. He excused himself with another bow, then turned away and set himself to pace the small deck.

Mrs Bulwer set her chin in the end of her muff. 'H'mmm.' But then she saw that Frances, to free both hands for attention to her loose hair, was gripping her bonnet and shawl between her bent knees. She sprang forward. 'Give those *to me*!'

Frances saw in her outraged face the reflection of her own lack of grace and propriety; she unloosed her knees and let her take the bonnet and shawl.

'Now, either go below, or tuck *all* your hair under your bonnet. It is better to look *skinned* than like a *tinker* woman.'

* * *

Louisa Harbin, very tall and thin, and clutching about her with long hands a furred and hooded mantle of dark blue, dragged her feet as she crossed the deck to her chair. She had just come up from below. Her big lips were compressed and her deeply lidded eyes all but shut. She sat down in a resigned but gingerly way, shut her eyes completely, and folded her hands in her lap. The fur trim on her mantle, from her habit of clutching it, was worn to the hide on the breast and inside cuffs. Mrs Bulwer clucked with her tongue and hurried over to her.

Peter Carey
Oscar and Lucinda

The big question for a writer is, how can you know this? In what corner of yourself can you find what you need to write truthfully about things of which, objectively, you'd have no knowledge?

Peter Carey

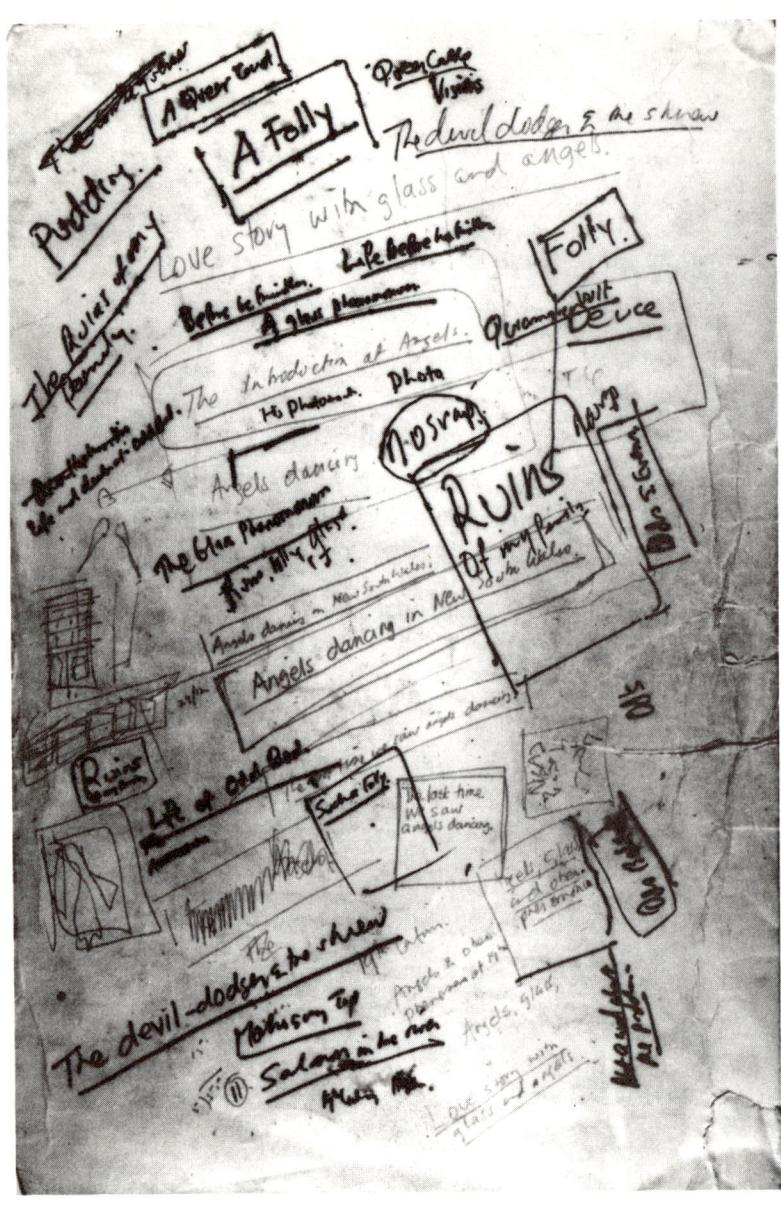

Peter Carey—Oscar and Lucinda

Peter Carey suggested that we explore his early drafts of *Oscar and Lucinda*, which are held at the Fryer Library in the University of Queensland. We had heard Carey talk in another interview about his writing process, in particular the process he calls 'cantilevering', and we imagined it as a very orderly way of working. What we found at the Fryer Library was an immense archive of many drafts and much rewriting within drafts—a whirl of material, meticulously indexed, of course—a gigantic jigsaw that surely only the mind of the author could put together. When we talked to him, we discovered something of how he did it.

Our interview took place in Sydney in August 1991.

INT: This first piece [Extract 1] seems to demonstrate the way you circle around various ideas in a stream of consciousness way...

PC: It makes me feel very vulnerable...You spend all that time trying to be perfect, trying to create this wall of...When you begin writing you're in a basic state of stupidity because you don't know anything. You end up spending two or three years so that you look good. And *here's* the bit where you're stupid! I suppose people often imagine that the process is much clearer, more calculated.

INT: Can you reconstruct how that circling happens?

PC: This isn't the surface of something else: this is it. Writing it is the way I think it. So I suppose I just follow the river of the idea on the typewriter. Then the river dries up and I can't think of anything else, so maybe I go back and run with it again, to see if this time it goes any further. And maybe in the course of that, another image comes up so I try that...

INT: Was there a pattern to it: the idea of a manufacture, then batteries, then glass?

PC: It's very romantic to say writing is like a madness, but it is a little bit. When the madness was over, I couldn't remember quite what happened, so I developed an answer which is deceptive in its simplicity. It's in all the interviews about *Oscar and Lucinda*—I was living in Bellingen, in the country. And there was a little church down the road that they wanted to take away. I looked at the landscape—only 200 years ago this landscape was full of Aboriginal stories.

I thought about that church I knew, how it might have arrived.

I wanted it to arrive intact—on a barge gliding like a dream into the landscape. It had to be prefabricated in order to be on the barge, and I knew about Victorian cast iron prefabricated technology. And then my architect friend said: Why don't you make it a glass church, because that's what the technology was for, to build glasshouses.

That's the story I'm used to telling, and it is probably the order in which it happened. I thought if I have a glass church then I have to have glass manufacture, so it comes from the need to have a prefabricated building, that means it's glass, glass is a good idea.

There were thoughts before this, however. Please don't ask me what they were.

INT: From the anecdotes you've told, that sort of accident happens fairly often—for example, the thing about the architect mentioning the glass church.

PC: But it isn't an accident, I'm obsessed, driven towards it—in typical self-centred writer fashion, always talking about myself and my own fantasies. So I don't think it's chance. I think I probably would have ended up with a glass church anyway—the cast iron was leading me towards it. But it was very nice that it was someone I like so much who could give me that gift.

INT: In another interview, you mentioned the influence of *Father and Son* by Edmund Gosse—did that fall into your lap by accident?

PC: I kept John Carey's review of the Anne Thwaite biography of Gosse.

INT: What was it about the review that struck you?

PC: Oh I don't know, something I remembered was about the Christmas pudding sizzling...

INT: How did you come across the review?

PC: When we lived in Bellingen we were given a present of a sub to the *Sunday Times*, and this was in it. I'd never heard of Edmund Gosse. My way into *Father and Son* was to read this review, then later I read the Anne Thwaite book, and much later read *Father and Son*. If I'd realised what a loved and treasured book it was, I don't think I would even have dared.

INT: When you're writing, are you in that obsessive state, where you're in the book twenty-four hours a day?

PC: In the early drafts, in the afternoon, I just don't think about the book, I just spend the mornings on it...Well, I don't know, whatever I say I can always think of ways in which it is not true.

INT: Are later drafts more obsessed?

PC: I could make that generalisation. In later drafts I think about the novel every minute of the day.

INT: At what point do you re-read what you've written? The next day do you begin your work by re-reading it?

PC: Yes, I'd read it back that afternoon or evening, and make notes, and when I began work the next day I'd read that annotated version.

INT: Sometimes, in the notes, you summarise what you're doing [see page 47].

PC: Where I give myself a talking-to?

INT: Yes, like a teacher writing the points on a blackboard.

PC: I do this all the time. I get really depressed: is it going to work? What am I doing? What is this about? So I just sit down and remind myself what it's about.

INT: Does this happen when things are starting to freewheel a bit?

PC: It can happen at any stage. I'm continually losing my way and losing confidence. You have a burst of excitement and think I've got this; then a day later I'm in a mess, nothing's in control, I've lost focus. So I sit down and say, 'This is a story about'. Then I think, okay, that's something I can write. I'm capable of writing that if I work hard enough at it.

INT: Did the characters change as you worked?

PC: Yes, for example, Lucinda kept on changing; what she looked like, how she was physically. As I tried to come to grips with who she was, and as I made notes, she changed—quite different sort of physical descriptions. At about this stage I imagined her as being really square and broad and square-faced, almost mannish, then I started changing that.

INT: How conscious are you of that process? Do you think, 'I have a problem here, this is inconsistent', or does it all remain intuitive?

PC: I give myself little lectures about things...That's conscious.

INT: As you change the character, what are you trying to find?

PC: Somebody who's somehow alive more. You know you do that thing with a character where there's a little...osteopath's click, and they can get up and walk around and you think, thank heavens, *I believe*! It's that terrible feeling that all the time you're writing you're not fully believing in it yourself; then you do something and you think, *I believe it*! You might have a contradiction that's built in, or something that you hadn't previously wanted the character to do and it appears contradictory. So you change the character to accommodate that contradiction, and in making the change, he or she comes to life.

INT: There's a lot of wonderful stuff in these early drafts you don't use. Do you regret having to leave that behind?

PC: No, I figure we writers do this stuff, we make things up, and if we can make stuff up we can make up plenty more. I quite enjoy throwing good writing away.

INT: Can you tell us about getting the voice? You seem to have had it in fits and starts from very early on.

PC: I really didn't think about voice too much. I would have been more worried about the point of entry into the story, the structure of the story, and the development and discovery of the characters. I don't think you'll find me giving myself a lecture about voice. It really is totally intuitive. I certainly didn't research nineteenth-century voices. I just kept on writing until it felt right.

INT: Were there any particular technical problems with this book?

PC: I think the things I was most concerned with were character and motivation. I wanted my characters to do some unusual things. Then I had to find out who they were, the people who did those things. I also had to have Oscar and Lucinda drawn towards each other, but at the same time to prevent them consummating their relationship successfully, because I'd already decided way back there that they weren't going to be allowed to.

As for how all this would affect readers emotionally—it's not that I'm unconscious of it, but I'm sometimes unaware of the amplitude of the emotions the work produces. There's no question of working on the emotion, of maximising it or minimising it. I've just got this thing (in *Oscar and Lucinda*) that I've got to do—characters that are drawn together just can't come together—so I've got to continually find reasons to keep them apart.

Structurally, the novel never changed much—I set up these little boxes, these chapters, and within each box the action always took place in the same rooms, the same places, the same people were there, but the meanings of the things that happened within those compartments continued to change completely.

INT: Do you have doubts about what you're writing as you're working on it and, if you do, how do you deal with them?

PC: Well, I worry about everything. That's why bad reviews are so devastating, there isn't a single thing a bad review will say that I won't have thought. I say: Oh, I've been worried about that. Oh, the characters are unconvincing—I knew they were. Or this is slick, or this is turgid, or this is whatever. Whatever it is, I've thought it. The whole business of writing is to live with doubt: to do what you don't know how to do, to place yourself continually in a situation of ignorance and inelegance. Finally you finish. You come to believe that the work is elegant, well structured and intelligent. You start to think you are gifted. Then you begin a new book and you see everything you write is awkward and shallow because it's not fully imagined. Someone who's good at observing from life might have different sorts of experiences, I don't know, but I feel my stuff is very made up. The people and things remain not real for so long into writing the book. I'm writing it and writing it, and they still haven't really come alive. It seems so artificial, so contrived, but anything you might think to say that might be critical of any work of fiction, anything, I would have thought it.

INT: This next extract [Extract 3] seems to perfectly illustrate what you call 'cantilevering'—starting the same piece several times and getting a little further each time.

PC: This would have happened all on the same day. That's just me trying to start the chapter, and now we have computers you lose this.

INT: What happens in this embellishment, why do you 'panic and scurry back', as you describe it in an interview?

PC: I don't know what I'm writing about, it's inauthentic. Somehow it's lying, somehow it's not true. So I go back and start again.

INT: Do you visualise it more clearly, or...

PC: Yes, it becomes more fully imagined. It's like this thin bit of wire that you want to encrust...so maybe that's all it is, just building it up so I can see it, believe it.

INT: Do you do a lot of that?

PC: Yes. All this is a first draft, you know I'd never thought this before. It might have been the first time I'd ever written about Oxford. That's research material that I've incorporated, about the breakfast, the nature of the breakfast. When I read it now I can see that I wasn't very confident. I felt I had no right to be writing about this world or this situation.

INT: So your reaction to lack of confidence is to take it further, to justify?

PC: Well, yes, that's one way of looking at it. But the first thing, even if it was a world I knew more, would have been to imagine it more fully. I'd want to discover where everything was, what the people looked like, so I could move things around.

INT: You mention in one of your interviews the difficulty of writing nineteenth-century historical material, the limits to the way you can impose your own experience on it.

PC: The big question for a writer is, how can you know this? In what corner of yourself can you find what you need to write truthfully about things of which, objectively, you'd have no knowledge?

INT: So did you find such a thing here, for instance? Is there perhaps something of your old school, Geelong Grammar, in here?

PC: Yes. When I was at Oxford with Robert McCrum, I needed to look at a room, a room that Oscar has. Robert went running up the stairs and went rat-tat-tat, 'Hello, Robert McCrum from the BBC, we're doing a film, can we look at your room?' So we looked at this guy's room, and I made some notes.

I said to Robert: Well, I think I can do Oxford, I'll use Geelong Grammar in some way. He looked at me rather doubtfully but that's why I thought I could do it. And the other thing is there's a whole lot of this that's just part of our imaginative life from literature as well, and that's part of the porridge.

INT: Can you say anything about the page of possible titles for this novel? [See page 34.]

PC: What it is, it's an attempt to make myself feel okay by getting a title. The thing of having a title—in the middle of all the uncertainty you think if you have a wonderful title then you'll feel better about your book. The titles are all different ways of focusing or looking at aspects of the story. I mean like there's the word 'deuce' which means the devil, and is also a playing card. I was playing with the notion of a folly...

I think the title's important, it does provide a context within which readers enter the book. I didn't want to throw false signals about the intention, so in the end the title was a very functional thing. 'This is a story about.' All this is just me trying to have a feeling of being in control. You know, I might get excited about something because it's got a nice name, it's like—you name your child and somehow you think that's going to pass on magical properties, that the child will be imbued with the qualities of the name: but a child defines the name, and in the end the book defines the title.

INT: Do you deliberately seek out inspiration in music or art or other fiction?

PC: I've done that a lot in my life. During the late 1960s, early 1970s, I'd begin work every morning by playing *Blonde on Blonde* or *Highway 61* to get myself sort of wound up with vindictiveness and spite. During *Oscar and Lucinda* I just generally read a lot of stuff about the period.

I find it gets harder and harder as you get older to find a work of literature which will do for you what almost everything did for you when you were a bit younger. Everything you read you thought: Oh! Ah! Now as you get older and at once more confident, it's harder to find something that works for you. I was just on holidays and reading *Don Quixote*, the first page really does it for me, but after another hundred or so pages it certainly wasn't doing it for me any more.

INT: Is there any part of the process that we haven't asked you about that you think is important to mention?

PC: I think that the one false signal that this discussion might give is that the whole journey was more straightforward than it really was. Some of the earlier notes were much more confused and less focused than this. The process is muddier than even this indicates, and I know that this is muddy. The confusions and the darkness ...this seemed more focused and direct than I think the process is.

There's this question people have, how should I *really* be doing this? Students always think when they're proper writers their self-doubt and their uncertainty will go away. I say to them, this is what you're choosing for your life. You think you feel bad now, you wait. Because that's the nature of writing.

Making Stories

Extract 1 from a very early manuscript

These early notes are described in the interview as 'following the river of the idea' (page 35).

<u>HIS FATHER INVENTED THE AQUARIUM</u> and started the mid Victorian craze for sea shore collecting.
This from Edmund Gosse's biography
Gosse's father
John Carey's review begins:
'As befitted a Victorian child, Edmund Gosse was racked by guilt. It shaped his life, making him anxious for love, addicted to overwork, and a keen donor and recipient of flattery. His parents were, of course, to blame. His father Philip had been a prodigy of self help, leaving school at 14, sailing to Newfoundland as clerk to a whaling company and subsisting on a single herring a day while teaching himself natural history.
O.K.: Aquarium to church.
<u>Father says Xmas pudding is idolatrous</u>. Asks total strangers are they saved. Reads religious tracts to wife dying in pain. Expects second coming every day. And his son was at once a rebel against him, but also an echo of, the aquarium magically turned into a church, but also, you see, racked with guilt that the things he enjoyed, the beauty of the country which he saw earlier than most, the drinking, dancing, song, women, everything filled him with guilt and his relationship with the almighty was in accord with all his other relationships — it was in the nature of a dangerous bet, in which agreement there were at once strict rules and also great affection, the affection shared by men on other sides but who despise those who live their lives outside such dangerous conflict
What a passion for life he had, what a battle with the god of his father,
<u>THROWING THE XMAS PUDDING OUT THE WINDOW.</u>
The mixing of religion.
<u>BEGIN BY SAYING THE CHURCH IS TO GO.</u>
Had dinner with the bishop of Grafton
for he was a religious man, but like a fellow who can only love combatively, abrasively,

[insert, handwritten on separate sheet]

Today, go thru the notes and <u>transcribe</u> into the note book anything that seems worth keeping.

---

what comfort he got from his book.
Dear God, he prayed, I am sorry to have done what I shouldn't. But here, look, isn't it a lovely thing to pray in, all full of your work, your mountains, your dreadful river.
Dear God, forgive me, I am a sinner, but look at it.
Etc. He prayed.
He saw the blacks. He did not know he was starting a legend.
When I was a young boy there was old black Jimmy who lived in a hut at yellow rock. He told me how my grandfather arrived.
He had tigers and circuses etc he said that day, jesus crucified.
He was drunk
So up the river
HE PRAYED TO GOD ABOUT HIS GAMBLING.
HE KEPT A BOOK.
HE RECORDED WHAT HE PRAYED AND WHAT HAPPENED.
On the basis of this he believed god was helping him and there was, in the choice of a church, some feeling of repayment
But there was also the question here of a bet, a side bet, that he could do it, he put up the church
Then they bet him he couldn't get it into place wi
He took this last bet.
Debtors prison.
It was not as they said he was a coward.
It was the shattered glass.
They dragged it up.
The fire that raged through the town, left it

SO THERE IS THIS STORY
It was not until my grandmother was an old woman that the church that had brought her impregnation and widow hood —a gambler—the coincidence of ovum and sperm.
That Captain Moonlight arrived and it was he who revived it. Put the blanks. Etc. He was an unusual man. Such was his following etc. What a preacher

Making Stories

I grew up with this. This valley. The buying and selling. Etc. Car dealers. Battery manufacturers.

They want to take the church away. The church has decided, the bishop has decided, that it is not VIABLE. Jesus Christ! Excuse me,
Well, the church is not viable, and petitions are being signed, for the Church of England

The role of religion. The stories, the guilt, religion was a strong force.
'Have you been saved?' My great grandfather is reputed to have said. He invented the aquarium. He was responsible for having thrown the Xmas pudding out the window.
My grandfather was the one who brought the church. If he hadn't done that, then the

THE GRANDFATHER IS THE ONE WITH THE GLASS.
HE TAKES IT HIMSELF
AFTER THE SHIP SINKS.
HE DOES IT HIMSELF.
ON LAND. HE NEVER CARED FOR THE WATER ANYWAY. TOO MANY BAD THINGS. THE WATER, AS IT TURNS OUT, IS WHAT DESTROYS IT
HE WAS A GAMBLER. HE HAD GAMBLED ON THE GLASS AND THEN NEW GLASS HAD TURNED UP.
HE WOULD NOT BE BEATEN.
THE GLASS HOUSE.
THE CHURCH.
THE QUESTION OF A GLASS CHURCH.
THE GLASS CHURCH WAS NOT HIS ONLY ODD INVENTION.
<u>HE WAS UNLUCKY ENOUGH TO MEET A CLERGYMAN WITH WHOM HIS FANCY RECEIVED REINFORCEMENT. HAD IT NOT BEEN FOR THIS HE WOULD NOT HAVE DIED SO YOUNG AND I WOULD NOT HAVE BEEN BORN.</u>
The glass.
My grandfather's position in business is cloudy. Gambling.
Gambling and religion.
READ PASCAL
The glass coming up the river. The type of glass. The finest. The sand that went into it. The wide over hang. The systems that he incorporated, <u>louvres, slides, ideas so</u>

Peter Carey—Oscar and Lucinda

that they could be removed, and reversed. That he would have to fight against stained glass—it was not necessary. He knew he would have to give in. He incorporated panels gothic in shape, which suggest as much as

The man who loved glass.
So: here is the fellow, he profits from Australia quickly, proving his adage that one need not use cunning, that one can—unlike Macarthur and those other villains, rogues, tricksters—benefit simply by wishing well. He fell in love with glass. It did not occur to him that he was wealthy. The problem of women. Sex, in 1890. He was beset with passions. The fun, the excitement, the theatre crowd, an actress, a dancer. Felt himself to be risking hell, the gambling
The indulgent streak in him too, in his appetite for food, not a glutton but a sensualist, his love of wine, smells, cigarettes, something to happen. A nervous energy, a love of life, so that, for all his christianity he WANTED MORE. MORE MORE. He would holler, MORE his voice comical, his face a sight, He was engaged, but the engagement was broken off when he appeared at her home, her father's home, drunk, alcohol on his breath
Alright:
So if his suicide is depression induced, a great vortex, a whirlpool then his character becomes, of course, more complex, more interesting.
I still can't see him.
He began like 'A', but now I don't know.
I am inclined to make him frail, but brave, an enthusiast, angel haired, blue eyed, sharp chinned, triangular faced the hair a great shock of red, the voice which should—by the appearance of the man—been fluting, was as mellow as an oboe, a long stride, slightly pigeon toed, the eyebrows hard against the eyes, beard-less
Glass.
Glass & the bible.

[margin note] COULD BEGIN HERE.
His view of god was not like his fathers, who threw a pudding out the window because it was idolatrous, but it was just as intense, just as important. He did not, as his

45

Making Stories

<u>father did, confront total strangers to enquire if they were saved or no. But, by jiminy, he had a tussle with the chap on many issues.</u>
<u>He bets God his life.</u>

[margin note] PIVOT
<u>He made the bet, a cowardly man too, a dreadful bet with God.</u>
his experience of clients being nervous, not wishing to break new ground

I. the grandmother inherited, to take to court. A seventeen year old took them on.
Glass.
The varieties of glass?
She brought it. The works, the skills, the sands, shifted it here.
Seventeen years old

<u>Go to the church and thought of her making toffee. Said things she should not, when she was old, a scandal.</u>
Sitting there. My father ashamed. I was beaten for listening. But that is how I know about the church you all wish to pull down, sitting

The story with the grandmother: the kitchen: the wood stove, the soap being made, the toffee, like glass

HOW IS ALL THIS KNOWN IF IT IS FIRST PERSON.
MAYBE THIRD WOULD BE BETTER.
BUT THE STORY.
<u>THEY ONLY KNEW EACH OTHER A NIGHT SO IT IS A WONDER THEY HAD TIME TO CONCEIVE MY FATHER, SO BUSY WERE THEY CHANGING STORIES</u>

My idea, last night, was to build a series of short stories which were all about the church which lead, chronologically, to the bare patch of earth, the stones, the thistles, to
But which starts with the carrier, 'A', his bullocks, the journey north what he needed the money for, why the church was built, the delivery to the wrong place, how he stepped off the chair.

Peter Carey—Oscar and Lucinda

Sad story.
Then the story of the bushranger priest, Captain Moonlight, and how he was admired, liked even. I don't know what the story is, but it's an interesting idea.

The architect who travelled with his bicycle, what's his name, Aubrey whatsit, arrives just

The aboriginal who saw the church come up river.
He was an old man, but he remembered. He lived then in the cabin at Yellow Rock, he played football, he saw the church floating up the river (cast iron, prefabricated) and he knew it was the end, the new stories pushing out the old.

SO WE HAVE THE BOOKENDS: THE FIRST STORY: THE DELIVERY OF THE CHURCH TO THE WRONG ADDRESS. AND THE LAST STORY: HOW THERE IS A BATTLE TO PRESERVE THE CHURCH AND IT IS LOST, THE STORIES ARE LOST. A PLACE WITH NO STORIES, NOT EVEN ONE ABOUT THE MOON. THERE IS ONLY ONE STORY, HOW THE CHURCH WAS BROUGHT HERE

Later the priest who was a bushranger. Captain Moonlight.
He was the one who got it going. What a preacher he was. Packed it out, until they found he was Captain Moonlight and they hanged him. Anyway, he was christened a presbyterian
Clergymen come and go. The historical society has the photos. The
And when I grew up.
The family business. Battery making. It was a prosperous town in those days. All the this and that. Battery making. The tailors, the plumbers, etc etc.

BUT I DON'T KNOW ENOUGH, YET TO WRITE IT.
Make it like Bacchus Marsh.
He has always lived there, the church maybe was the church of his childhood. The dairy farm. I played football. Dances. There was a football oval, big lads, rough games.
We had some fun.
The opponent is a city man.

Making Stories

Ha, perhaps, the city fellow wants to put in a steiner school, does he. Why would he do it

THE THEMES STIRRED UP BY THIS SITUATION ARE INTERESTING. Time, loss of values, meaning of christianity, lack of cultural base etc...but there is not enough
It feels too dull, drab, lit with flat light
Maybe the battery story could come into it
There is a battery.
All my life I have tried to do the right thing. I am not a good man, I know, but I have tried.
I will give you an example. My business is the manufacture of car batteries and I may have to explain a little to you about their manufacture. It is not necessary to be bored. We are talking, after all, about electricity

It is a miraculous thing. It is what makes us think, feel, everything. The Ark of the Covenant. Etc. Although I had no religious intent, of course, in setting up the manufacture of batteries.
It is simply something that can be done well. The batteries I made lasted ten years. Nowadays they expect blah blah.
How the thing is, who they employ, how it is done. The casing, the lead. There is a lot of weight in a good battery.

(Reproduced courtesy Fryer Library, University of Queensland.)

Extract 2 from the published version

Oscar and Lucinda, pp 374–7 and 380–4

'And are you curious?' she asked, pulling and pushing, challenging him even while she promised to confide. 'About the reason for my tears? Are you curious a little bit?'
He was curious, of course he was, but he had a lover's curiosity and he feared what she might say. He imagined the tears were somehow connected to the fat letters she left lying on her marble mantelpiece. He imagined they were produced by Dennis Hasset. He was curious. He was not curious at all. He had a lover's selfishness, was grateful for the intimacy the tears had made possible, was resentful of what they seemed to threaten.

They looked at each other until the look became a stare and both of them lost their nerve at once.

'Yes,' he said, 'of course I am curious.'

He wet the corner of the handkerchief again and tenderly removed the smudge from her nose. She tilted her head a little and closed her eyes.

She told him how the men, her employees, had offered him a fellowship they had denied to her. Her mouth changed while she told it. It became small. He was aware of the cutting edges of her lower teeth.

He was sorry for her. He was a fool, and had been party to a great unkindness. He was sorry, so very sorry, and he said so. He was also privately elated that the tears were not to do with Dennis Hasset at all, and although he tried not to grin, he could not help it.

'Well,' he said, 'you should know why I came bounding after you.'

'Not to dry my tears.'

'Are you curious?'

'Oh,' she smiled, 'I am curious, of course.'

He acknowledged her irony with a bow of his head. 'I chased after you to tell you I had never seen anything, in all my life, quite as splendid as your works.' He frowned.

Lucinda coloured, but it was not clear what she felt.

He pressed his clenched hands beneath his knees.

She said: 'Oh dear.'

He sighed and said: 'Yes.'

'Yes what?'

But he had only said 'yes' in response to what he hoped 'Oh dear' might mean, and he was not brave enough to be explicit. 'Perhaps,' he said, picking up his battered hat from the floor, 'we should take tea.' He was thinking of the Café Français, a place with marble tables.

'I will show you,' she said, standing and smoothing down her velvet skirts. What this meant was most uncertain.

He did not ask her 'what' or 'where' but followed her as she left her office. His mind was out of focus at the edges, sharp at the centre of its lens. Her walk was unexpectedly jaunty, crisp, clear, echoing. On the landing she opened a door marked 'Acclimatization Society of New South Wales'.

Oscar thought: Mr Smith.

'Gone,' she said, tapping the sign. 'Vamoosed. Mine now.'

She unlocked the door and swung it open. He waited for her to enter, but she would not. She stepped to one side and made a gesture like a theatre usher. They collided and tangled in their own politeness. 'Look,' she said impatiently, 'just look.'

What she asked him to look at was Mr Flood's 'proty-type', that construction which, only a second before, had occupied the crystal centre of her life. But when she stood beside Mr Hopkins in the doorway she no longer saw the cleverness of Mr Flood with his singed, hairy arms and his dividers and tables predicting 'actual shrinkage'. She did not see the ingenious collar-and-rod construction of the trusses. She saw only a dumpy little structure with a pitched roof like a common outhouse.

'You may approach,' she said drily. 'It is not sacred. It is merely', she said, imitating Mr Flood's pinched nasal tones, 'a "proty-type".'

But Oscar did not see as Lucinda imagined. As the dust danced in the luminous tunnel of the western sun, he saw not a dumpy little structure, not a common outhouse either, but light, ice, spectra. He saw glass as those who love it perceive it. He understood that it was the gross material most nearly like the soul, or spirit (or how he would wish the soul or spirit to be), that it was free of imperfection, of dust, rust, that it was an avenue for glory.

He did not see an outhouse. He saw a tiny church with dust dancing around it like microscopic angels. It was as clean and pure and free from vanity. It was at once so beautiful and yet so...decent. The light shone through its transparent, unadorned skin and cast colours on the distempered office walls as glorious as the stained glass windows of a cathedral.

'Oh dear,' he said, 'oh dearie me.'

When he turned towards her, Lucinda saw his face had gone pink. His mouth had become quite small, as if the thing which made him smile was a sherbet sweetmeat that must be sucked in secret.

He said: 'I am most extraordinarily happy.'

This statement made him appear straighter, taller. His hair was on fire around the edges.

She felt a pleasant prickling along the back of her neck. She thought: This is dangerous territory you are in.

He was light, not substantial. He stood before her scratching his head and grinning and she was grinning back.

'You have made a kennel for God's angels.'

Whoa, she thought.

She thought: This is how the devil looks, with a sweet heart-shaped face and violinist's hands.

'I know God's angels do not inhabit kennels.' He stepped into the room (she followed him) and crouched beside the tiny glass-house. It was six foot long with all its walls and roof of glass, the floor alone in timber. 'But if they did, this surely is the kennel they would demand.'

'Please,' she said.

'But there is nothing irreligious,' he said. 'How could we have a sense of humour if our Lord did not?'

She smiled. She thought: Oh dear.

'Do you not imagine', he said, 'that our Lord laughs together with his angels?'

She thought: I am in love. How extraordinary.

'How could God, who is all-knowing, not understand the foundation the joke is built on? I mean, that here is something the size of a wolfhound's kennel which, thanks to your industry, is a structure of such beauty and joy as to be a habitation fit for His angels.'

He stood still now, having, while he spoke, danced like a brolga around the little glass building. He held out his arms as if he might embrace her and then brought them back across his chest and hugged himself and hunched his back a little.

She thought: He will ask me, not now, but later.

'And haven't you done something?' he said. 'Haven't you *done* something with your life? I must confess to envy.'

The setting sun bounced off the red-brick wall of the next-door warehouse. It was this that made the little room so pink. The light refracted through the glass construction on the floor and produced a spectroscopic comet which they stood, neatly, on each side of. Lucinda duplicated his stance without meaning to; that is, she hugged herself, kept her arms locked firmly around her own body while she felt the space between them as if it were a living thing.

* * *

My great-grandfather was in love, and although he managed to hide all the signs of his despair from Lucinda, he was miserable. He made little jokes about the natty gents in checked waistcoats, laughed, patted her arm, but whatever happiness he felt he saw only as a sign of all that would be denied to him.

This was because he had an idea in his head, and I do not mean the idea that he had promised to reveal to Lucinda at the dinner table. This was another idea, quite separate. The idea that caused the real trouble was the one that Lucinda herself had lodged in his head – that she was in love with Dennis Hasset. She had done everything possible to make the idea stick. She had left the swollen envelopes on her mantel for days at a time. She had told him she was in love. She had spent hours of her Sunday at her secretaire. The letters grew so fat that they required excessive amounts of red wax to seal them properly.

The idea had taken hold, and such was the stubborn set of Oscar's mind that it would not easily be knocked loose. So it did not matter that she took his arm. It was the prior action, the snatching away, that stayed in his mind. It was here the truth seemed contained, and in the second act, the taking of the arm, he saw only pity.

Oscar did not like Dennis Hasset. He had not met him, but he did not like him. Not that he imagined the man had bad qualities. Quite the reverse. He imagined him good, clever, handsome, generous, a manly man who would be attractive to a lady. He could think of nothing to do to press his claim in competition, nothing except to display an excess of goodness, of selflessness, as if this behaviour, this loving self-denial, would provide him with the rewards that selfishness could not.

It was this that lay behind the dangerous wager he now planned to undertake in the dining room of the Oriental Hotel.

There were only two other tables occupied in the cavernous black-and-white-tiled dining room. A farming family occupied a table pushed gracelessly against a fluted pillar. A single gentleman in a frock coat sat beside a window; he read from a chapbook while he ate.

Lucinda was not hungry. She ordered as Oscar did. Her mind was occupied with the problem of how to undo delicately the clever knitting of her lies concerning Dennis Hasset. She could not concentrate on anything as ordinary as food.

She thought: This is what it is like when you love a man. She watched him as he buttered his bread and cut it into nine small squares. Should not this hitherto alien act now feel dear to her?

'Do you know what I envy you?' she said. 'It is that you are not constrained.'

She meant: The way you walk, walk in here, your clothes like that, and do not give a hoot what opinion the waiters or the diners may have of you.

He smiled, his piece of bread held between thumb and forefinger.

'You do not mind who sees you or who hears you or what they think of you. You know your own value, I think, and this puts you in a strong position.'

'And you?'

'Oh,' she rearranged a small pin in her hair. 'I am too careful.'

He thought about this for a moment or two while he chewed his bread, and as he had the habit of chewing thirty-two times, this gave him the appearance of great sagacity whereas he was merely wondering, whilst he counted, whether he should disagree with her own assessment of herself and cite her Pak-Ah-Pu and wonder if this was, really Miss Leplastrier, the habit of a careful woman.

But he said instead: 'It does no harm to be careful.'

They sat in silence. He seemed not to be discomforted by it. She was. The silence made her so-called love for Dennis Hasset seem too heavy and insurmountable an obstruction. It made her feel dull. It made her too aware of the waiters watching them. She did not like the Oriental Hotel with its crawling adoration of wealth. She began to resent the dining room and think how she would never have come here on her own initiative.

'What a lovely place it is,' he said, gazing around.

She thought: Do not be irritated and do not judge. He is not Them and he is not You. He is himself, uniquely so. When he admires, he admires as someone who cannot afford this luxury, not as someone who takes it as their right. Be like your papa who would want to know how the fluted pillars were made and what sort of fish that man is eating, and where it was caught and whether it is sweet to taste.

'Shall I tell you my idea?' he asked her.

'Oh, yes, do, please.'

'It involves glass.'

'A subject close to my heart.'

'We sometimes guard the things close to our hearts.'

She did not look at him. She said: 'You do not need to tread so carefully with me.'

'Yes,' he said unhappily. He saw no invitation to intimacy in this. His preconceptions made such an interpretation impossible and so he understood her back to front.

Lucinda heard his tone. She thought: I have been too bold. I am always in too much of a rush.

'And', she said, working against the current of a depression which now rose up and seemed to take possession of her mood, 'of glass, tell me, what was your idea?'

The waiter brought their consommé, not in a soup plate, in a deep bowl. Did he always have consommé? She had always thought it food for invalids.

'You could manufacture conservatories.'

'Is this your idea?' she asked, her heart now truly leaden.

'Oh, no,' he grinned.

'I would *loathe*', she smiled, 'to manufacture conservatories.'

They both looked at each other, their soup spoons raised above their bowls. In that moment she felt ridiculously happy. She felt he loved her after all. She could not stop smiling. 'So what', she said, laughing, 'is *your* idea?'

He sipped his soup. He had a nice sipping mouth. She liked the way it came to meet the spoon. She desired the mouth. She breathed out very quietly.

Making Stories

'You must tell me,' she said.

'Indeed.'

But he did not tell her. Instead he bent over his soup bowl and went at it with speed. Once, half-way through, he looked up and raised an eyebrow. Lucinda felt that mixture of irritation and affection so well known to Wardley-Fish.

'There,' he said, wiping his mouth with a fastidiousness perhaps induced by the quality of the napkin, 'now I can speak without my soup going cold.'

'You are a practical man,' she laughed. She felt a little unreal – a thrumming sensation behind her eyes.

'In some respects, yes, I am,' he said. 'How does your correspondent enjoy his living in Boat Harbour?'

She shut her eyes against the question's slap. She was shocked to feel its cold hostility. And even though hostility was not intended, she was not mistaken in detecting it.

She straightened her cutlery. She said: 'Well enough.'

'And does he have a church built yet?'

She thought: Fool, fool, do you think I care for Hasset?

She said: 'They hold service in a room above a cobbler's. They threw his predecessor into the river.'

'Oh dear.'

'Perhaps', she said, 'they will do the same with him.'

Oscar looked up sharply, but Lucinda was finishing her soup. When he at last saw her face it was like a room swept clean of meaning.

A waiter took away their bowls.

Oscar said: 'Mr Hasset should have a church.'

She did not wish to discuss Hasset. She said nothing.

Oscar did not like to think of Hasset either. It was the first time he had spoken the name out loud. When he said it he saw a hoe or a mattock, neither of them implements he had any fondness for. And yet he must say the name for he had an idea involving it, an idea that involved such a dreadful laceration of his own feelings that it is really hard to credit. And yet it was all born out of habits of mind produced by Christianity: that if you sacrificed yourself you would somehow attain the object of your desires. It was a knife of an idea, a cruel instrument of sacrifice, but also one of great beauty, silvery, curved, dancing with light. The odds were surely stacked against him, and had it been a horse rather than a woman's heart he would never have bet on it, not even for a place.

'And what would his feelings be, do you imagine,' he said, 'if, when Mr Hasset awoke one morning, he looked out of his window and saw a church?'

Peter Carey—Oscar and Lucinda

Lucinda opened her mouth to reply.

'Made of glass,' said my great-grandfather. (See! This is the sort of man I am!)

Extract 3 from an early manuscript

This is an example of what Peter Carey calls 'cantilevering' (page 39). This is from an early draft.

It was Wardley Fish's opinion that his tutor was a Suck-up. And this, surely, was behind his 'forgetting' to breakfast in his rooms. This, of course, was not Wardley Fish's interpretation. He did not go in for interpretation at

It was Wardley Fish's opinion that his tutor was a low grade Suck-up, a cultivator, a secret scholar of Debrett's. And this, surely, must account for Wardley Fish so completely 'forgetting' to attend breakfast in the silver-haired little fellow's rooms. This was not Wardley Fish's interpretation. Wardley Fish did not go in for interpretation at all. It made him feel uncomfortable. It would turn him silent and sullen and he would glower around the room, refuse the muffins and feel every one knew him to be stupid. These metaphysical tea parties filled him with horror.

It was Wardley Fish's opinion that Mr Temple, his tutor, was a low grade Suck-up. And it is not unduly psychological that it was this which made Wardley Fish so completely 'forget' to attend the breakfast in the tutor's rooms. It was not just that he forgot it in the morning when he woke to the clatter of his Scout cleaning the ashes from his fire. He had not forgotten it at 5 p.m. the evening before, because he had seen his tutor at the gatehouse and the tutor had mentioned the matter and Wardley Fish had made some enthusiastic remark. But he must have forgotten it half an hour later, for it was then he placed his breakfast order for the next day. He instructed his scout to bring him, at nine o'clock, a breakfast of Yorkshire pie, plovers eggs, grilled turkey leg, and a large tankard of ale to wash it down with.

Making Stories

It was Wardley Fish's opinion that Mr Temple, his tutor, was a low grade Suck-up. And it is not unduly Psychological to imagine that it was this, the tutor's smarminess, which made Wardley Fish so completely 'forget' to attend the breakfast in the tutor's rooms. He did not merely forget it in the morning. He forgot it the night before —ten minutes after discussing it with his would-be host—when he instructed his Scout to bring him a breakfast of Yorkshire Pie, plovers eggs, grilled turkey leg, pickles, and a large tankard of ale to wash it down with. And it was only when he had eaten this breakfast —there was mustard too, but I forgot to mention it—and had settled himself in front of his grate and had called for a second tankard that he 'remembered'.
'Blast,' he said.
An odd word for Wardley Fish. It is the sort of word he might use if he imagined his mother listening.
In any case he did not look cynically or self-critically or even self indulgently at his 'forgetting'. The psychological view did not occur to him. He did not interpret in any way at all. He gazed out the drizzled glass to the vague outline of the roof above the second quad and reflected that the Scout would, by now, be in the buttery drawing his ale. It was too late to stop him, so he would wait for the ale, drink it, and then consider what he could do.
At length the Scout brought him the ale. Wardley Fish barely saw him. Only after he had left did he think of him and only because, due to some delayed olfactory echo, he caught a slight whiff of urine and knew the frantic little fellow had been running too fast again—he had splashed one of his slops buckets on his trouser cuffs. When he had finished his second tankard he decided what he had known

It was Wardley Fish's opinion that Mr Temple, his tutor, was a low grade Suck-up. And it is not unduly psychological to imagine that it was this which made Wardley Fish so completely 'forget' to attend breakfast in the tutor's rooms. He did not just forget in the morning. He forgot the night before when he instructed his Scout to bring him a breakfast of Yorkshire pie, plovers eggs, grilled turkey leg, and a large tankard of ale to wash it down with. And it was only when he had settled himself in front of his grate and had called for a second tankard that he 'remembered'.

'Blast,' he said. The psychological view did not occur to him. He did not interpret in any way at all. He thought only that the Scout would, by now, be in the buttery drawing his ale. It was too late to stop him, so he would wait for the ale, drink it and then consider what he should do. Wardley Fish did not go in for interpretation. It made him feel uncomfortable. It was the tutor's passion, a passion almost the equal of his interest in anyone whose father was in Debrett's, had a thousand acres or more or a seat in the cabinet. The tutor's metaphysical breakfasts made Wardley Fish turn silent and sullen. He would become taciturn, and then sullen. He would glower around the room, imagine insults and go away convinced that every undergraduate in Oriel knew him as stupid, good for a third and a living in some forsaken corner of Wales.

The Scout brought him the ale. Wardley Fish barely saw him. Only after he had gone did he think of him and only because he had caught a slight whiff of urine and known the poor fellow must have splashed one of his slops buckets. When he had finished his second tankard he decided what he had known he would decide all along i.e. to hell with Temple. He would find his friend Bishop.

(Reproduced courtesy Fryer Library, University of Queensland.)

Extract 4 from the published version

This is the same scene as in Extract 3: from *Oscar and Lucinda*, p. 103.

It was Wardley-Fish's opinion that Mr Temple, his tutor, was a low-grade suck-up. And it is not unduly psychological to imagine that it was this, the tutor's smarminess, which made Wardley-Fish so completely 'forget' to attend the breakfast in the tutor's rooms. He did not merely forget it in the morning. He forgot it the night before – ten minutes after discussing it with his would-be host – when he instructed his scout to bring him a breakfast of Yorkshire pie, plovers' eggs, grilled turkey leg, pickles, and a large tankard of ale to wash it down. And it was only when he had eaten this breakfast – there was mustard too, but I forgot to mention it – and had settled himself in front of his grate and had called for a second tankard that he 'remembered' he had promised to breakfast with his tutor.

'Blast,' he said.

An odd word for Wardley-Fish. It was the sort of word he might use if he imagined God was listening.

In any case he did not look cynically or self-critically or even self-indulgently at his 'forgetting'. The psychological view did not occur to him. He did not interpret in any way at all. He gazed out through the drizzled glass to the vague outline of the roof above the second quad and reflected that his scout would by now be in the buttery drawing his ale. It was too late to stop this, so he would wait for the ale, drink it, and then consider what he should do.

Wardley-Fish did not go in for interpretation. It made him feel uncomfortable. This was the tutor's passion, a passion almost the equal of his interest in anyone whose father was in *Debrett's*, had a thousand acres or a seat in the Cabinet. Mr Temple's breakfasts made Wardley-Fish turn silent and sour. He would become taciturn, and then sullen. He would glower around the room, imagine insults, and go away convinced that every undergraduate in Oriel knew him as stupid, good for nothing better than a third and a living in the corner of some High-Tory bishopric.

At length the scout brought him the ale. Wardley-Fish barely saw him. Only after he had left did he think of him and only because, due to some olfactory echo, he caught a delayed whiff of urine and knew the frantic little fellow had been running too fast again – he had splashed one of his slops buckets on his trouser turn-ups.

When he had finished his second tankard he decided what he had known he would decide all along, i.e. to hell with Temple and his claret-stained whiskers. He would find his friend Bishop and go shooting at Otmoor.

Helen Garner
The Children's Bach

I never have a theoretical idea for a book. What I write usually emerges from things I've witnessed, experiences I've had myself, or that people around me have had. It emerges organically... Writing isn't like other artforms in that it's at second remove from the physical. It has to be so conscious, writing; but there are some days when your inhibitions go away...I wish could write like that more often.

       Helen Garner

V: "My friend went & had colonic irrigations. The lady who did them found stuff inside her that she'd eaten 10 years ago."
D: "How could she tell?"

*

Vicki is a hypochondriac:
"I feel as if part of my brain has come away."
"I feel as if all my period didn't come out."

Eliz to V. "They just look on your card, and if you're a hypochondriac it shows."

Vicki starts to hang round Bunker Street. They hear her old pushbike crash against the rubbish bins & she springs up the concrete steps. Even at breakfast time. Stays an hour. Eats a poached egg Dexter has just cooked for himself; makes herself useful & pleasant. Laces Arthur's boots for him. He submits with a patient smile. He can do it b'self.
V: "Can I walk down to school with you? Do you mind?" "yes," Vicki.
A: (absently) "You do mind?"
V: "I mean, yes, you can come."

Vicki and Dexter:
She stared down at his face which was quite still, eyes closed, half-smiling. She gazed at his face which the moonlight had transformed, all the lines were wiped away, she was looking at a stranger, his skin was smooth, he looked like a calm-faced, tranquil woman. He was nothing to do with Dexter: he was a placid creature just found, it was hers, no-one else even knew it existed. The mysterious Buddha face, sphinx, mermaid, on the pillow: him not at all, yet nobody else either. She did not touch the face: only looked.

Other way round. Athena dozes. She hears Vicki singing in the kitchen, washing the dishes. She feels looked after. When D does not ask her whether she's sick. Makes a milky soup—

Helen Garner—The Children's Bach

When Helen Garner agreed to contribute to *Making Stories*, she sent us a notebook that she had used in the early writing of *The Children's Bach*. The notebook was divided into five sections according to the names of the major characters of the novel—Dexter, Vicki, Athena, Elizabeth and Philip. Each section had entries that were written directly in, or pasted or taped in. Some were typed, and some were handwritten. The order of these entries seemed entirely random (see Extract 1).

They were fascinating notes—scraps of dialogue, lists, cryptic glances at the characters, sometimes a moment captured in a phrase or sentence—but it wasn't at all obvious how they could become a novel. Then we talked to Helen Garner.

Our interview took place in Sydney in December 1991.

INT: What came before this notebook?

HG: A smaller notebook that I carry in my bag all the time. I never go anywhere without it. I write in it little crumbs that I pick up from everywhere. Recipes. Titles. Things I overhear in the street. Quotes from what I'm reading. Details of people's appearance that I happen to notice. That kind of thing.

INT: Nothing more abstract?

HG: I never have a theoretical idea for a book. What I write usually emerges from things I've witnessed, experiences I've had myself, or that people around me have had. It emerges organically. I keep these small notebooks—I was going to say at random, but I mean without any particular aim except that I can't bear to let things get past me. Philip Larkin says somewhere that 'The urge to preserve is the basis of all art'. That's pretty much my approach. Small things are so fascinating and precious that I can't bear to let them go. So I write them down as they strike me. I don't invent a book out of thin air. I need—or I did at the time I wrote *The Children's Bach*—a bed of detail for the thing to be based on before I can start to make something up.

INT: When would you jot things down?

HG: Any time. I've become completely shameless. I take notes right in front of people now. It's not that I'm writing down anything particularly revealing about the person. It might be just an attractive turn of phrase—like someone saying 'euchred' or 'jiggered' instead

Making Stories

of 'tired'. Often, though, it's got nothing to do with what's being said. People might be talking about one thing that triggers off in me a thought about something quite different.

INT: Do you think the notebook helps you to notice more?

HG: No. It helps me to remember in detail what I notice. I'm a pretty good noticer already. Using a notebook touches on what T.S. Eliot might have meant when he talked about the 'objective correlative'—an image or a detail that summons up in a rush a whole attendant mood, or vibe. For example, there's a café I used to go to over in Darlinghurst when I lived in Sydney, and in that café at certain times of day late in the winter, I used to see some men, heavy guys—pimps or petty crims I suppose, blokes you wouldn't want to mess with—they would sit leaning against the back wall of the café and staring out on to the street. The sky at the end of the day was green. It was spooky. There was a terrible feeling of desolation on those late afternoons. That scene, those heavy blokes, I couldn't find a place for, anywhere, in what I was writing at the time; but the mood of the scene imbued a whole story, the one called 'A Vigil' in *Cosmo Cosmolino*. That's the way I can use the notebook now that maybe I wouldn't have been able to earlier, when I was sort of hooked on detail—I mean anxiously and obsessively collecting detail to use, as I did in *The Children's Bach*.

On another level, it shows you that even when you think you are idle, just walking around gaping at the world, you are actually working quite hard, in that part of yourself which is not amenable to organisation or routine or even conscious control. If you write down a dream, you take certain brief notes, and much later when you think you've forgotten the dream, you read the notes, and suddenly they trigger the rush of memory—suddenly you're in the land of the dream again, in its spookiness or its bliss or whatever its emotional tone was.

INT: Have you always used notebooks this way?

HG: Writing in the notebook is in itself a skill that I have developed more subtly over the years of doing it. These days I feel much less tied to it. I don't feel any more that I need to be so terribly exact, so precise in what I write down—like a good little girl taking neat dictation. I'm more likely now to take a stab at the right note, so that when I read it afterwards, the same note will sound again, and remind me of a whole sequence of events, or moods. I think I'm learning to trust myself more, and not to be so anxious about getting it right on the spot.

INT: How did you go about using these notebooks when you were writing *The Children's Bach*?

HG: By then I would have filled up three or four of these small notebooks. Getting a grant meant that I had real writing time—I could start to collate this mass of raw material into a usable shape. I set up the typewriter and got out the notebooks and started to type them up, on to ordinary A4 paper. It's kind of laborious, I suppose—what word processors were invented to relieve people from. But I loved it, it was the sort of task that really suited my nature. Fiddly and obsessive.

I would have thought about Athena and Dexter first—I always start a book with the characters—then the two sisters, and Philip. I was left with reams of A4 paper, four or five entries on each sheet. Next I went to K-Mart and bought a big foolscap 'five subject notebook' with spirex binding. I labelled each section with a character's name, then I got my scissors and cut up the A4 sheets, and I filed and pasted the bits under whichever character they seemed vaguely to suit. It was amazing how many of them were attachable to the characters. As if the book had been writing itself inside me all that time I was only faintly aware of wanting to write it. I sorted and filed and pasted madly. With UHU glue. It's the best.

It wasn't a closed-off process, either. Just say I overheard a bit of dialogue in the street, I might think: Would any of my characters talk like that? And if they would, I'd slip it into their part of the book. And if they wouldn't, it's still floating in a folder somewhere.

INT: Can you tell us more about that process of picking and choosing from the notebooks?

HG: I've got so I know that there's no point in trying to force something in. In every book there'd be some little treasure that I couldn't bear to let go of, but I'd always find I had to let go of it in the end: that I couldn't move forward *unless* I let it go—that's the trap of working the way I do, or did back then. But if it doesn't fit, it doesn't fit.

I do notice, too, that the very fact of having written something down, years and years before, somehow fixes it in my mind without my having to look it up. So that one day I'll be writing along, not even trying to remember it, and it will pop into my mind exactly when I need it. Just a detail. A turn of phrase.

INT: Do you deliberately create a scene around a phrase, or do you happen to remember the phrase when you're writing a scene?

HG: Let me think. Once or twice I've got a whole story out of a single sentence or two. 'We heard he was back. We heard he was staying in a swanky hotel'—I got 'The Dark, the Light' out of that. But usually it would be that I'm writing something and I'd think...aha! This will go in *here*.

INT: How do you go about structuring your novel?

HG: That works almost completely organically. I'm no good at planning. I just start. That means I'm rather slow. When I was writing the screenplay called *Two Friends*, I made a structure for it which may or may not have worked—opinions differ—but I found that having a structure as strict as that one speeded up incredibly the process of writing. I almost felt anxious about it. It was so fast that I felt I couldn't be doing it properly. Whereas with *The Children's Bach* I didn't know what was going to happen. I just knew that I wanted this family and that there would be a little boy who had something wrong with him, so you could only reach him through music. I hardly had any more idea than that, and of the possibility of other musicians...I hardly remember, that's the odd thing, because I don't plan it. It just kind of emerges. I start at a certain point and I keep going. I try it this way and I try it that way—it's a very anxious process. It's terribly enjoyable, but a high level of anxiety goes along with it—at any given moment I don't know where I'm going.

INT: Do you rewrite actual sentences?

HG: Oh, yes. Specially now. At the time I was writing *The Children's Bach*, my sentences were short and stumpy, but lately I've been trying to lengthen them, to make them more...capacious and sinuous. Flexible. I spend many wonderful hours shifting clauses around and taking out adjectives and putting more in. Somebody once said to me that adjectives were the small change of language. At the time, I thought, Oooh! Well, I won't use any then. But now I use thousands of them. I love them.

Whenever I read Christina Stead I get an electric thrill from the way she breaks all the rules. She can string seven adjectives together in a row—in *Letty Fox, Her Luck* I practically pass out with envy and admiration. She holds the noun up to the light, and uses the adjectives to make it shine *this* way and *that* way, shifting and shifting. Of course you never get the sense, with Stead, that she's even given a moment's thought to any of this. It's beneath her. Did she ever rewrite? I envy that naturalness—as if she sat down and out it poured.

Helen Garner—The Children's Bach

As I get older my vocabulary seems to be shrinking. It's alarming. Where there used to be a word there's now a blank. So when I'm reading, especially eighteenth- or nineteenth-century things, I always keep a bit of paper handy and write down any interesting or strong words that strike me. I tack them up near my desk so that if I'm writing wimpily, I think: I wonder if I've got a word on this list that I could use to replace the flat, weak one I've written. It's like a personal file. Words like taxing. Afflicted. Costly. Trifling. It's like having a collection of pebbles or marbles in my pocket. I can get them out every now and then and examine them. Often there's one I can use. It's always a word that I already know—I don't mean impossible or new or obscure ones—but a word that didn't spontaneously appear in my writing. I find it extremely useful, to keep jolting myself like that.

If I have an idea when I'm actually sitting at the desk writing, and it's not an idea that I'm ready to use yet, I'll dash it off on a bit of paper and stick it up with masking tape in front of me, and then later on I might come round to it. Or maybe I won't.

A terrific thing happened when I was writing the screenplay *The Last Days of Chez Nous*. It went through a lot of drafts, and I guess I was at about fourth draft stage. I had a card for every scene, a little filing card, a whole stack of cards—I don't use a word processor—and I needed to simplify the pattern of the story. I laid the cards out on the floor in the order they were in the current draft, and I was standing there, staring at them, panicking, when suddenly a breeze blew in through the window. It blew the cards—not into a better configuration...if only it had!—but it fluttered them all over the room. At first I was aghast, but something made me stop and think, and then I realised it was a gift. From nature, or wherever these gifts come from. I thought: Ah—*this* is what was the matter. I was stuck in that configuration. I'll get rid of it. I'll rethink the whole shape of the narrative, without the rigid old grid. The wind was just a light puff, on its way across my room from the balcony. But it was a wonderful moment of illumination. That's why I don't plan very much. Because if I do, I start to wield the plan against my instincts, and it acts as a clamp. It becomes a duty, or a trap. It prevents me from being flexible, or alert to a fresh possibility. A friend of mine said to me once, in her Polish accent: 'A plan is to be had, and srown away.'

INT: When you're much further advanced than this notebook, when you're ready to start the narrative, how do you hold that number of bits in your head?

HG: Well, I suppose I don't, really. What's in my head is a whole lot of possibilities, not very formed. Every day in a first draft, I'm anxious. Every day I've got no idea where I'm going, it's like scrub-bashing. I feel filled with anxiety, until I get about seven-eighths of the way into a book. Until it forms itself into a curve and I feel that it's probably going to be alright. Then I start to love it. Then I can't get to work soon enough each morning, because I don't know what's going to happen next, and I won't know until I write it. So it's terribly anxiety-making, but I can't seem to find another way of doing it. The anxiety seems to be a necessary part of the process.

INT: So you start off every day not knowing where the writing will take you?

HG: Some days I do know, but only if the day before I've had to stop before I've finished the idea. I find my whole week goes in a pattern. Monday and Tuesday are hopeless, Wednesday I'm just starting to see something, Thursday is always the best day of the week, and Friday I'm just tidying up the mess from Thursday. Every week goes in a curve. I look forward to it.

INT: How do you know when the structure is right? How do you make that judgment?

HG: It's all by feel and instinct. I've got to feel satisfied. It's hard to describe...It's a sort of architectural feeling that I get, a sense of balance and the right density. It's shifting weights around. By the time I hand in a draft to my publisher, to Hilary McPhee, my main problem would tend to be the narrative pace. It moves too fast. I always have to slow things down. David Malouf said to me, once: 'You're a natural sprinter.' Hilary will usually say: 'It's too fast here, and here you've lost it, it's too cramped.' Not cramped in that there's too much there but cramped in that I haven't spaced it out. When I handed *The Children's Bach* to her that's what she said. I had to loosen the structure—relax it a bit. Hilary is very sensitive to what you're trying to do, even before you know it yourself. I'd show her stuff in a very primitive draft. She's got an incredibly delicate touch. You can hand her something that's just a dog's dinner, and she'll be quite witty and light—you feel only encouragement and exhilaration; you go away from her thinking: Whacko, I can't wait to get back to work. And when you do get back to work you realise that she's actually given you very tough criticism; she's taken it right up to you. But she does it in such a way that it hardly hurts at all. She's able to show you the potential of the mess. That's her brilliance. I had the most wonderful stroke of luck in stumbling onto her early on.

INT: How did you slow down *The Children's Bach*?

HG: I can't exactly remember, to tell the truth. I probably added a couple of little scenes, or maybe I extended some. *The Children's Bach* is made up of fairly small segments, and I think I either put in a few extra ones—or maybe I had to expand the sequences about Athena going to Sydney with Philip. I can't remember now, in detail.

INT: Can you talk about the process of arriving at your characters?

HG: Most of my characters are initially rooted in a real person, or part of a person. Often the reason I start writing something is because I'm interested in working out why somebody I know acts in the way they do—or, more accurately, I'm interested in making up a story about how someone I know might act if I put them in a certain situation, one that I invent.

But I've just finished writing a character, in this new book *Cosmo Cosmolino*—a bloke named Alby. I invented him totally. Well...as totally as a character is ever really invented, in fiction. Anyway, he is not based on or inspired by a real person, and I found that writing him was the greatest bliss and joy of anything I've ever done. And then when I created him I had to fight him for control of the book. He almost got the upper hand. I thought: Bugger you—I'm in charge here! He marched into the book and turned everyone around him into wimps. He was like an energy thief. We had a titanic struggle. I *think* I won. Nothing like that has ever happened to me before. I've always felt I was in control of things.

INT: When you do draw from a real person, do you at some point consciously camouflage their origins—or does that happen anyway?

HG: I used to think I should apply camouflage. When I tried, my attempts were primitive and clumsy. These days it happens by itself. At a certain point, the whole concoction sort of gels. I lose the demarcation line between 'reality' and what I'm inventing. And then I'm free. It's no longer a person, then. It's become a character. The more experienced I get, the more confident I feel about this.

INT: In *The Children's Bach*, was music an organising principle for the book, or an inspiration?

HG: I had my first piano lesson a couple of years before I started writing it, when I was 40. I can't really recall making a conscious decision to use music as an organising factor. I think it developed organically, like everything else. It's partly because nearly everybody I know is interested in music. Music's probably the greatest pleasure and interest of my life, apart from books and people. Also, about *The Children's Bach*, I did actually know a child who was autistic; music was his only connection with order, the only way he could be reached. In some moods he could only be calmed by a certain piece of music that he loved. He used to sing just as the child did in the book.

Learning the piano myself made me aware of the struggle, the almost *moral* struggle that playing music entails. Even limping through pathetic childish piano pieces as I did—and still do—can teach you a lot. It doesn't matter how hopeless you are. Even in the tiniest phrase, there's the struggle to perceive form, to establish order. Even in your own clumsy fingers. The struggle to discipline my body to make music—it's enlightening.

INT: Is there a collection of music called *The Children's Bach*?

HG: Yes. I've got a book called *The Children's Bach*. It's got little pieces in it that look easy but aren't.

INT: Is the structure of the novel like a Bach piece?

HG: No. Oh, yes—oh, it'd be going too far to say it's contrapuntal. But I wanted all the characters to have a voice. People read the book and sense an order in it—I'm talking about reviewers—and they grope around for images for the order they sense in it.

INT: Is writing a process of more or less groping, for you, too—or do you have days when the writing comes, if not automatically, then spontaneously?

HG: Writing isn't like the other artforms in that it's at second remove from the physical. It has to be so conscious, writing; but there are some days when your inhibitions go away. Those days come to me only in short bursts—oh, I suppose the occasional short story might come like that. I wish that I could write like that more often, you know, just sit down and trust myself.

That character Alby came down from heaven and landed on my page. I found such ease in him—I don't know why. It was totally accidental. A Jungian psychologist might say that Alby was a version of my animus, he seemed so intensely familiar to me. It was as if I were he. It was the most wonderful feeling of freedom. I felt I could not make a mistake with this character. All I had to do was control him. It was almost not like work, it was like play, it was wonderful play. I suppose if you were a grand artist like Bach, or Picasso, that's what work would always be like—wonderful play—and you'd feel so free, and guided by some huge force. I got a tiny hint of it when I handed myself over to Alby. But to me that feeling of freedom comes only in very small bursts. You start a paragraph sometimes and suddenly: Boom-boom-boom-boom-boom! Out it comes, all these ideas are streaming through you and you can hardly keep up. And then it's over. A page is the most I'd get out of it. Perhaps I get scared. But who was it, Flaubert, I think, advising someone who was writing in a limping sort of way; he said: Don't worry, no one's going to come into the room behind you and snatch it off your desk and publish it! Take a risk!

I always feel ashamed of my clumsiness. I couldn't bear it if anyone came in and saw the mess on my page. You've got two selves, I think. One of them's the deep one that can do the work, and the other one is constantly discouraging you and saying: Oh come off it! Who do you think you are? It's so deep inside yourself, that sneering voice. It's pre bad review. Bad reviews merely slot into that voice.

INT: We're asking everybody what they do about doubts.

HG: Some days I look at what I'm doing and I think: This is pathetic. How can I have thought this was any good? That's when the bottom drops out of everything. Some days it's so awful I have to put my pen down and lie on my bed, or go to the movies. I feel like a phoney; an appalling phoney and *someone's going to find me out*. I'm going to be exposed...that's my fear. They'll say: who wrote *this*? She calls *this* a book?

INT: What do you do to get over it?

HG: It depends on where I am in the book. Some days when you feel like that you just have to slog on. You have to say: I'm doing the best I can. If it's feeble, it's feeble. And you just have to go on. I try to keep going. I was rather encouraged by Annie Dillard in *The Writing Life*. She said there's no point, while you're actually *doing* it, in asking yourself whether the work's any good. Just keep going. Keep going. That's the best advice. Unless you feel that you're so full of hatred of what you've done that you're about to burn it, in which case you should probably go for a walk around the block. You've *got* to keep going. Because if you don't, nothing better can happen. That's the way I look at it. I feel panic and shame a lot of the time. I reckon a lot of writing is bluff. Because you don't really even know what...a story is.

INT: You've mentioned Jung—do you often find those external influences useful to your writing?

HG: I went to a Jungian analyst for a while though I hadn't read much Jung. What I learned from the analyst was how to approach dreams in a different way. Before I went to him, I'd read a little bit of Freud, and if I had any idea about my dreams, it was on rather ignorantly Freudian lines. I saw largely their sexual symbolism, which, when you think about it, is not very useful. Not for a writer. Well, I don't find it useful. What I learned from that brush with Jung is the usefulness of dream imagery, and the richness of it. I started to take the imagery of dreams more seriously instead of seeing them as a sort of scum or froth lying on top of whatever was happening in my life. I started seeing the beauty and richness of it; and soon I wanted to get that actual quality into the writing. Not just to make characters have dreams, but to try to get that strange, crazy dream-richness into the texture of the writing itself. Of course, I found it terribly difficult to do.

I've got a line from Jung pinned on to my wall. He's talking about analysis, of course—about what to do when someone brings a dream to him: 'Long experience has taught me never to know anything in advance, and not to know better, but to let the unconscious take precedence.'

I stuck it on my wall to remind me that when I get in a panic and get blocked, it's because I'm not paying attention to what's happening inside me: I'm listening to something external, an external idea of what I should be doing or how I should be writing.

INT: Do you use music while you're working, or have pictures you look at?

HG: Oh, certain bits of music, I feel that if I hear them everything's worthwhile. Those Bach Toccatas, that are so thrillingly energetic—if I'm down in the dumps I go and listen to that kind of music. Muscular and extremely patterned. But not while I'm actually working, no.

I looked at a couple of pictures when I was doing *The Children's Bach*. The picture of Tennyson and his wife and children, that I describe on the first page, that had a strong effect on me. I didn't stumble on it until quite late in the piece—I was about a third of the way into the book when I found this remarkable picture of a family—the body language of the people in it! The photo seemed to echo what I'd already written.

Recently too in Sydney I saw some paintings by a New Zealander called Maria Olsen. They were dark paintings of huge, cistern-like tanks, very mysterious. They were exactly at the point of overflowing. Water was slipping and slithering over their sides. They were straight out of a dream *I'd* had. It made me very excited to see that I wasn't alone, with that imagery—that someone else found it satisfying, and meaningful. My initial reason for writing is that I need to shape things so I can make them bearable or comprehensible to myself. It's my way of making sense of things that I've lived and seen other people live, things that I'm afraid of, or that I long for. It may be that this limits me—working from such a close personal need—but there you are.

I've noticed that when people review Australian literature from outside the country, they expect to have Australia—and our lives here—presented to them as a spectacle, with every social class represented, and several generations, and all the regions, not to mention deserts, scuba diving, stock market crashes, tycoons and so on. I can't be bothered even *thinking* like that. I can't, and I don't want to. I'm working absolutely from the inside out.

INT: When you're deep in writing, do you feel you're inventing or discovering?

HG: Both. Perhaps inventing is a more advanced stage of the same process. I'm not sure I can distinguish between them. Inventing implies more consciousness—more will. But first comes a faith in passivity. You have to know how to *wait*. David Malouf says that the main thing a writer needs is patience. Strange leaps happen in your imagination—they happen—I don't think we can take the credit for a lot of things that happen in our imagination. After the fact comes the labour. It's taken me years to learn to trust my intuitions and act on them, specially after a university training of the kind we got in the 1960s, when we really believed that artists 'knew' what they were doing when they worked. In the face of that, your own efforts looked pretty puny! As if I thought that somewhere there was a book of rules about how to write, but I was too embarrassed to ask where it was.

I've become very interested lately in spirit—or rather soul. A few years ago I started going to church. I imagined that everybody else in the church knew quite clearly what they believed, and why they were there. I thought I was the only person present who had dragged herself along to church out of an obscure longing for something nameless and inexpressible. It didn't take me long to realise that most churchgoers are like me—not knowing, but searching. Finding something out is always more interesting than knowing it already.

I'm sure that the urge to religion and the urge to art are deeply linked—the longing people feel for the thing we have so much trouble naming—grace, meaning, wholeness.

When I was writing *Cosmo Cosmolino*, I went to church at Pentecost. The readings from the Bible on that day were all to do with images of the Holy Spirit: a mighty wind, fire, water, and birds—all the poetry of how the Holy Spirit manifests itself in the world. I went reeling out the door in bliss. All these images were ones that were in the book I was writing. I'd been struggling away trying to find imagery for hope and significance in people's ordinary lives, dumbly dragging them up from what I'd seen and felt—and here they were in the *Bible*! I felt as if a bomb had gone off in my head. They must be thundering great unconscious archetypes that our lives touch on and gain energy from, and that's why they're in art and in religion, over and over.

But at a certain point in the process of writing, you have to think. You have to do sort of thinking that hurts, as Iris Murdoch calls it. It's hard to think. It's about the hardest thing in the world. It's definitely not my strong suit. You learn to listen to your intuitions, but then you have to learn to build on them. To use your intelligence, consciously, as well. It's a mysterious process. My grandfather said to me when I was very small: 'Helen, you are quick on the uptake—but that is *not enough*.' Sometimes I wonder if that's been the theme of my life.

Extract 1 from an early manuscript

This is an extract from the notebook mentioned in the interview. We have reproduced the sections on Dexter and Vicki.

```
SECTION ONE: DEXTER
   Is Dexter a gardener?
```

'I picture the human memory,' said Dexter, 'as a huge, dim basement full of filing cabinets. Two old blokes in

Helen Garner—The Children's Bach

grey dustcoats are smoking roll yr owns & leaning about with their hands in their pockets. Down comes the message, through the dumb waiter gadget in the corner. 'The name of the fox terrier pup I had that got run over. The height of a telegraph pole. The patron saint of map-makers. Twelve sevens.' They heave themselves upright, tread out their butts: 'all right, all right! If you must know...' & they plod away down the dark aisles.'

Athena's father calls Dexter a blow-hard.

He has also been, without thinking about it, a one-woman man. The seventies passed him by. Herpes? Never heard of it. It's only the firm network of the past that means anything to him.

His memory. He commandeers other people's experience, remembers their dreams, tells the story always in the same words.

His memory-contests (quotations) with Elizabeth. E. always won.

He quotes Dr E.A. Floyd. 'Some people pronounce it Purcell. That's an Amedicanism.'

He hates modern things: postcodes, people who write '7 April' instead of 'April 7th'. New York addresses which contain not a single word. 'X's address is a nightmare'.

He was the sort of person who'd put on Ravel's Bolero first thing in the morning.

'Don't fight!' said Dexter. He clenched his fists & jumped up & down on the spot. 'I want you to be happy! Have you tried weeding?'
  'There's no dirt here. All bricks.'

D is deeply sociable. A has to make an effort.

'Pudding!' cries D & bangs his spoon on the table. Vicki is disgusted.

Making Stories

D and his father can't stand it when people fuss in restaurants abt paying the bill. 'They're still coupled in conference about who had the rice!'

D mimics old lady at Viet demo:
'Fuckin' mu-u-urderers!'

Dexter reads out the article by the divorced man.
'"I continued to parent because..."
He lets out a groan of contempt. 'Prrrrnting. I continued to prrrrnt,' he said with relish in a grotesque American accent.
'When I'm commissar for language I'll line up people like him & machine gun them'.

'We were outspent by the Labor Party dollars-wise by a factor of 4 to 1.' Lib who was elected.

D: 'That's right. Smash everything. Smash smash smash smash. Then what.'

To Morty   : 'I hate the way you pronounce the word fuck.'
M (stung)   : 'There's not much range, is there? Fuck, fewck, ferck. What do you expect.'
D   : 'It's the shape of yr mouth.'

D : 'Would you mind if I sang a few more stanzas?'
EL : 'Yes. Don't. I don't like hymns.'
D : (hurt): 'you're so rough on me.'
     (Breaks seat)

'University tests prove...'

Dexter wanted to live gloriously

Dexter hears his father saying (at a party? at the party at wh. Ath tries to play the recorder?) 'Of course, the main thing about Chopin is...'
D. whispers, 'Oh, shut up.'

Dexter woke up in a muck sweat.

Helen Garner—The Children's Bach

He is an academic but not the modern killer kind. Baillieu: Leavis—'Morty, can you find a verb in this sentence?'

He stuck up for the Soviets long after Stalinism had turned others away.

'I am <u>NAHT SHOUTING</u>!'
—One-upmanship
—the trick wine cellar
—kicks up his heels like Charlie Chaplin

When the business w the German starts, he panics. 'This must be modern life'

J. Sutherland at the Southern X:
Dexter & Eliz at E's sister's wedding:
'How's X getting along, Morty?'
'I don't know. I haven't had any contact w her for 8 yrs or so.'
Dexter is shocked.
'But Morty! You <u>must</u> keep in touch with your family!'
'why should I, for X's sake?'
'Because there's nothing else. Without our families we're nothing. We're just dry leaves blowing down the gutter.'

They have got a TV that Athena's parents gave them, but they've hidden it in a cupboard & never used it. Arthur doesn't even know it's there.

DEXTER CRANKED OPEN A TIN OF PEARS.

D: Can I sing another stanza?
E: No. I hate hymns.
D: (he is staggered. Reels. His chair splinters)

DEXTER COOKS. From the kitchen a volley of oaths. He stands in a puddle of oil.

THE TENNYSON PHOTO IN THE BOOK ON EDWARD LEAR

Tennyson, his wife and their two sons 'walking in the garden' at their house on the Isle of Wight. It is a

Making Stories

really shocking photo, in a way. They are all (except perhaps the man) so bundled up in enormous, voluminous, dramatic garments. Eye-lines:
Tennyson into the middle distance,
his wife, holding his arm and standing very close to his side, gazes up at him, one boy holds his father's hand and looks up into his face,
the other boy holds his mother's and looks at the camera with a weak, rueful expression. Behind them, out of focus, twinkles the windy foliage of a great garden. Their shadows fall across a lawn: they have just taken a step. Tennyson's hands are large square paws, held awkwardly at stomach level.
The wife's face is gaunt, her eyes set in deep sockets. It is a photo of a family. The wind puffs out the huge curved sleeve of the wife's dress, and brushes the long hair of the father's boy back off his face which is turned towards the drama of his parents' faces: though he's holding his father's hand, he is separate from the group: light shows between his buttoned-up torso and his father's legs.

Dexter feels fatherly towards Vicki (but later sexual)

They're marriage encounter people, and everywhere they go they hold bloody hands.

On their way home they came out of the rush hour station. D called Arthur's attention to a dead bird on the ground. They stood in a line staring at it.
'Quite a young one, too,' remarked Dexter.
'Just about to begin life,' said Arthur.

Dexter & the sunset:
At sunset someone shouted outside her window. She opened it and saw Dexter and someone else on the pavement looking westward.
'Look at the sky!' shouted Vicki.
It was fiery down low, with little scalloped yellowish clouds high up against a thick grey backdrop.
'How do they do that?' said Dexter. 'Make the smaller clouds a different colour?'

Helen Garner—The Children's Bach

Dexter claimed he had never been in love. When he made this remark, Eliz gave a knowing, bitter laugh.
—What's so funny?
—You'll know, one day.
—I don't see why people think falling in love is inevitable. Anyone would think it was some kind of disease, or plague. People only fall in love because they want to. I don't want to, therefore I'm not going to.
—But weren't you in love with Athena? said Vicki, scandalised.
—No, said Dexter. Not in that tortured way you read about.
Vicki looked quickly at Athena, afraid she'd be hurt, but Athena is smiling and listening.

V did believe in love, or 'lerve' as Dexter scornfully called it; and she felt a dread, looking at his mocking and yet innocent face, of the moment when it would sweep down on him and knock him for six.

Dexter's kids in class. How rain calms them and wind drives them out of their minds.

Dexter hears someone else—Philip after he has visited Vicki?—singing in the shower, Oh I'm the kind of guy / who is always. . .Dexter never listened to commercial radio and did not recognise the famous song revived, but he wondered, What kind of 'guy' am I?

Dear Mister Fox, I am writting (sic) this letter because Mary was sick on the 19th of November pains in the stomach

Dexter teaching. A dull boy at the back cries out, Hey! I <u>understand</u> this!

The control that Billy wields over their singing round the house.
A: I've given it up, really. Have to teach myself again.
D: Learn to be spontaneous.

Making Stories

Dexter sings: 'I'll sing you a song of the fish of the sea, O, Rio!' in a big round pompous tuneful voice.
'All the birds sing up in the trees.'

Dexter remembers sitting, in a first year French lecture, in front of a Hungarian boy who, while they waited for the professor to arrive, tapped him on the shoulder & showed him [his copy of] the Hugo poem they were about to study, the epigraph of which was a phrase from Macbeth: 'Horror, horror, horror,' 'Look, Dexter,' said the Hungarian boy. '<u>Anyone</u> could have written that!'

She walks along beside him, gasbagging about her life.

SECTION FOUR: VICKI

<u>Three young blokes, 20 or so</u>. Plain, white, one of them plump.

Wasn't it awesome, when it came over the flats.
You can tell this isn't New York. If this had happened on Manhattan, everybody would be saying 'Oh, my Gahd.' Did you notice? Not one single person said 'Oh, my Gahd.'

'Our mother was American. But she died.'

Dexter calls her 'the young savage'.
V: When I'm miserable I feel like wearing tight clothes.

'Great. The rubbish is out. Athena must be back.'

Her surprise to find a pleasant, strong body under Dexter's unfashionable clothes.

[margin note] VISITING MOTHER
Watching from the front window she sees Athena's friend arrive to visit. The slow ritual of getting out of the car. The car door held open against the hip. The unstrapping of small bodies, the blue plastic nappy bag, the Maya temple colouring book: horror, horror, horror.

[margin note] Vicki to Athena
'You want to know what kind of a person Elizabeth is? She's the kind of person who doesn't hesitate / slow down when she approaches an automatic door. She buys herself a pair of jeans, & gives them to you straight away b/c they're stiff & she's too impatient to wear them in: then 3 mos later when they're all broken in & perfect, she asks for them back.'
Her expression. '(E's) <u>important</u> walk.'

Vicki is at the swimming pool when the dust storm comes. She is lonely. She hears the 'serious young insects' making their jokes, their voices trembling with excitement. '<u>Oh my Gahd</u>. If this was happening in New York, everyone would be saying <u>Oh my Gahd</u>.'
She wants to know them. They are talking about Eliz's & Ph's band.

She does circles over her i's instead of dots.
<u>What sort of a girl is she</u>?
—she suffers terribly from boredom
—she put hot coals in a plastic bucket & it melted
—she tips coffee grounds & tea leaves down into the sink
[added in margin]
She can't get used to the cold. Drunk, she burns her hand on the pipe of the pot-belly stove.

She wore her scarf like a noose

Vicki is revolted by what she calls the 'cappucino froth' on Dexter's piss.
'Why can't he pull the chain?'

Vicki gets her ears pierced.

What Vicki saw.
She had sat twisted with boredom on gilded chairs while Jerry watched her mother trying on expensive clothes.
(The gigolo)
(her mother's high heels, w metal chains for ankle straps)

Making Stories

Vicki: 'I don't remember ever knowing Eliz. till I was 12. [margin note] (younger.) 'And I hated it when she visited because Mum fought with her' etc.

Vicki copies Ath's handwriting

Vicki had been ~~was~~ the teenager twisting on the chair [margin note] (in salons) beside the vain, smooth-skinned man who advised her mother which jacket to buy.

Vicki is scared of spending money. Her mother was extravagant.
'Monn-e-tary' instead of mercenary.

V: What do you do, without TV?
A: Lots of things. Read. Play the piano.
V: Oh yes—I heard you plinking away in there and I thought, 'Poor Thena!'

In the spring wind, Vicki takes William for a walk in the park.

Vicki is <u>new company</u> for Athena. She has nothing else to <u>do</u>, follows her around.

V likes the toilet. Bks in there? The first train at dawn. HOT NIGHTS: They drag their mattresses outside & sleep on the grass.

Eliz: 'Bunker Street is her <u>god</u>'

Vicki knew Athena liked Philip, because whenever he came round her nose went red.

Vicki's naive pleasure in her haircut. All smiles.
'Now I feel <u>terrific</u>. Is that red mark at the back of my neck still there? Do you know what it is? She cut that squared-off bit at the back with the shears.'
'Clippers?'
'Yes! Clippety clip! And once she was going clippety clip right into my skin!' She gave a high, excited laugh.

Helen Garner—The Children's Bach

On Vicki's first morning: she opens the bathroom door & sees a rosy haze of steam, pierced by bars of sunlight, a haze in which Athena's pale body—elongated, shanky legs, rounded belly & slightly drooping breasts—is stepping smoothly out of the shower, reaching for the towel.
'Sorry!' cries Vicki. She steps back & slams the door, moved like someone who's just seen a great painting.

[margin note] READINGS' WINDOW
Vicki's unhappiness at Elizabeth's. She goes looking in Readings' window (where she runs into Athena who is only fantasising) THIS IS WHERE THEY MEET AGAIN: Athena at first doesn't recognise her.
Vicki: 'Look at this one:
To let: one room, limited daylight only, $18 pr wk, bond $50, rent covers gas and electricity. NB house not communal.

Athena sees Vicki's nascent sense of humour. When V moves in, she wants A to look at her notes from an excursion. A is not interested, V insists. A realises V is trying to show herself.

V: 'My friend went & had colonic irrigations. The lady who did them found stuff inside her that she'd eaten 10 years ago.'
D: 'How could she tell?'

Vicki is a hypochondriac:
'I feel as if part of my brain has come away.'
'I feel as if all my period didn't come out.'

[Margin note] Eliz to V.
'They just look on your card, and if you're a hypochondriac it shows.'

Vicki starts to hang round ~~Urquhart~~ Bunker Street. They hear her old pushbike crash against the rubbish bins & she springs up the concrete steps. Even at breakfast time. Stays an hour. Eats a poached egg Dexter has just cooked for himself; makes herself useful & pleasant. Laces Arthur's boots for him. He submits with a patient smile./ He can do it h'self./

Making Stories

V: 'Can I walk down to school with you? Do you mind?'
A: (absently) 'Yes.'
V: 'You <u>do</u> mind?'
A: 'I mean, yes, you can come.'

Vicki and Dexter:
She stared down at his face which was quite still, eyes closed, half-smiling. She gazed at his face which the moonlight had transformed, all the lines were wiped away, she was looking at a stranger, his skin was smooth, he looked like a calm-faced, tranquil woman. He was nothing to do with Dexter: he was a placid creature just found, it was hers, no-one else even knew it existed. The mysterious Buddha face, sphinx, mermaid, on the pillow: him not at all, yet nobody else either. She did not touch the face: only looked.

[margin note] other way round.
Athena dozes. She hears Vicki singing in the kitchen, washing the dishes. She feels <u>looked after</u>. D does not like her when she's sick. Makes her a milky soup.

Vicki tries for the tone of Elizabeth:
'I'm so elegant now, I ought to be lined up & <u>shot</u>.' How this pricks Athena's heart.

She opens a cupboard & a rubber glove falls out in a gesture of appeal.

'My toes are so cold they feel like marbles in my boots.'

They are talking about skin cream. Vicki feels Elizabeth's hand. 'Oh! Your skin is so <u>soft</u>!'
E: 'It bloody well ought to be, the amount of money I spend on skin cream.'
(They all feel each other's hands).
V: (to Elizabeth, pretending to be hurt) 'You haven't said mine are soft.'

Vicki finally unloads the stories of Elizabeth: screaming in the restaurant. GET THE DATES RIGHT.

Helen Garner—The Children's Bach

The curtain story from the red diary (would this work, because of dates?) Perhaps this was the shock for Vicki: that before she died her mother was already weakening. All the crying: 'I cried all night. When I woke up in the morning my eyes were so swollen that I looked like a <u>cane</u> toad.'

Billy was already up when Vicki woke. He stamped /and shuffled/ about the house, making his grieving, wailing cries, sometimes sliding into song, puffing and humming for a moment, then giving a series of light screams.

The siren: he covered his ears with his palms and uttered high shrieks of distress or pain: he seized Vicki's wrist in a tight grip (his hands were muscular and warm) and at the same time savagely bit the meaty part of his own thumb.

Athena was already dressed, standing by the table. Billy got up off the bed and approached her. He put out his hands to the waistband of
her grey jumper, which had a wide black stripe, and folded it up, carefully, so that an inch of bare skin showed between her jumper and her trousers. He did this slowly and with great deliberation, so that the jumper was turned up equally all round. The others watched him without speaking.

Vicki imitates Eliz's broad social manner. This mollifies E. Vicki sticks out her hand to Dexter, to say goodbye. 'I've enjoyed being with you,' she says. Later she says to Eliz. 'I've changed my mind about Dexter. I think he's rather handsome.'

V is privately amused that A offers her seat in the bus to an older person. To V, A is already in the category to whom seats are offered: no age at all, just old.

The notes they leave for each other, the funny drawings and silly rhymes, the embarrassing singing, the vegetable garden, the apparent fluster over the generous order,

Making Stories

the rushes of activity followed by sunny calm: Vicki was in love with the house and the family. 'Bunker Street is her <u>god</u>,' says Elizabeth.

'<u>Moss</u>? Pfft. She absorbed <u>pollen</u> through her <u>skin</u>?' Girl in shoe shop commenting on radio news bulletin about girl ship-wrecked and found three years later in the jungle of Sumatra covered in moss but still alive

V to Eliz, describing a genre of contemporary horror movie:
'You know?—she drives up to this house & gets dismembered.'

Vicki hangs up phone after conversation w Christian, & thinks in disappointment, 'She didn't say "God bless you".'

In clothes shop: if the saleswoman rebukes her for touching, she will retort bitterly, 'Oh, don't be <u>silly</u>.'

Vicki at the baths. Ath. notes that she has shaved her pubic hair. 'It's my birthday! I made a point of getting up early before 3 o'clock so I could get down here before dark!'

Vicki goes to the University.

Vicki rides to the Fitzroy Gardens to see the Italian weddings.

Vicki enjoys the company of young kids. She sat at the table for hours & giggled with them, drawing & colouring in, making up silly words. 'The two mermaids murmured to each other: mur-mur.'

Vicki goes to a 'hat party.' She tied a diaphanous scarf round her head, stuck a yellow rose in it, & put a lot of makeup on her flat, smooth, pale face. She looked striking, & flustered because of the lipstick she had rubbed into her cheekbones.

Helen Garner—The Children's Bach

Extract 2 from the published version

The Children's Bach, pp 26–30 and 33–8

Athena's life was mysterious to Vicki. She seemed contained, without needs, never restless.
'I'm bored,' said Vicki. 'Un-bore me, Thena!'
Athena laughed. 'I don't even know what boredom is.'
But how could she not know? thought Vicki, watching jealously out the front window the arrival of Athena's friend to visit with her two children: the slow ritual of getting out of the car, the back door held open against the hip, the unstrapping of small bodies, the unloading of the blue plastic nappy bag, the toys, the pencils, the Viking helmet, the Maya temple colouring book; the endless patience with the whining, twining children; the slow talking about nothing in particular; the friend gasbagging about health and sickness while Athena stood ironing at the board, keeping her head half-turned to show that she was still listening.
'The woman next door,' said the friend, 'went and had colonic irrigations. And the lady who did them found stuff inside her that she'd eaten *ten years* ago!'
'How could she tell?' said Athena.
'*Anyway*,' said the friend, 'she rang up and told me he'd gone off with some *child*, a girl of eighteen, So I said to her, "Get some interesting knitting. Something with a complicated pattern. And stay home and just *sit it out*." And that's what she did.'
They were talking like this when Vicki left to have her hair cut, and they were still talking like this when she got back, the only difference being that the table was now covered in dirty cups and cake crumbs.
'Look!' cried Vicki. 'Now I feel *terrific*. Is that red mark on the back of my neck still there? Do you know what that is? She cut the squared-off bit at the back with those shears.'
'Clippers?' said the friend.
'Yes! Clippety clip! And once she was going clippety clip right into my skin!' She gave a high, excited laugh.
The two mothers looked at her with their calm smiles. She felt as jerky as a puppet.
'Last time I had my hair cut short back home,' Vicki chattered on, rushing to the round mirror in the corner, 'I looked so ugly that I cried all night. And when I woke up in the morning my eyes were so swollen that I looked like a *cane toad*!'
'You certainly don't look ugly now,' said the friend, in her slow drawl.

'I know!' said Vicki. 'I'm so elegant now that I ought to be lined up and *shot*!'

The friend laughed, but Athena heard Vicki trying for Elizabeth's smart tone, and it squeezed her heart.

Vicki began to hang round the Foxes' house in Bunker Street earlier each day. They heard her old pushbike crash against the rubbish bins at breakfast time. She sprang up the concrete steps, checked her hair in the glass, and stayed an hour; ate an egg that Dexter had poached for himself; tried to make herself useful and agreeable, though she was domestically incompetent; she tipped tea-leaves down the sink and blocked it; she put embers from the pot-belly stove into a plastic bucket and melted it. But she began to know where things were, she was cheerful company, she laughed at Dexter's jokes, she played with Arthur. She laced his boots for him, though he had been able to do it himself for years.

'Can I walk down to school with you?' she said. 'Do you mind?'

'Yes,' said Arthur, with his nose in a cereal packet.

'You do mind?'

'I mean yes, you can come.'

When the mail arrived and Athena opened envelopes, Vicki watched and said, 'I never get any letters.'

Athena suppressed an impulse to say, 'You can read mine.'

Vicki loved their lavatory in the corner of the yard, its shelves made of brick and timber stuffed with old paperbacks, broken tools, camping gear and boxes of worn-down coloured pencils. She loved the notes they left for each other, the drawings and silly rhymes, the embarrassing singing, the vegetable garden, the fluster under which lay a generous order, the rushes of activity followed by periods of sunny calm: Vicki was in love with the house, with the family, with the whole establishment of it.

'Bunker Street is her *god*,' said Elizabeth.

Dexter was flattered. 'I feel sentimental when I see you, Morty,' he said. 'Why don't you bring this Philip round here?'

'Philip? What would I bring him here for?'

'He's your bloke, isn't he? Aren't you going to get married one of these days?'

Elizabeth shouted with laughter. 'Marry *him*? Forget it! He's already married! And anyway can you see me as a married woman?'

Dexter clenched his fists and danced up and down on the spot. 'But I *want* you to be happily married!'

Elizabeth raised her eyes to the ceiling.

'I don't understand the way you live,' said Dexter. 'What are the rules? Does he – you know – betray you?'

'Of course he bloody "betrays" me,' said Elizabeth. 'When you've been with someone that long, what else is there to do?'

Dexter flung out his arms and turned to Vicki who was at the mirror by the piano trying to tie a scarf round her head.

'I hate modern life,' he said. 'Modern American manners.'

'It's just love,' said Vicki, turning and twisting to get a back view of herself.

'Love!' roared Dexter. 'I've never been in love, then. In *lerv*e. I don't even know what it is. What's so funny?'

'You'll find out one day,' said Elizabeth.

'I don't see why people think falling *in lerv*e is inevitable,' said Dexter. 'Anyone would think it was some kind of disease, or plague. People only fall in lerve because they've read about it in some cheap American magazine, because they *want* to, because they're bored and have nothing better to do. I don't want to, therefore I'm not going to.'

'But weren't you in love with Athena?' said Vicki, scandalised.

'No,' said Dexter. 'Not in that tortured way you read about.'

Vicki looked quickly at Athena, afraid she would be hurt, but Athena was smiling and listening.

'You're not really a scarf person, are you, Vicki,' said Elizabeth. Vicki yanked the scarf off her head.

'Who's the pianist round here?' said Elizabeth. She flipped up the lid and struck a note or two.

'Athena plays, don't you dear,' said Dexter.

'Well, I'm learning,' said Athena. She was keeping her back to the room.

'How about playing us something?' said Elizabeth.

'Oh no – I'm hopeless.'

'Come on. No false modesty.'

'No, really!' said Athena. She turned from the sink with the knife in her hand. 'You don't realise what an elementary stage I'm at.'

'You can't be that bad,' said Elizabeth. She opened the book. '*The Children's Bach*. God, listen to this – how pompous. "Bach is never simple, but that is one reason why we should all try to master him." Show us how you've mastered him, Athena!'

'Oh, please don't make me,' said Athena. 'Please. I can hardly play at all.'

'It's true,' said Vicki. 'She can't. You play like a mouse. I heard you plinking away in here the other day and I thought, poor Thena!'

Athena turned back to the sink.

'Yes, dear,' said Dexter. 'You ought to practise when you're the only one home.' He turned over a page of the newspaper. 'It's a bit dreary having to listen to someone picking their way through those pieces.'

He sat reading at the table with Billy on his knee. Vicki folded the scarf. Athena shifted the potatoes about under the dribbling tap.

Elizabeth braced herself. 'Vicki wouldn't remember this,' she said, 'but our mother had a saying. She told it to me when I realised my voice wasn't going to be quite as fabulous as I'd hoped. *If only those birds sang that sang the best, how silent the woods would be.*'

'Clumsy syntax,' said Dexter. '*Woods* and *would* right next to each other.'

'Say it again?' said Athena.

'*If only those birds sang – that sang the best – how silent the woods would be.*'

'She must have been a nice woman,' said Athena.

'I don't know if nice is quite the word,' said Elizabeth. 'She was the sort of person who'd put on Ravel's *Bolero* first thing in the morning. And she had a voice like somebody falling off a mountain.'

'Shutup, Elizabeth,' said Vicki. 'She *was* nice! She was! Just because *you* didn't –'

'She used to like ironing,' said Elizabeth. The easy stuff – you know, tablecloths, hankies. She got cancer.'

'I know,' said Athena. 'Vicki told me.'

'She wouldn't go into hospital,' said Vicki.

'That must have made things hard for you,' said Athena. What selfishness, she thought. *I* would have been more sensible. 'Why on earth wouldn't she go?'

'Well,' said Elizabeth, 'I suppose that would have been admitting to herself that she was going to die.'

It was a patient and courteous answer to an ignorant question. Athena felt ground drop away from under her feet. She hung over a black gulf, she heard the wind. Her self was in tantrum, panicking. *What? Me* die? Life go on without *me*? Impossible! It was briefer than a pulse. It was over before she had time to gasp. She held the hard potato in her hand. For the first time she looked at Elizabeth properly, with open face.

* * *

So Vicki came to live with the Fox family at Bunker Street. They moved the junk out of the small room behind the kitchen; it overlooked the vegetable garden and the shed and the rabbit's cage and the Hills Hoist and the European trees, thick with new leaves, that grew along the banks of the Merri Creek. Athena and Vicki painted the room yellow. 'I'll be like a chicken in an egg,' said Vicki. Elizabeth thought the yellow was rather ochreous, but in her relief she kept this opinion to herself. She went home on the tram and was surprised to find a small lack in herself, a blankness where the unwelcome responsibility had been. She flung the pink quilt out to air over the windowsill and went into the city to buy herself a pair of shoes.

Early in the morning Vicki lay with the striped sheet over her nose. Billy was on the loose in the house, a forlorn seeker. He stamped and shuffled down the hallway, in and out of rooms. He puffed and hummed as he went, he tested his voice in a series of light screams, he lapsed again into his grieving, wailing cries. He stopped outside her door. She lay still. He laughed under his breath and shoved at the door with his shoulder, grunted, gave a breathy screech, and wandered away again on dragging feet towards the room where his parents would be sitting up in their big bed reading, like two figures on a tomb. Vicki sprang up and ran across the kitchen to the bathroom. She pushed open the door. The room was not empty. She saw a rosy haze of steam pierced by bars of sunlight, a haze in which Athena – lanky legs, rounded belly, drooping breasts with pearl-grey radiating stretchmarks – was stepping out of the shower and reaching for a towel.

'Sorry!' said Vicki. She stepped back and slammed the door. She was shocked and moved, like a tourist who, bored in a gallery, has turned a corner and come face to face with a famous painting. She sat down on a kitchen chair with her towel across her lap. The window had twelve square panes. Last night's dishes stood in order in the rack.

Dexter insisted on cooking the spaghetti. He stood before the stove in a puddle of oil. The women hid in one of the bedrooms but his volleys of oaths, his tremendous singing drove them as far as the bottom of the yard.

'Morty!' he roared. 'Remember that little old lady we used to see at the Vietnam demonstrations? Must have been 1966. "Fuckin' mu - u - urderers!"' He burst into the drinking chorus from *La Traviata*.

'Hey Dexter!' called Vicki from the back garden. 'Come and have a look at this!'

'All right all right all *right*.' He appeared at the top of the concrete steps.

'Look at the sky!'

It was fiery down low, with scalloped yellowish clouds high up against a grey backdrop.

'Marvellous!' said Dexter. 'How do they do that? Make the smaller clouds a different colour?'

The three women stood in a row on the path and looked up at him. Their attention! He loved it. 'That's what they should have on TV every night,' he shouted. 'Not that violent American rubbish. They should have the Sunset Report. Brought to you by the Federal Department of Nature Appreciation.' He held up his wooden spoon like a wand and dropped the rest of his body into a limp arabesque. Their laughter flowed up the steps to him.

'Where's the nearest pub?' said Elizabeth. 'I'm going to buy a bottle of gin.'

Poppy brought a book. When everyone had been introduced she took the end chair and began to read with her hands round her face like blinkers.

'This is the last time I let you do this,' said Philip.

'Do what?'

'Read in company.'

'But it's boring!'

'It's rude.'

Poppy smiled and shrugged. Athena stood by the door and watched. Philip, glancing about him for support, caught her eye. He was surprised: she looked *dignified*; her limbs were narrow, her hips were wide, her hands were large and cracked. Her hair looked as if she had cut it herself, pulled it forward and chopped at it. She blushed, and he kept her glance in his and nodded several times: it might have been the courteous nod that accompanies formal introduction, except that they had already been introduced. Elizabeth strode in with an armful of bottles and a bag of ice. Vicki ran out for a lemon off the tree and cut it up. The kitchen was full of people smiling, shifting an elbow or a foot to make room, saying 'Sorry!'

'What book are you reading?' asked Arthur in his loud, sociable voice.

Poppy turned up the cover to show him.

'I've seen you on TV,' shouted Arthur.

'Who, me?' said Elizabeth.

'No, him.'

Philip shook his head. 'Couldn't have been me, mate.'

Poppy looked up from her book and directed a blank, level stare at her father.

'Yes I have!' said Arthur. 'On Countdown. You had longer hair and a sparkly shirt.'

Elizabeth laughed. 'Sparkly!' Philip dropped his head and smiled. They began to eat.

'He doesn't actually go on TV,' said Poppy. 'He makes up songs, and he does sessions at night. Is there meat in this?'

'If you go on Countdown you get a lot of money,' said Arthur. 'They pay you a *lot* of money.'

'Oh, they do not,' said Poppy.

'Some Countdown people were making a clip in the park once,' said Arthur urgently. He was bolting his food. 'They said I might be able to go in it. They were going to pay me about two hundred dollars.'

'Bullshit,' said Poppy. 'Countdown don't make those clips. They just put them on TV.'

'I want to get one ear-ring,' said Arthur.

'Don't be silly, Arthur,' said Dexter.

'A boy at school's got one.'

'Why don't you get a tat?' said Elizabeth.

'A what?'

'A tattoo,' said Philip. He put down his fork and rolled his shirt sleeve up to his shoulder. It was a very small butterfly. Muscles and green veins rolled under his skin; his forearm was covered with fine black hairs. Arthur was so thrilled he could not speak. He gulped down the rest of his plateful. Athena could not help staring at Philip. Whenever she took her eyes away she felt him looking at her. It seemed they took it in turns.

'Have you been to America, Philip?' said Vicki.

'The sort of singer who lounges across a glass piano,' said Elizabeth.

'I like to have tortellini of a Friday,' said Philip.

'She was wearing these daggy flares,' said Elizabeth, 'with embroidered insets.'

'I got my hand jammed between two speaker boxes,' said Philip. 'My finger burst like a sausage.'

'You know?' said Vicki. 'One of those horror movies where she drives up to this house and gets dismembered?'

'I got to Reno on the bus at eight o'clock in the morning,' said Philip. 'People were stumbling about the streets in full evening dress.'

'She had all the colour and dynamism of a parsnip,' said Elizabeth. 'You could not by any stretch of the imagination drum up any feelings of sisterhood for her.'

'We've got a rabbit in a cage,' said Arthur.

'I walked in to our first gig,' said Philip, 'and they were sticking red cellophane over the lights. I thought, Oh *no*.'

'I went through centuries of torture,' said Elizabeth. 'I'd emerge exhausted from the Crusades and the Black Death only to realise that I still had to drag myself through the entire Spanish Inquisition. I never touched it again.'

'They only cost twenty-five dollars,' said Vicki, 'so I bought two pairs.'

'Does anyone want more spaghetti?' said Athena.

Dexter got up and cranked open a tin of pears.

'Sing something,' said Poppy to Elizabeth. 'Sing "Breaking Up Is Hard To Do".'

'Oh, not that,' said Philip.

'You do the come-ah come-ah,' said Elizabeth to Philip.

They sang. Billy flung himself about in Dexter's arms, loopy, with rolling eyes. Their rhythm was solid, they slid their eyes sideways to meet, and smiled as if to mock each other for their unerring harmonies. Athena saw they were professionals. The piano is such a lonely instrument, she thought: always by yourself with your back to the world. This music, thought Dexter irritably, is American music. He remembered Dr A. E. Floyd's quavering voice on the radio: 'Some people pronounce it Pur*cell*: that's an Ameddicanism.' The song ended. 'Now *we*'ll sing,' said Dexter. He put down Billy, who wandered away; he made Arthur come and stand beside his chair, and they sang 'The Wild Colonial Boy'. Arthur had the long song wordperfect. He stood to attention and threw back his head on the high notes. Vicki watched with a cold eye. 'I suppose,' thought Elizabeth, 'that he is trying to keep something alive.' It embarrassed her to see the righteous set of Dexter's mouth between verses: she looked away.

Drunk on performance, Dexter hardly let a pause fall before he cried, 'And now I'll sing "When I Survey the Wondrous Cross".' '... And pour contempt on aw-haw-hawl my pride,' he bawled. He drew breath and looked around him, smiling, with tear-filled eyes, his right arm still extended in its melodramatic curve. No-one spoke. Poppy turned a page.

'Mind if I sing another stanza?' he said.

'Yes,' said Vicki. 'I do. Hymns are boring.'

Had anyone ever crossed Dexter before? *Had* anyone? He jerked back as if he had been struck. His chair splintered under him and he saved himself only by flexing his legs and grabbing the corner of the table with one hand.

The gin bottle was empty.

'Why was that teenager so rude to that man when he was singing?' said Poppy on the way home.

'Who knows,' said Philip.

'But I like the mother,' said Poppy. 'Athena's perfect, isn't she.'

'Perfect – you reckon?' said Philip.

Elizabeth looked at him. 'She'd have to be, to live up to the name.'

'The goddess of war,' said Philip.

'I didn't mean *that* perfect,' said Poppy.

'Of war and needlecraft,' said Elizabeth.

Kate Grenville
Lilian's Story

My first thought was: Okay, this is good raw material for a book; now I have to make it into a flowing narrative...The biggest struggle I had was to recognise that those fragments were not preliminary notes, they were the structure of the book itself.

Kate Grenville

23

Aunt Kitty was a phálosopher and a happy widow. Uncle Forbes had passed away in theirty second of terribly anguish, his fingers clutching the shirt over his ~~heart~~ chest so that it tore in a long shred. He was a serene corpse. It was a long time ago, Aunt Kitty said confortably as she poured barley water.

Visits to Aunt Kitty were always queer.
~~In the early~~ days, when ~~Laura~~ had visited Aunt ~~Bea with her mother,~~ Kitty things ~~were not too far gone.~~1 Sometimes ~~her aunt~~ Aunt Kitty would be wearing six different dresses, one on top of the othter, starting with the longest so that each uneven layter of hem could be seen like a book of carpet-samples. ~~Or the dusty coffee-table would be poled with empty snail-shells from the garden.~~ and Mother hummed on the way home as she did Visits were short, ~~on those days~~ but visits continued to be made. not often I'd like to eat my past, Kitty Aunt ~~Bea~~ might say over her ~~cup of tea~~ barley water. do, and smiled to herself. Just spread on thin bread wwith the crusts ~~cut off and~~ pop it into my mouth. ~~Laura's mother would laugh and glance at her daughter to make sure she had not thought this important.~~ Mother's Kitty's Laura's ~~mother;s~~ laugh, in Aunt ~~Bea's~~ house, had a ~~rough loud~~ edge it never revealed at home. It was easier to imagine her posing with the stuffed donkey when she sat, Kitty's legs carefully crossed, on Aunt ~~Bea~~ soft from which kapok puffed out each time she moved. Only here was it possible to imagine her sillier.

Making Stories

As her contribution to *Making Stories*, Kate Grenville gave a hand-written manuscript extract that at first glance read very much like the published version of *Lilian's Story*, except that the narrative seemed a little out of order. She said that, despite this similarity, they were in fact the very first pages she had written.

I knew that the novel had gone through many, many drafts, and I had always assumed that the drafts were spent finding and maintaining the distinctive story-telling tone of *Lilian's Story*. They weren't. But in our interview, Grenville explained why she felt she needed to do so much re-working.

My interview with Kate Grenville took place in Sydney, March 1992.

S.W.

INT: How did the writing of *Lilian's Story* begin?

KG: It began in a sort of soup—lots of completely disconnected things going on in my mind. The first was that I'd just finished *Dreamhouse* and was sick to death of living in that cynical bloodless world. I wanted to live in the book of a positive, vital, cheery kind of world for a while. Another was that I was just about to come back to Australia after seven years away, and I was starting to think about the place, through the distorting—or maybe clarifying—lens of distance. And one of the images of Sydney that I came across, turning over images in my mind, was Bea Miles, a famous Sydney eccentric of my growing-up days. A bag-lady, but a cheerful soul. What I was reading had nothing to do with Sydney, though: I was reading the letters of Jane Austen and Flaubert.

Well, all those elements were going on, and I was making desultory notes as I was reading the Jane Austen letters, and suddenly a sentence leaped out at me from the page: 'In the nights we invent a few hard names for the stars.' I wrote it down and found myself writing the fragment about Bea Miles sitting on the beach [the beginning of Extract 1].

At that stage I knew hardly anything about the real Bea Miles, and I certainly didn't know that I was beginning to write a book about a person rather like her. She and the sentence from Jane Austen connected, that was all I knew, but if I'd been asked then, I probably would have said she was going to be a minor character in the book—as she is in the third-person fragments [see Extract 1, pages 110, 115].

Kate Grenville—Lilian's Story

At that time I didn't allow myself to think any further than: here is a character, a setting and a tone that interest me. If I stir the waters around, I may come across other interesting things. And out of that may come the subject of a novel.

The more I wrote about her...well, two things started to happen. The first was I realised that the voice she spoke with was the voice I wanted to write in. I knew I was going to enjoy that voice. The other was that, slowly, I realised that she was going to be central.

INT: Did you do any research into her life?

KG: Not until much, much later. I researched her after I'd written many drafts, in fact. Because in the beginning I wanted to...see, I wasn't all that interested in the real Bea Miles, but in what she represented to me. As I wrote more and more, she—at least my idea of her—began to embody ideas I'd been vaguely mulling over for quite a while—about how a woman gets to write her own life, rather than have it written for her. How a woman gets to turn her back on all the things women are supposed to want, and invent another set of priorities. How it feels to be a big loud rude active woman instead of a little meek polite one. *Dreamhouse* had been a book about passivity and lack of self-knowledge—the exact mirror image of that.

Looking back now, it's almost as if I had written one side of the equation in *Dreamhouse* and wanted to write the other side. But I was pretty sure that if I found out too much about the real Bea Miles I would be locked in then, to her. My own imagination would be blinkered. So I wrote perhaps three drafts of the book, and then I went in to the State Library and read about her a bit. *Lilian's Story* overlaps with the life of Bea Miles in a few places, but that's all—it's not really about her at all.

I just kept on reading Jane Austen's letters and Flaubert's letters, and every time I got to a bit I liked the sound of—I didn't analyse why, or wonder how I might use it as part of a book, particularly—every time I got to a bit I liked, I'd use it as a starting point for a short piece of writing. It was almost free association, but free association within the magnetic field, if you like, of the image of a big powerful woman whose empire was the streets of Sydney. I riffled through a lot of reading in that kind of opportunistic bower-bird way: my feelers were just out for anything that took my eye.

Some lines—that line [Extract 1, page 110] about 'Beatrice was briefly beautiful'—came to me as lines are said to come to poets, like a rather tantalising offering of a beginning, then you're on your own. I would have written that sentence down and then used it as as sort of contemplative device, not caring much what it meant, but more just musing around the possibilities suggested by it.

I wanted to get away from any sequential or logical process. It was an invitation for the mind to leap around rather than walk. It was just a stab in the dark.

INT: What other kinds of elements did you 'stir around'?

KG: My own memories of childhood, particularly schoolyard memories, went into the stew—I suddenly realised how I could use those in a way that made them not just boring old self-regarding autobiography. I could give them to this woman who was starting to take shape in my mind and they could be transformed. Also as I wrote the book—I was back in Australia then—people told me stories about Bea Miles, and with some of those I thought yes, I can use that. For example the 'short and curlies' fragment [Extract 1, page 111] was actually told to me by the man who'd been that projectionist thirty years before.

As I started to home in on the idea of Bea Miles a bit more, as I realised that I could use her as my central character, it was natural to start to look at Shakespeare. Bea Miles was famous for quoting Shakespeare outside the Public Library—sonnets were threepence, a scene from a play was sixpence. *The Tempest* was the play I used most obsessively in the book.

INT: Which part of *The Tempest*?

KG: Oh, at first I'd just flip through it in a very wicked way, until I came to a good line. But after a while, I realised it was the perfect play to use, because it's about someone inventing a world. Later on I realised it had all kinds of other things that I came, very slowly, to see as important to the book I was writing. The book's full of lines from *The Tempest*. 'Every third thought shall be my grave' and 'I would fain die a dry death'—they're just wonderful lines. Shakespeare—even at his most serious moments—his writing has that glee in the sheer putting-together of words, and reading him heightened my own sense of what you should be able to demand of words.

There were other things, too. While I was writing the book I went to the National Gallery and I saw paintings there that just ...exhilarated me. *Blue Poles* was one, and that Tiepolo ceiling where you're looking up the bums of all the cherubs, and some of Nolan's Ned Kelly pictures. They were so *bold*! I kept repeating the word, I remember, in a sort of astonishment. That Kelly one where the picture's dominated by a black-and-white check floor with just little characters round the edge—I thought, what a terrific and outrageous thing to do. I suppose it shows how backward I am about visual art that I found those so exciting. But I did. I remember coming back and throwing myself back into the book with renewed energy—it wasn't that there was anything I could use directly from the pictures, it wasn't even really the pictures themselves, but that sense of risk-taking.

INT: As well as pieces of narrative, this extract also shows you more or less talking to yourself...would you have done that at the end of a day's work?

KG: It might have been at the beginning of the day's work: if I'd written myself out the day before, then the next morning I wouldn't have known how to begin and I might have started by writing out some of these plot possibilities, which I might have been thinking about on and off during the time I hadn't been writing. Or, I might just run out of momentum during a writing session, and all these musings to myself are possible ways to get going again.

INT: As you say, Jane Austen's letters and Flaubert seem a long way from Bea Miles—what was it you found so useful in all those other writings?

KG: It was my way of getting the voice. That very first line about the hard names for the stars—it's true that I could give that actual thought to Lilian—but mainly it was the tone of it, the tone I wanted to be able to write in, that kind of expansive, confident, slightly self-mocking voice. I knew I wanted to write in that voice.

INT: Is it a process of finding and using a voice that transfigures your own perception?

KG: Yes, because it's not my own voice. I had to find it. That was the great breakthrough with *Lilian's Story*, which I hadn't had with other things I'd written. I found a voice that was not my own, but which I could use with joy and confidence. But finding that voice was not enough, I kept losing it.

INT: How did you re-find that voice, day by day?

KG: I kept having to remind myself of it. I had a shelf full of those books—the Austen and the Shakespeare and so on—and I kept refreshing myself at them. It wasn't always that *they* had quite that tone I was after, but somehow reading them put *me* in that tone of voice. There were certain phrases that I kept using because they were so evocative, and each time I used them I felt that I could still use them again. I began to think of them as being like mantras, things to contemplate. When I was really despairing of the whole thing, I would go back to a phrase that I knew in previous times had sparked off a good paragraph or two, and I'd try it again. You can see that happening in the extract [page 113]—'every third thought shall be my grave'—I was obviously having a bad day that day and couldn't get very far the first time; I wrote a paragraph and came to an end. Then I went back to the phrase again, and whereas the first time it had sparked off a thought about making sandcastles when she was a little girl, the second time it's about when she's an old woman waiting for death. I would have written those within minutes of each other.

Sometimes those mantras led to meaningless and truly self-indulgent dead-ends but I let them go. I thought: the thing at this stage is to get the language, the feel, not the meaning, I can work later on what it might mean and get rid of the nonsense.

INT: Did you do a lot of rewriting?

KG: Once I got the voice each time, once I was on tune, the stuff just flowed. I didn't actually rewrite the words very much at all. I threw out chunks, but it wasn't a matter of rewording sentences.

INT: So if it flowed, does that mean you wrote it very fast?

KG: It didn't feel fast. I had a sort of daily quota—after I'd written five pages, I'd say to myself: If you want to finish now, you can. But until I'd written five pages I wouldn't allow myself to do anything else. I followed Flannery O'Connor's idea that you should make yourself write simply by sitting at the desk. You're not allowed to do anything else, but as long as you cover those pages, it doesn't matter what you write. Using that idea I wrote an awful lot of rubbish about the view out of my shed window, the washing on the line, but it nearly always turned after a page or so into something usable. And it gave me great faith in that method. It's as if the putting-together-of-words part of your brain has to be activated, and it doesn't matter what activates it, a shopping list would almost do.

But there were many days when covering five pages was like drawing teeth. I'd get going and then come to complete stop, and have to start again in some completely different place, perhaps using one of my faithful mantras. Some days even that didn't work and the five pages were just junk.

It felt difficult to write. The voice flowed, that's true. The difficulty was partly that I had a paucity of incidents. I didn't know what I could make to happen. I had the voice to say it in, and a sense that I would arrive at underlying ideas that would give it some substance, but I was always scratching around for things actually to happen. When I'd think of something or come across something, it'd give me a great burst, I'd write very quickly then for a while, after which I'd be stuck until I could think of the next little node-point—a place where I could get a couple of characters together, perhaps, and something happening.

INT: The fragments are mostly about the same person, obviously the same characters, and they have the same mood and the same tone. I have the impression that you didn't have much trial and error with that part of it.

KG: Not too much, but there were lots of false starts in the early fragments. For a long time I thought it might be a third-person book—looking at the Bea character from the outside. You can see [on page 115], where I have a go at telling it as a third-person story from the point of view of Bea's niece. But that just didn't work, mainly because it didn't let me use the voice I'd started to enjoy so much, the voice from the letters and Shakespeare.

But I went back to it and tried again a couple of pages later. It's the great problem with writing a book this way, you keep running out of steam and keep on artificially pumping yourself up to get up a head of steam again—there is no organic reason why you should keep going, there's no plot. That's why it jumps around like this. I came to the end of that childhood stuff [on pages 114–15], for example, and thought: Oh, maybe that's not going to work after all, let me have another go at the one I abandoned before, with Laura and Aunt Bea. I got a lot further with it that time—half a page—before deciding again that the tone was just awful. But in fact this *is* in the final book, the same scene but from Bea's point of view. I hit the right tone occasionally, but it's a bit tentative, and I can also see leftovers from the *Dreamhouse* tone—that bit about noxious corruption [on page 108] is straight out of the early drafts of *Dreamhouse*. The tense seemed to make a big difference too.

INT: So you would've liked a plot?

KG: When I have a plot from the beginning it can be a disadvantage, because it takes some of the element of surprise out of it for me. It can all slide along in a rather flat way. I seem to prefer to be plotless until quite late on, because that way I discover things I wouldn't otherwise.

When I ran out of steam in *Joan Makes History* I could fall back on some real event from history, whereas with *Lilian* I had to fall back on finding something colourful, something just beautiful in its own right, not connected to anything bigger. But you can't always write a book like that—every book has its own personality, and I seem to have to find a slightly different mechanism for keeping up that excitement in every book.

In fact, plot ideas gave me a lot of false starts. Some of those false starts had nothing wrong with them—they just didn't feel like part of this book. At some point I began to feel as if I was beginning to uncover several other books as well as *Lilian's Story*. Page 111 in the extract is one of them: those dots represent my awareness that there was a whole mass of stuff there waiting for me about history, who's in it and who gets left out. I could see that this was going to turn into another problem area, another preoccupation. I made a sort of mental note to come back to it. That sentence with the dots eventually became *Joan Makes History*.

INT: I remember that you had a lot of trouble at the end of *Lilian's Story*, ending it.

KG: That's right. Literally I couldn't think what the last scene could be, that would somehow be right.

I suppose part of it was that I knew that the only appropriate ending would be something like death, but with a first-person narrator it's difficult to manage that. I don't remember writing a lot of different versions of the end, although I might have. The problems must have just gone on in my head. When I did sit down to write, it came out very easily. Now I think about it, a friend told me at some stage that story at the end about the visit of the important religious person and Bea being whisked off for the day. Either I remembered it at just the right time, or he told it to me at just the right time—but in any case, I saw then how I could use it as the end.

INT: As you've said, you didn't start your story at the beginning and work in order. Can you talk about the shifts in your thinking about how to order the fragments?

KG: My image of Bea Miles was of course of her as an old woman, because all the famous stories are about Bea Miles as an old woman, and the few times I had seen her she was an old woman. So I suppose that's why these drafts start with her in her prime. But pretty early on it began to be apparent to me that the project of the book was to work out how she got there. So I began to work...well, I didn't *work* backwards, I *leapt* backwards then, to her childhood. It was a sort of pincer movement. I was fairly confident about writing her schooldays because I knew that I could use so much of my own. The mature Lilian I was fairly confident about too; I was confident that I could make that work because of the tone I'd got from Austen and Shakespeare. But the real mystery of the book was what happened in the middle. Something happened at some point that caused her life to take this particular turn. So in the writing I did a pincer movement from the two parts that I was confident about, the beginning and the end, and gradually began to tentatively feel my way into that middle part.

Everything I'd written previously, I'd written much more consciously than this book, and I'd thought very early about things like the motivation of my characters, and where the plot would go, and I'd had chapter-plans and all the rest of it.

When I did this first writing for *Lilian's Story*, I'd just finished two years of studying in the University of Colorado writing program, and finally—now that it was over—I had come round to the idea that maybe you could write books in a much more open-ended way. Maybe even that you should. Each day when I sat down to write, I'd have no idea, till I got going, whether I was going to write a scene from the end of the book or the beginning, or something that didn't seem to belong anywhere. That's why there wasn't so much a shift as a sort of pogo-sticking from one bit to the next, depending what happened to fall under my hand.

The shift actually came much later, I suppose, when I realised that the fragments were going to fit together—and it was now time to try and order them. Try and provide some sort of narrative thread. I would have had maybe a hundred pages of fragments at that stage.

INT: Was there much reshuffling?

KG: I don't remember the rearranging as being a great problem, because after I decided to tell it chronologically, the fragments fitted together fairly easily. During that rearranging I could begin to see the gaps in it, the bits where I hadn't written a fragment that the jigsaw needed. So by the same rather hit-and-miss method I wrote more fragments—trying not to shape them too knowingly to the gap I wanted to fill, although at the same time kind of holding in my mind that gap, and what sort of things might conceivably fill it. A kind of knowing and not-knowing at once.

The biggest struggle I had was to recognise that I had to go with the material in the way it had come to me. What I had was a pile of fragments, and my first thought was: Okay, this is good raw material for a book; now I have to make it into a flowing narrative. So I smoothed it all out. Instead of having each one being a jumpy little scene of its own, I made them flow together, and I even wrote little transitions to force them to flow when they didn't. And of course something terrible happened—it just all went dead. The same material—it just flattened out. That was the biggest struggle I had, recognising that those fragments were not preliminary notes, they were the structure of the book itself.

INT: That process of moving things around would seem to be a process of great logistical difficulty. Did you have lots of bits of paper that you reshuffled?

KG: I probably should have, but I was writing in exercise books at this time. I'd write it by hand in the exercise books in whatever order it came, then I'd number each fragment, and write instructions: now go to page 17, number 4, that kind of thing. Every once in a while I'd type out what I'd been writing, according to those instructions. Then usually I'd need to rearrange it again, and I'd cut up the typescript and hang bits together with sticky tape. I'd end up with a sort of fringe effect of little strips precariously taped together.

INT: You've spoken of enjoying that voice that you discovered—were there doubts, as well as the pleasures?

KG: There were endless doubts. The pleasure reigned supreme whenever the writing was just a private thing that I was doing for myself. The doubts started in as soon as I began to think of the world out there actually reading what I was writing. For the longest time, I didn't think *Lilian* was a book that would ever in any form be published—it was just something I was doing for my own pleasure, and one of these days I would start a real book. It was a secretive and almost shameful groping—I felt a shame at my own inability to work out what I was doing with the book. It felt very self-indulgent.

I used to read the book pages—reviews—and that fed the doubts. It's the job of the reviewer to analyse and judge, but those ways of thinking may not be at all useful for a person actually engaged in writing. If you ask yourself what your book's about you get all twisted up—at least that's my experience—and if you ask whether or not it works you'll always find fault with it. Getting into the critic or reviewer state of mind makes me timid as a writer. I start to play it safe and the writing gets strangled with sheer caution.

INT: How do you get around that?

KG: I find it a continuing problem. The best I can manage at the moment as a way of dealing with it is a sort of sleight-of-hand. I find going back to handwriting is good, because handwriting is very personal, very private. You can feel with handwriting that no one else is going to read it. Whereas on the typewriter or the computer it suddenly has that public look about it.

I also find writing in fragments is good, because while it's in fragments, I can tell myself: Well, this is obviously not the book, this is just the raw material, no one will read this but me. And of course I've stopped reading the book pages.

INT: What keeps you writing in the face of all these doubts?

KG: If you write for the reasons I think I do, as a way of contemplating problems—scratching the itch of something you don't understand—there's an inbuilt reason to keep going, no matter how strong your doubts are. There's an internal pressure to go on, not because you think what you produce is going to be worth it, but because you need to know something that you can only know by writing it.

INT: You've mentioned a lot of coincidences and chances that helped to shape the course of the novel...

KG: I had that sense of casting a very wide net, bringing in a whole lot of stuff to look at, and sorting through to find what I could use. I think—I may be wrong—but I think that whatever had happened to me, and whatever I had read, there would have been something in it that I could have turned to use. I think that's because the net that the book covers is so wide. It was something very broad that I wanted to explore, so it was a very broad band of input that I could have turned to use. Obviously things like someone telling me about the Pope or whoever it was visiting the hospice was a most wonderful thing, but I feel that if it hadn't been that it would have been something else. I would have remembered something else, or read something else.

INT: That sense of: If it hadn't been this event, it would have been another event, suggests that the book would have become *Lilian's Story* whatever chances had happened.

KG: I think so, because I think I so much wanted to explore the notion of a self-defining woman—that was such a powerful

Making Stories

    pre-occupation in my mind—that I probably would have found a way of doing it.
    But there was an element of magic about writing the book. There were times when I felt in direct relation to that voice, and that the book was—as they say—'writing itself' through me. But I don't think in fact that it *is* magic. I think it's that my image of that person released something latent in me, released one of the voices in me. Lilian's voice felt very natural to me, although it's not a voice I ever use in my own life. In taking on that persona—that voice, actually—I discovered an astonishing freedom. Perhaps that's the compulsion of writing: the freedom to be, not somebody else, but another of your selves.

INT: Like when you go to a fancy dress party and you hire a costume that appeals to you...

KG: Yes! You've chosen that particular costume because somehow you know unconsciously that that's the one that's going to liberate some part of you.
    It's as if something that's always been there, in the real world—Bea Miles for example—connects with something in your psychological make-up—in the way two atoms might be attracted to each other because one is missing an electron and the other has an extra one. To me, it feels as if all you can do is stir a lot of atoms around and see which ones connect, and a long time later start asking why.

Extract 1 from an early manuscript

These handwritten fragments, prefaced by dates of Jane Austen's letters (see interview page 97) are the earliest notes for *Lilian's Story*.

```
Thurs 15 Sept 1796 p 14
Sun 18 Sept        "   p 18
Sat 27 Oct    1798 p 24
Sat 17 Nov    1798 p 28
                   50 invent a few hard names for the
                      stars
```

In the nights we build fires from the wood ~~that~~ frayed by the tides and invent a few hard names for the stars. <u>Hebdomedary,</u> old Francis suggests after a long silence. Or <u>cornucopia</u>. ~~The wood~~ When the flames reach in and singe the wood it spits salt and embers that pulse on the sand

Kate Grenville—Lilian's Story

before ~~they die~~ dying. Evelyn and the baby make damp noises to each other and when ~~that~~ the tiny ~~tooth~~ blunt-gummed mouth begins to smack at the air we hear Evelyn's buttons release a breast ~~and Blue~~ Tommo works each night to bury ~~both feet and both hands in~~ his limbs under the fine cool sand, ~~that~~ with its stores /of/ cigarette butts, as if for the future, ~~but~~ and then sits as if /invisible or/ guiltless, examining the water.

   These summer nights are our times for telling the stories of our lives, either the ones we had or the ones we wished for. We watch by cold starlight and hot flames as tears slime down Francis' cheeks. ~~My~~ <u>The wife</u> he'll say and look for the bottle /beside him/. <u>Me little girl</u> he'll say and the cork will make a hollow /mocking/ sound ~~of contempt mockery~~. Those who spend their days ~~with coins sliding~~ ~~smug~~ ~~the power of~~ smiling and worrying at each other, and their nights behind walls and windows, would claim that Francis has never had wife or daughter, and never wanted anything but the loving boy he never quite had, but we listen and throw another plank onto the flames, and later one of us might hold him a little as he shudders under the dew. Across the water, as black as the inside of an ear, the windows of those in the old country seem to be sending us code as the branches of their domesticated trees bend ~~in front~~ down across the light, and up again. ~~In~~ When our memories or inventions fail us we ~~listen to the sem~~ watch the yellow semaphore and the baby clutches out feebly as if to put the flickering lights into his mouth. <u>Snug as a bug in a rug,</u> Evelyn says, but it is not ~~possible to know~~ clear if she speaks of the baby or those ~~in th~~ secure in their houses across the bay. Behind us a few more handfuls of plaster drop from the laths of the ceiling of <u>Rosecroft</u> and another litter of rats is born, squeaking.

   In the old country, across other bays and tides, I have known the image of myself, a young girl with glossy bangs, in the dim reflection of a window closing out night. I know the chill on the shoulders after bending too long over the piano, wondering if the draught meant someone had come in. When ants were discovered seething through the sugar in the curled silver dish, Mother had hidden her open mouth behind a hand and looked at me. I had accepted her accusation, of course, and like those others I too was /slowly/ transported to a beach on the lip of another ~~new~~ strange land./ The privilege of the first settlers is to impose names of their own invention on the new world./

Along the tide-line where we sit, our faces glowing and our backs pimpled with cold, the litter of everyone else's lives seemed washed up for our inspection, washed obsessively by the harbour's tides. People drink a great deal of plastic-bottled orange juice and toss the grey plastic over the side. From the evidence of this beach, dozens of men each day must lather their faces with the white cream from the spray-can but then in a clumsy movement knock it overboard and stand, faces lathered foolishly, their lips cherry pink among the white, as the can bobs further and further away. Of course there are condoms, too, children's sandals, and sometimes a small animal corpse in a sack. We do not investigate, but Tommo will lift the ~~sack~~ sodden sacking—he snickers as he does this but ~~my feeling~~ I interpret this as ~~a most efficient one way of breathing out~~ not inhaling—and toss it ~~far out~~ far into the bushes behind the beach. Once or twice, squatting among those bushes in the dark, I had been aware ~~of the~~ that death ~~knows~~ experiments with every kind of noxious corruption.

Evelyn holds the baby so tightly /that/ sometimes it ~~has to~~ wheezes and Francis has to say, <u>Steady on easy on there love</u>. Her eyes are crossed from the fear that they will take the baby away, ~~and dress~~ dressing it in institutional white ~~that they will~~ and teaching it that no-one comes when you cry. ~~Tommo, who has exposed himself so often in the daylit parks~~ Although I have never had a ~~baby~~ child, and certainly never will now, I am sometimes permitted to ~~take~~ hold the ~~child myself~~ baby while Evelyn takes her turn in the bushes, and I push my withered nipple into its mouth. ~~As if politely, the~~ As Francis watches ~~and~~ a trickle of saliva finds it way out of the corner of his mouth. Tommo, too, ~~who~~ as far hidden in the sand as possible, stares and stares. He has never had a woman but exposes himself daily and

For many years I wished my name was William. ~~It was only after~~ Finally I realised that I was William, and it was of no importance that my father had decided I should be called Beatrice.

energetically in all the parks and returns to our beach sighing with happiness. His other crimes are long behind him.

It was a wild and stormy night when I was born. The horses in the stables kicked down their stalls...(other details from Shakespeare). The infant mewled
and blinked ~~away~~ stared and the doctors assured her mother that a caul was a lucky sign. <u>A girl</u>? the father exclaimed outside in the tiled waiting-room, tiled as if for /horrible/ emergencies. This seemed a contingency he was not prepared for, but he ~~emerged~~ rallied within a day and ~~came to where the mother~~ announced that night: <u>Beatrice. She will be called Beatrice</u>. There was probably nothing remarkable about the baby Beatrice ~~for~~ but for her
The mother lay in her white bed, her hands palms turned up, staring at the moulding of the ceiling ~~and~~ with the expression of astonishment and pain she wore for the next eighteen years. <u>You didn't tell me</u> she whispered to her friends as they patted her crocheted bed-jacket, and she began to suffer her overlapping series of illnesses and indispositions. ~~The friends left, placing the baby in her mother's arms in a picturesque~~ The friends picked up the baby from its crib beside the bed and placed it in the mother's arms. <u>A lovely picture</u>, they ~~smil~~ agreed, and ~~Rose who had seen the doctor only the week before and had not yet told her husband,~~ left.
Sunlight slanted between the curtains so that a band lay across the bed like something alive. In the folds of the white coverlet shadows filled with textures that did not quite move, were not quite filled with ~~seething~~ sharp things seething up into the light. <u>This is my bed</u>, the mother reminded herself. <u>My own bed in my own house</u>. ~~So why was it that~~ <u>My coverlet made by Aunt Rose</u>. Still the carpet flamed where the sun fell over it and on the ceiling the reflection of the waves outside, the ~~endl~~ tirelessly shifting water of the bay, flickered and danced on and on like a conversation. The ~~lea~~ thick leaves of the eucalypt rubbed up and down against each other and the kookaburra pealed hysterical cacklings. The baby was slipping further down off the rise of the mother's breasts ~~and~~ but the mother did not move. Her lips made a smile, though, as the

Making Stories

baby ~~disap~~ slid quite silently off the bed and the mother lay, smiling and staring unblinkingly at the flickering ceiling, listening to the raucous screeching of the bird, until ~~at~~ Alma came in, her hands reddened from ~~the old~~ chopping meat, and saw Beatrice's tiny fingernails scraping weakly over the blue patterns of the carpet and her wet mouth opening and closing on air with tiny faint whimpers.

(Main story—Bea's journey? picaresque? back to some childhood place? to die?)

Beatrice was briefly beautiful. A photograph with a crease across it records this moment, although Beatrice herself, now thickly grey-haired, winkled, ~~crepey~~ scaly of neck like a goose, refuses cameras. The tourists are sometimes intrigued, wish to carry a part of her back to Toowoomba or Bulli: <u>Oh yairs, the loony in Martin Place, ~~remember~~ Crazy as a two bob watch of course</u>, they say, and try to remember the words she spoke, but if they had a photograph at all it is of a woman in an ~~ancient bleached~~ colorless torn dress with both palms spread in front of her face. Tommo, though, will go so far as to break into a run to be caught on film. Lounging on the steps of the Town Hall eating what he has found in the rubbish bins or scrounged from the kitchen door of the Greek's, he smiles at all the cameras pointed towards the elaborate stonework. Later, at home in, perhaps, Bulli, husband and wife will ~~blan~~ see with dismay the figure which in the heat of the moment and the excitement of so much wrought stone they had failed to notice.

(plot from S. as the present action? Lear?
Or—she's in love with businessman? Follows him, thinks she sees his response, has whole fantasy with him.
She thinks she's S. Reincarnated. What plot wd lead from this?
Crisis that made her like this, marriage? Work forwards through molestation of girls to living as a man to the present where she thinks she's S.)

I was like any other short girl with a broad nose and wide mouth, and now I am like all old women.

Beatrice waited for the ferry, having the chipped wooden bench on the wharf to herself as usual

Many a girl on early death has been praised into an angel.
Mr & Mrs Manhood
The serenity of the corpse is most delightful
Seven years are enough to change every pore of one's skin

<u>Get her by the short and curlies</u>, the cinema manager had ordered the reluctant projectionist, <u>Get her on out of there</u>. I was under the dusty plush seats by then, seeing up the slanting wooden floor where row after row was bolted to the floor and chewing gum stuck in gobs was the only irregularity. My hands were strong, my bare feet braced on one row of seats, my grip firm on another. He crawled towards me on his stomach in the dust and spilled lemonade ~~like myself~~ his young face bursting with mortified blood. <u>Go on lad</u>, we heard. He crawled closer so that I could smell the milk on his breath and see how his nostrils flared at the dust. His eyebrows grew together over his nose. <u>What's your name</u>, I said, and saw him shape the word: <u>Terry</u> before he realised what he was doing and bit the word off. <u>You were born to be hanged</u>, I said, pleasantly enough, <u>Your mother will be proud</u>, and when his red face lunged at my hand and his teeth came close to breaking the old skin, I found it necessary to crawl back away between the seats, standing up and throwing a milkshake container at the manager. ~~On~~ Out on the street cars were embracing and men picked their noses while they waited for the lights to change. Chrome ~~yelled~~ blared in the sun. The asphalt showed the marks of heels as sharp as daggers each time the ~~secretar~~ office girl took a step closer to distributing her nine greasy packets of egg salad sandwiches, Pecks Paste sandwich and meat pie with sauce. The lights changed suddenly, a mother snatched back a child, the ice cream cone flew out of the small hand and ~~was~~ lay melting between the cars. There are moments when the cranky tears of a hot day sound like a machine seizing for lack of oil in its works.

Making Stories

 Bea has brother. Parallel in beginning, then diverge. He becomes pillar. Talk show host? TV producer? (S. Parallel?)
 Chronological structure—just beginning and end in present, 1st person, B as old derro.
 Iris. PM's son. Pickled. Witch story / Refractions. Miss H an ongoing character? A pre-shadowing of what B will become. Story thread in childhood section is B and 'witch'. Tile-stealing. Speaking in street. Ideas from Deb's outline of the witch story—school etc? Section could end with Miss H's death. Miss H at swimming pool with man? Tommo being the flasher on the submarine? Snake-eating, catching etc with the brother. And girlfriend—another recurring character. Iris recurring also. Rapprochement perhaps as B gets disillusioned & older & drinks? But still on the right side of sanity and society. But when I dies another phase ends—start of B's life as S. B dressing as man (Meg's film about this). Tries to get brother to cross-dress also, or forces him to? Another sibling with voluntary deafness—Rick's brother? Father uses <u>words</u> so sibling becomes deaf & B takes them over by parroting S.

 pickle
 Tempest Act V. sc I Every 3rd thought shall be my grave

 Seven years are enough to change every pore of one's skin. ~~But those first seven years.~~ But it had not been enough for Beatrice's father, that man of moustaches, and excessive ear-wax, to produce a son. Even another daughter, he finally felt, might go some way to proving something. His wife ~~dreaded~~ had begun to dread the slippery shine of the peach nightdress on her shoulders. Over his shoulder she watched ~~what~~ the world of the ceiling. There arms with spines like tyrannosaurus gestured angrily and closed like teeth gnashed against each other. Even on those calm nights when the white house ~~looked~~ froze under moonlight, ~~the~~ and the palm trees stood splitting moonlight like knives, she could see the shadows coming towards her over the ceilings. In the room below, Beatrice lay across the bed in ~~her~~ the cowboy costume. The barrel of the gun lay against her mouth and shone with saliva as she mumbled through dreams like dull lessons. Feelingly, she said loudly, and sat up. Above her her father a large cooling wax-like bead of sweat fell from her father's forehead. Her mother felt it trickle down her cheek, a clammy tear. Don't move, he said, and ejaculated convulsively into her. Don't move. In one movement he had withdrawn and ~~clamped~~ clapped the square of waxed paper between her legs. Keep it in.

    Every third thought is my grave while, with my toes, unconscious in the sand, I dig furrows big enough to bury mice in matchboxes. John had a way with sandcastles I never had, patience to furrow and burrow through the whole edifice so that, lying on my stomach,/looking through,/ I could see a patch of his brown face with a smear of sand on his chin, on the other side. His moats were models, each drawbridge another blow for democracy. The flag on top, a gum-leaf poked into the damp sand, did not waver but turned loosely in its socket against the breeze from the waves. I could see his ~~crawling~~ blue play-suit crawling with its yellow bucket between the sea and the castle, filling the moat endlessly as it drained as quickly back to sea. Finally I would clamber so far up the rough cliffside that it seemed I would be able to crush him with one strong leap outwards. Father, though, sauntering out from under the umbrella /to check on his son,/ would be a tougher nut to crack.

    Every third thought is of my grave. Frank will go first, I think, however. Some dank June night when we hear the tankers mooing to each other like full udders in the fog, when the crumbling walls of Rosecroft do nothing to keep out the cold, when the fires we build there on the floors have burnt down and there are no more laths handy—on ~~some~~ one night or other like that, ~~he will groan, hiccup a last~~ Frank will die. Frank was once a wealthy man, he says, and has written a will, he says, leaving his estate in its entirety to me, he says. Two or three glasses more and he may well claim to be the lost scion of the House of Windsor.

    Frank will go first, perhaps in my arms, perhaps rolled tightly into his own corner of the room in Rosecroft. Where the ceiling has not unclenched the plaster, there are still swags of flowers and crisp bows up there, dusted with soot from our fires. In the corners, under the rubble and faeces, the boards of the floor still gleam in spots where ~~some~~ the maid on hands and knees, kneeling on the thickness of folded sheet, her cobbled soles exposed pathetically to the door, polished until she could make out ~~a dark~~ the murky threatening shape she knew to be her ~~head~~ face.

(Rosecroft belongs to Bea? Fire burns it & her down?)

After Father died, maddened by so many piles of clippings from so many newspapers and so many scribbled notes to himself, Mother and John and Beatrice lived in silence in the house. It was as if we all hoped that, by our silence, we could fool the harpies who had engulfed Father.

(later scene of Father in madhouse)

Mother became very healthy. John and I saw for the first time how full and stately a woman our mother was and believed for the first time the sepia photograph of her standing erect and proud, one hand on the saddle of a stuffed donkey, a waterfall frozen behind her, in a dress made of chips of light. <u>That was when I was younger</u>, Mother would explain, apologise when visitors picked up the silver frame and commented on the halo-effect the photographer had achieved around the hand resting on the donkey. <u>And sillier</u>. Beatrice would watch her mother titter. Upstairs in <u>The Study</u> another ~~pile of newspaper would slide to the floor the weight of age~~ clippings would slip off the desk in the chink of sunlight that came between the tattered curtains. Dust puffed up from the carpet as the paper settled in for another few years' rest. <u>Mechanic drills seven holes in wife</u>. Even after newspapers become yellow and as brittle as bark they remain legible. Bark is also legible, ~~those~~ that elegant curvaceous script dark against the grey sheen, but only a few have learned to read it.

<u>I am to be married, Aunt Beatrice</u>, Laura said. <u>I think</u>.

<u>Books should have toilets in them</u>. ~~Una's voice~~ Each word seemed stopped short, bitten off, by the dead misty air of the cubbyhole in the cave. Una coughed to hear that sound, too, flatten and soak into the crumbling stone walls. Pam's giggle floated a little further. When it was swallowed up in the silence she laughed again on a high

pitch like anxiety. Whaddya mean, toilets? The last word rang out around the cave for an instant. They both glanced quickly into the gloomy tapering end of the cave where the cool slippery sand underfoot smelled richly, moistly. Pam made Una go outside the cave when she took down her shorts, ~~so that~~ and would hum loudly to cover the rushing of steaming urine on the sand. I mean like people really do, you know ~~use~~ go to the toilet and eat and that. Oooh Pam's nose wrinkled. Pam sucked the end of her plait and brushed the blue ribbon against the end of her nose. Ooh I don't wanna. Her eyes were unblinking. You're loony, she finally said. I gotta go home now.

Miss Poole at school agreed. It was one thing to draw careful pictures of Sir Joseph Banks Discovering Bottlebrush, or maps of New South Wales with a red arterial maze of Governor Macquarie's Roads. It was something else to have to think of what Mrs Banks and Mrs Macquarie would have been doing, and what everyone might have had for tea. Muffins? London Broil? Damper? Mrs Poole had never been quite sure what damper was but was sure it was not pleasant. Nor did she wish to hold up the whole class for such questions. On the boys' side of the room, John blushed and Stewart made a noise like a fart with a piece of his father's best rubber-band. Miss Poole was sweating lightly under her powder and Ashes of Violets, ~~and decided that~~ ~~Gwen sh~~ it was time that Gwen ~~stammering Gwen would~~ should read aloud. Page 53, Gwen. Under the picture. Gwen could not be prevailed on to stand and read, nor would she read from a sitting position, and continued to shake the silky mouse-brown fringe that hid her face and make tiny anguished gestures with her fingers on the pages of the book, until the bell rang for recess.

~~It was easy to answer~~ What happened in 1813? It was easy to answer that Blaxland, Lawson and Wentworth crossed the Blue Mountains for the first time. But it was more interesting to imagine...

In the early days, when Laura had visited Aunt Bea with her mother, things were not too far gone. Sometimes her aunt would be wearing six different dresses, one on top of the other,/starting/ with the longest so that each uneven layer of hem could be seen like a book of carpet-samples, ~~but that was easy to overlook~~ or the dusty

Making Stories

coffee-table would be piled with /empty/ snail-shells from the garden, each painted red or blue. Visits were short on those days, but visits continued to be made. <u>I'd like to eat my past</u>, Aunt Bea would say over her cup of tea. <u>Just spread it on thin bread with the crusts cut off and pop it into my mouth</u>. Laura's mother would laugh and glance at her daughter to make sure she had not thought this was important. Laura's mother's laugh, in Aunt Bea's house, had a rough loud edge it never revealed at home. It was easier to imagine Laura's mother posing gravely with the stuffed donkey, when she sat, legs daintily crossed, on Aunt Bea's sofa from which kapok puffed out every time she moved. Only here was it possible to imagine her <u>sillier</u>.

(Reproduced courtesy Mitchell Library, State Library of New South Wales.)

Extract 2 from the published version

Lilian's Story, pages 1–13

IT WAS A wild night in the year of Federation that the birth took place. Horses kicked down their stables. Pigs flew, figs grew thorns. The infant mewled and stared and the doctor assured the mother that a caul was a lucky sign. A *girl?* the father exclaimed, outside in the waiting room, tiled as if for horrible emergencies. This was a contingency he was not prepared for, but he rallied within a day and announced: *Lilian. She will be called Lilian Una.*

Later, the mother lay on her white bed at home, her palms turned up, staring at the moulding of the ceiling with the expression of surprise she wore for the next twenty years. *You didn't tell me it would hurt,* she whispered to her friends as they patted the crocheted bedjacket, and she was already beginning to suffer her long overlapping series of indispositions. The friends picked up the baby from its crib beside the bed and placed it in the mother's arms. *A lovely picture,* they agreed, and left.

Sunlight slanted between the curtains so that a band lay across the bed like something alive. The carpet flamed where the sun fell over it, and on the ceiling the reflection of the waves of the bay outside flickered on and on like a conversation. Eucalypt leaves rubbed against each other and a kookaburra pealed in hysteria somewhere. The baby slipped further down off the breast, but the mother lay smiling and staring at the ceiling, listening to the bird, until the baby fell to the floor. When Alma came in, reddened from dusting the banister, she saw Lilian's tiny fingernails scraping weakly over the patterns of the carpet, and her wet mouth opening and closing on air.

If it was mine, Alma thought, and picked the baby up. She said to Cook, later, *If it was mine I would take better care*, but Cook was having a mood and plunged her ladle into broth without speaking. Lilian cried and was fed, cried and was changed, and so many nappies kept everyone busy.

Four years are enough to change every pore of one's skin, but were not enough for Lilian's father, that man of moustaches and excessive ear wax, to produce a son. He was beginning to feel that even another daughter might go some way to proving something. His wife began to dread the slippery shine of the peach nightdress over her skin. Behind his shoulder she watched the shadows coming towards her across the ceiling, and in the room below, Lilian lay across her bed with a pair of white bloomers on her head, mumbling through dreams like dull lessons. *Feelingly*, she said, and sat up.

In the room above, a wax-like bead of sweat fell cooling from her father's forehead. *Don't move*, he told her mother, and convulsed. *Don't move*, he said again, and clapped waxed paper between her legs. *Keep it in*.

Mother's Story

MOTHER WAS A woman of pale colours: lilacs and lavenders and the grey of galahs. She cut roses in the mornings and laid them in the flat basket I was allowed to carry. *Alma will take care of it*, she soothed when I dropped a vase that shattered into astonished pieces around my feet. *Alma!* she called, and rang the little brass bell. *Alma is a maid*, she explained when I asked. *And I am a lady. You will be a lady one day, but now you are a little girl.* Her eyes became curved when she smiled, and close up she smelled of flowers. *Your father is a gentleman, and is writing a book.*

In the parlour there was a photograph of her standing erect and winsome, smiling, one hand on the saddle of a stuffed donkey, a waterfall frozen behind her, in a dress made of chips of light. *That was when I was younger*, she explained and apologised when visitors picked up the frame and commented on the halo effect the photographer had achieved around the hand resting on the donkey. *And sillier.* I watched Mother titter. She had little to say about the wedding photograph next to it, full of people looking anxious for the camera, in which the train of her lace dress had succeeded in drawing her feet into its coils. *He courted me,* she said, *and we married in St. Andrew's.* Father's story was almost the same. *I found your mother charming,* he said crisply, *so I courted her. We were married in the rain.*

Father's Story

ALBION WAS A man of moustaches and of shiny boots that squeaked when he walked. His boots on the stairs filled the house, his hand with the powerful black hairs gripped the banister hard enough to make it tremble. *Lilian, do not bang your feet like that,* Mother exclaimed. *What do you think you are doing?* I tried explaining, *I am being Father, Mother,* but she did not hear, only said, *A lady glides, Lilian.*

When I asked him, Father said, *Your mother is a wife and mother. And a lady. And I am a gentleman.* He hoisted me up onto his shoulder and from such a height the floor shone in a strange way and the ceiling made me dizzy. *And you are a young lady whose bedtime it is.*

Some mornings Father went to an office and returned in the evening with a newspaper under his arm. At the office he *kept the business afloat,* and came home smelling of the ferry. *Someone has to keep the business from going under,* he said when I asked him about that office. *So that you will have something to come into.* I thought, and asked, *Will we live in a boat?* I was looking forward to the sound of waves against a hull at night, but Father sighed and slapped the paper against his thigh. *Anything is possible, Lilian,* he said, and went up to the study.

Yes, Lilian, he agreed when I badgered him. *I am writing a book, but first I am gathering my material.* Father's book kept him out of sight in his study, but I could hear newspapers being read and shears slicing through paper when I tiptoed close to listen.

In the chilly dining room in the depths of the house, sounds echoed in startling ways from the cedar chiffonier with the decanters, from the sideboard with the thick carved legs, from the floor that Alma, on hands and knees, polished, panting, until she could make out a murky threatening shape that she knew must be her face. The legs of mutton stiffened in their fat, potatoes shrivelled as they cooled, and Alma's breathing was loud as she tiptoed from Mother to Father to me with the mint sauce. Mother ate slowly, chewing thirty-two times as someone had recommended, refusing mint sauce. Father's knife sliced vigorously across his meat and his voice ricocheted off the walls.

I waited until he had forked such quantities of meat into his mouth that he had fallen silent, chewing hard, staring at the salt-cellar, before I spoke. *Will your book have pictures, Father?* I asked, and Mother shook her head warningly at me from the end of the table. But Father laughed a thin laugh: *Ha! Ha!* and Mother pressed her fingertips into a headache. *No, Lilian, no pictures will be necessary. Norah, leave the room if you are suffering.*

I was slow for my age, bad at hints, and perhaps shouted in my excitement, *But, Father, what is your book about? Is it about pirates or burglars? Or adventures in balloons?* I had not finished, had hardly begun my list of all the things a book might be about, when Father began to shout back at me, *No, no, no, no, no!* until I was silent, showing egg in my open mouth, and Mother with a hand over her face had pushed her plate away. *Swallow that egg,* Father commanded, *and do not be dreadful, Lilian.*

Alma stood at the sideboard and her breathing was loud. She looked hard at the bowl in her hand as Father glanced around the room and I swallowed egg. *Alma, how many times must I tell you not to dust?* Father asked suddenly, as if he wanted an answer, and waited for one as Alma stood with her bowl of peas in butter and looked congested. *How many times?* If I had been able to count so far, I would have tried to give him the answer he was waiting for. *Alma, do not dust,* he said at last, when the silence had wrinkled around us all, and went back to his mutton, and Mother had to say, *Not in the study, that is, Alma,* and Alma nodded over her puckered peas.

The Treasures of Albion

THAT STUDY OF Father's was a silent and dusty place. Sun leaned in between the curtains and travelled slowly across the piles of newspapers on the floor. Dust hung in a nervous way in the beam of sun and there was not enough air, so that I panted and saw the dust motes dance. Stairs creaked outside although I knew Father could not be home, something rattled somewhere, a branch scraped along stone, and I knew I should hurry out and not come here again. But the pile of newspapers on the floor was a good height to climb and sit on, swinging my legs, and I hummed into the silence in a brave way.

It was a while before I had hummed enough to go over to the desk and look at the papers there, clippings from the newspaper pinned together in heaps. I picked them up and read with a slow finger underlining each word: "Rising Eggs a Menace," one said, and the next, "Brick Man Fondles Nephew." I looked at the handwritten notes, too, that spoke with Father's voice: *Norway has seventy thousand miles of coast and a population of ten million*, and *This year I have smiled seven hundred and four time*s. In the end, I could not keep up my humming in the face of these facts and was frightened at the way the silence roared in my ears when I stopped. I could not remember just how the clippings had been arranged on the desk, whether *Dew falls faster in summer* had been on top or not, and when in my fear I knocked against the pile of newspapers and sent so many old headlines sprawling, I could not arrange the pile just as it had been.

Someone sneaky has been in my study, Father said at dinner that night. *Someone sly. And has interfered with my research*. I had to say to myself, *I am sneaky*, and felt hot with shame. I could think of no excuses, but refused more pudding in penance. *But since you are so interested, Lilian, I will tell you*. Father's research was so many facts that Alma had cleared away every plate and fork, and Cook could be heard distantly above the sounds of washing up, and Father was still going. There were the lengths of rivers and frontiers, the populations of cities, why bats were blind, the distance all the eggs in the world would go if laid end to end. I watched the jabbing finger and counted as he ticked off so many facts on his fingers that I thought he might have to start on his toes. *The fact of the matter is this*, he said. *In point of actual fact, the facts are these*. I regretted having been sly. *Take for a moment the following fact*, he demanded, and lifted a finger into the air as if testing for a breeze. *Consider this fact*.

There could be nothing secretive about so many facts. My fingers read the smooth starched patterns of the tablecloth, I sucked at a grape seed caught in a tooth, watched a morsel of something dangle in Father's moustache, lost count of facts, and Mother nodded and nodded and squinted at another headache approaching her across the room.

In my room later, I put the bloomers on my head and played nurse or cook or milkman and talked to my patients or saucepans or cows. *The fact is this*, I whispered sternly, but could not think of any facts. *I want you to consider the following facts*. At last it occurred to me that I could invent my facts, but even with the authoritative white bloomers on my head, I knew I lacked Father's talent.

I was a child of unpromising lank hair and small eyes. In photographs I was caught looking sideways, looking sly, in fact, and unhappy at standing in frills while a man shouted, *Don't move*. In those photographs my hands were too large for me, as if I was trying on someone else's. But Father photographed well. His moustache came out nicely, the knob of his cane gleamed, his boots were planted on the rug in a masterful way. His moustache was the model of moustaches for me, thick and drooping, giving his face a look of manly melancholy. I saw other moustaches on other fathers, but they looked like nothing more important than hair. Above his moustache, Father's eyes were sleepy in the photographs and his hair lay slicked down against his skull so that the flatness of his head was apparent. In my early paintings, I drew his head as a square brown box on his shoulders, and drew the facts coming out of his mouth. *What are those lines, Lilian?* Miss Vine asked at school. *Has he been speared, dear?* and I would have to try to explain, *Those are Father's facts*, Miss Vine.

There Is Everyone Else to Consider

MOTHER BELIEVED IN conversation. *A lost art, Lilian, you must sit and learn*. She sat in the parlour on breezy afternoons when everything in the garden shook and swung in the wind from the bay, and poured tea, and I sat but did not learn. Ladies arrived and removed their gloves, smoothing them on their knees, and withdrew long pins from their hats as they watched Alma breathe too loudly. Mother did not have headaches on the days the ladies visited. She laughed and talked quickly as if there was not enough time for everything but she would like to try to fit it all in, just the same.

Lilian, how old are you now, dear? a lady with a big black bust asked me. *And are you enjoying school?* I thought she should know how old I was, since she asked my age each time she came, but perhaps she was absent-minded. She had a silver watch pinned to her heart, where she could not forget it. *I am going on five*, I said for the sake of a change, although I was only just four, *and school is good*. School was naps on mats in the blowfly afternoons, and cutting out coloured paper. It was painting in a smock and learning about King Arthur. *I have only been at school a little while*, I admitted. *But Mother taught me to read*. I was proud of that, and pleased when the lady with the black bust made her mouth an O and gave a surprised sound, and several other ladies looked. *She is already reading*, the lady with the black bust said, and all the ladies smiled without showing their teeth.

I wanted to astonish them further and brought out of my pinafore pocket the pebble with a vein in it like rainbow cake. *What I found*, I explained. *I had to get wet for it*. In fact, I had had to wade into the bay up to my thighs, and then a wave had taken me by surprise and drenched me. Now that it was dry, the pebble was boring and I could see that the ladies were about to lose interest, so I popped it into my mouth and then held it out, shining like a jewel in my palm. *Look, it is very valuable*, I crowed. The lady with the bust did not make an O again, but smiled without showing her teeth and said, *Norah, what a little tomboy you have*, and the other ladies nodded, and they began to comment on May's hat, and the pebble dried.

I asked Mother later, *What is a tomboy?* but she was fatigued by so many ladies and said, *I will explain later, Lilian, but now I will rest*, and lay back on her couch.

Among the Sisters of Albion

THERE WERE THOSE ladies who visited, and there was Aunt Kitty who lived in a house with blood-red stained glass beside the front door. Mother and I walked to her house on the next bay and listened to the bell jangle inside when Mother pressed the brass button. *Why, my dears!* Aunt Kitty cried out at us as if amazed, *come along, come along*, and hurried us down the hall to the parlour. There was a tinkling and a continual tiny chiming around her from so many necklaces and shivering earrings, so that I had to tell her, *You are like a chandelier, Aunt Kitty*, and she laughed on a high note. *Try how it feels*, she shouted, and began to drape me with her necklaces, but I was shy. Her hair at the back was slithering out of its combs, but her face was pink, her eyes shone, and everything made her laugh and hurry. *Come on, quickly now*, she said, and hurried Mother onto the couch, hurried a doll into my hands, hurried to fetch barley water and biscuits.

I am a happy widow, Aunt Kitty said, and whenever I asked she told me how Uncle Forbes had passed away in thirty seconds of anguish, clutching the shirt over his chest so that it came away in a long shred. *It was quick*, Aunt Kitty finished by saying, *and he was a serene corpse.* She poured more barley water and said comfortably, *It was a long time ago.* I watched her swallow a mouthful of barley water and say, *And now I am a happy widow, and a philosopher.*

Mother sat on the couch and laughed at the kapok that puffed from a rip when she moved. Aunt Kitty shook her jewellery at her. *It will come to all of us*, she said, *and I will try not to mind.* Mother laughed again and laid her glove over the rip in the couch. Her laugh in Aunt Kitty's house was louder and longer than her laugh at home, and it was easier to imagine her with the stuffed donkey when she sat with her glove over the rip in Aunt Kitty's couch. Here it was easier to imagine her being sillier. When Aunt Kitty exclaimed from nowhere, *I'd like to eat my past*, Mother nodded and smiled and waited for more. *Just spread it on thin bread and butter and pop it in my mouth.* They laughed till they spluttered, but I was restless, the doll Aunt Kitty had given me was stiff and boring, I did not like barley water. *Then go and play with a pup*, Aunt Kitty cried, gesturing at the back verandah, *and let us ladies be important.*

Kitty is my cross to bear, I heard Father saying downstairs at times. I hung further over the banister but could not hear if Mother answered. A teacup fell against a saucer and I imagined Father dabbing his moustache with his napkin and lining up the spoon in the saucer. *She is my trial*, he sighed. *And error*, he added, and laughed his jerky laugh. Blood rushed to my head from hanging so far over the banister and the stairs came up at me in an odd way, but although I wanted to hear more, no more was said.

David Ireland
A Woman of the Future

It's in the planning part where you're got the power to change everything. You're a little dictator with a tiny little kingdom. What you say, goes. The rest of the world may be rich, and have armies at their beck and call, but you've got this little book. There are no committees. No one's going to get in there and interfere.

        David Ireland

Succeeding Waves Chapter 6
of History

Ill use metaphor (circle? pts up/
pts dwn?)

2 of Successive developments
changes,

returning always
Hopeless life + heaven
" " + heaven — "make this better"
no heaven
Still hopeless -- sees human are - stuck after South fac[e]
- + hoarse

Making Stories

We had read that when David Ireland was employed in various jobs, he jotted down thoughts and notes for novels on cards he kept in his pockets. When we looked at his manuscript for *A Woman of the Future* in the Mitchell Library, we found small memo sheets and other workplace documents (see page 125), now pasted down sequentially by the library, and compiled into volumes. They were covered with rough notes of all kinds: quotations, thoughts, jokes, speculations, sometimes sketches or diagrams. It was obvious from the use of different pens, for example, that they had all been jotted down at different times, with later additions. Seeing writing at such an early stage was fascinating to us: all the material was unformed, a world still in flux. A mind was at work, but a book had not yet been shaped.

But we still hadn't realised the full significance of those small pages with their rough notes. Then, before we started our interview with him, David Ireland showed us his work-in-progress: a dozen or so plastic trays contained notes written by hand on tiny cards (some as small as a finger), bundled together with elastic bands in scores, perhaps hundreds, of groupings. It was, obviously, a very complex system of ordering thought. He told us about it. Our interview took place in March 1992 at David Ireland's home near Goulburn.

INT: Are your boxes of notes an integral part of the way you write?

DI: Before I ever wrote anything, back in the 1960s, I was making notes at random, as they occurred to me. I didn't think at all of what they might amount to. They're thoughts I had, things that occurred to me, so I put them down in case they were useful later on in some way I couldn't foresee.

Many of them were made at work, or when I was reading something entirely unrelated. Some were made in that space of time between the first and the third schooner, which was—*was*—a time when many ideas were stirred into life. (I never made notes where I could be seen.)

I would've started them in my early 20s, when I knew I wanted to be a writer. They were more than a resource. I felt I had something behind me, a support, or a mountain I could stand on. Whatever I wanted to write about, there'd be some notes there or a word that would trigger off other words.

INT: What sort of things went into these notes?

DI: Some of them are simply thinking on to the paper. I put down odd things I noticed—like, at my first five-day-a-week job, string being wasted.

INT: Did you keep them in any sort of order?

DI: They weren't kept in any order. Most often the paper was there on the desk and notes were added as they occurred to me, whether or not they had anything to do with the earlier note. But don't forget that any apparently unrelated ideas can go together.

INT: So when you first started writing, you used those notes as a base?

DI: I only started writing anything when I had a critical mass of notes, which eventually amounted to twenty-four thin notebooks and five thick ones.

When I was experimenting, in those years before I wrote anything that I thought was any good—the sort of stuff I churned out at odd times and threw away—I typed on to sheets of paper, doing the story in the order one reads it. Soon I found that when I had 50 or 200 pages, I couldn't keep up with what was going on. I'd think: 'Yes, that was on page 30. Go back'. And it might be there, or it might not. I'd waste time, finding out just where it was. Or, I might think, 'I don't want to go on from there', and I'd have to cut the piece of paper off. I actually did that, a few times, cut strips of paper up.

As well, there were so many things I had to insert, so many new ideas, corrections, deletions, changes, that it was impossible to organise the additions without cutting the sheets and separating out the bits. Also it was very difficult finding space to lay out a hundred sheets in such a way as to get a comprehensive idea of the whole.

I realised I needed to be able to manipulate the ideas before I set them in concrete on the page. If I stopped trying to write it all down in the order in which one reads, and instead separated out the bits first, I could arrange and rearrange as much as I liked. The answer had to be small and easily handled. Cards.

INT: So you had the notebooks, and cards...What came next?

DI: Before the planning, there's a period which to my mind is very much akin to closing my eyes on a train journey, and having the shape of the book come up in the dark sepia colour behind the eyelids. That's the time when I'm actually deciding what I'm going to do. I get into a funny gear inside. It's also a very delicious time too. Things seem to float in and out. You don't have to rub them out, or anything like that—an unspoken command and they disappear.

At that stage, I can't tell you any of the detail of how it ought to be. I can't see it in detail: just a shape. I can't see the words at all. I have to do things in accordance with the feeling.

With that rough shape in my mind, the next step is a selection process. Any finite number of notes can be expanded into an indefinitely large number of books. That follows Leibnitz: any finite number of observations may be accommodated within an indefinitely large number of different explanations.

What I did was like this. It's my vision of the ideal rubbish tip. The amorphous mass of rubbish, some of it recyclable and useful, is spread out. A magnet for iron is suspended over it and the iron is extracted. Then a 'magnet' for copper, glass, cardboard, plastic and so on. (Even though magnets for these materials haven't been invented yet.) Similarly with my masses of notes.

For *A Woman of the Future*, for example, the general idea of a girl from nought to eighteen years is suspended over the notes, the ones germane to that idea are extracted and cluster around the idea, and the rest fall back on the pile.

I try never to stint a book, never to save material for later in case I run out. I put in as much as I can, knowing I'll always be able to generate more ideas.

At that stage, I'd have bundles of cards roughly sorted out into groups by the magnet process.

With *The Chantic Bird*, for instance, I had seventeen bundles of cards, for the boy's seventeen years and the seventeen sections of the book. Each bundle consisted of incidents, adventures and ideas I wanted to inject. I had them on little luggage labels cut up. I'd put them out on a table, and I'd see that there was a gap between that and that. It would usually be obvious what I needed. It would usually be another incident, because, somehow, in mucking things around, I'd have two incidents jammed up together. I could add in ideas, generate new cards for themes I wanted to repeat—or flavours, as I thought of them—and transfer cards from one section to another. Or I might say: 'Is it time to reiterate one of the little micro themes I've got dotted throughout the thing?' And maybe it would be. Or maybe I'd get those two incidents right away from each other.

I used the same system for *The Unknown Industrial Prisoner*. This

David Ireland—A Woman of the Future

took over 300 sections, from memory, so it had to be laid out on a floor of a room cleared of furniture. All at a glance, more or less.

INT: When you say 'generate'. . .how did you generate those pieces that you began to see you needed?

DI: It's a constant going over what I have, with a view to improving it, filling in gaps, taking out silly bits, making the whole thing run. I can usually detect—I think—discontinuities that stick out, such as a big jump, and I say: 'Oh, I've got one card here, when I really need two or three.' This is done many times until, looking at it as a whole, all I want to be in it is in it, and it's ready to be written. I have only the sketchiest idea of the book in mind beforehand. I learn about it as I'm writing it.

I only ever have one manuscript. The 'second' draft is when one round of cuts, corrections and additions has been made. This goes on for dozens of rounds until the whole thing is less unsatisfactory. The book takes more and more shape, the more you order it. You go over it and over it and over it.

The brain work I find really fascinating is that planning part. It's in the planning part where you've got the power to change everything. You're a little dictator with a tiny little kingdom. What you say, goes. The rest of the world may be rich, and have armies at their beck and call, but you've got this little book. There are no committees. No one's going to get in there and interfere. I don't have to refer to anyone. This is an area of my own.

INT: You must have an intense sense of structure, of patterns.

DI: It must be so. I can't explain why. All I can say is that I love detail. In everything. If I've got the freedom to ask people about something they're saying, I love the details. Sometimes it's a bit annoying for them to have to explain—they think I'm grilling them.

I remember a lot. I can call up things from many years ago. I can see a scene, I can see things as they were. I suppose it's all got to do with my mother telling me: 'David, you're dreaming again!' I'd be standing there, seeing, but not seeing, things passing through my mind. It seems to me that the things I know, or feel, are constantly present, and I just have to pick them out. Things are swirling, like gas. Phrases or words come into my head.

INT: So in the planning stage, that's where the big imaginative leaps come.

DI: They come simply because it's planned. Because that new thing comes in there and you say: Ah! Goodness me! You can see that after a placid bit, for instance, suddenly there's something that's a violent contrast.

I used to envy other writers who'd say: 'Then I find the character taking over, going off in this direction,' and I'd think: That sounds much more creative than me. I'm just an old plodder that does this brick and that brick, puts this here and that there. But that's me, that's what I have to do. I don't like that other business, things taking off. They take off in the planning stage for me. If they go in at such an angle that they conflict with this and that, well they've either got to be brought back or modified or got rid of. I go over each stage so many times that any new directions have made their appearance long before I do the writing. But I have absolute freedom to move around. Nothing's decided. Everything's in suspension. Not until everything's right, not till I feel good about it, is there a framework clapped down. (When I say I suspend commitment till the end, I mean commitment to the details. I'm quite committed to the idea—I'm quite whole-hearted about that.)

INT: It sounds as if you don't actually sit down and write the sentences of the novel until quite a long way into the process.

DI: Exactly. That's where I probably sounded very evasive in answering questions from people to whom I had to give account of my time when I was receiving grants. They say: 'Would you like to explain what you've been doing in the last year?' You have to say: 'Yes, I'm writing,' when no, you're not. You're planning and writing. Or when you're having an interview from the papers, a book's out, and you're on the next one, and they ask, 'How much do you write a day?'

INT: That's not the right question.

DI: No. I've sometimes said, 'Well, if I'm going well, and it is at the writing stage of the book, I might do a good three pages.' But it's an evasion, and not quite the truth. Because a lot of the time I'm not writing, I'm thinking and ordering.

INT: How do you move from the process of ordering the cards, to the actual writing?

DI: When it's time for writing out, I lay each section of cards in order, and go ahead, beginning at the top. Easy. I type straight out what I call the first draft. That is the draft which will be altered, corrected and so on, the basis for all the later revisions.

INT: Does this draft get written in the same order that the final novel reads, from the beginning to the end?

DI: Yes, once the bits have been assembled and have stood up to the many attacks I make on them.

INT: Are there times when it's drudgery?

DI: The way I work keeps the job full of interest. The only drudgery is at the final typing end of the process. That, and the proofreading. But by then the book is done and I've turned my back on it.

INT: The notes we extracted were from *A Woman of the Future*. Can you tell us about the particular evolution of that book?

DI: I got the idea of *A Woman of the Future* from the newspapers. For several weeks there were guys putting themselves forward as reviewers and saying that Australian writers can't write in a woman's voice. So that really *got* me. It sounds very trivial now, but it wasn't to me then. If you're a writer, you should be able to do these things. It's quite affecting really, to remember that.

With *A Woman of the Future*, each time I thought about it, I'd write something on whatever piece of paper was handiest. I pressed into service everything I could find in my notes that I thought could be useful.

I didn't know what Alethea was going to do till about three-quarters of the way through. But it was changes that I wanted to talk about. I had the feeling, without knowing it, that she was going to change. And that she was Australia—I wanted to tell people that. I felt she would have to change in a dramatic way. I didn't want to worry about what the change would be. I could keep that in suspension.

When I'd extracted the notes that belonged to Alethea, I used the same method to separate out the bits that might apply to her at various ages. Then I looked at them to see what they lacked.

The notes on Alethea herself I didn't have in my stock, so I had to generate them—her birth, school times, etc. Similarly I had to generate her mother and father, neighbours, schoolkids and teachers.

When I say I '*generated*' a piece for *A Woman of the Future*, I would have thought: I'm going to have to make these people change. So I might have got a piece of paper and written the sorts of

Making Stories

changes down—someone sticking to the floor, or someone not being able to stop moving or someone having something growing out of them. That was a lovely time.

INT: How did you decide about the ordering of the fragments in *A Woman of the Future*?

DI: First, by the general order of Alethea's increasing age. The name, Alethea, comes from Alethia: inability to forget, dwelling on the past. I see the irony in that she dwells on the *future*. But she is, after all, Australia.

I put the ideas bit, the Servers and Frees and the bits on the approaching death of socialism and communism, fairly early in the book so the reader didn't have to wait long for explanations.

The positions of the fragments I left to the feeling of the moment, going over them dozens of times, trying them elsewhere, putting them back or nearby. There are always many revisions. But I enjoyed the final order and that was what mattered. To talk—in order—of cows, a lecturer on freedom, a cocky, the open society, a family of 'idiots', a drunken mother, and Jesus fainting on his cross, is my idea of how a bright, mentally agile young girl could be portrayed. I like complex things, and details, and also juxtapositions, so Alethea had to, also.

INT: Did you use a way of physically arranging the fragments so you could see the overall structure?

DI: I had to mark each age section off into bundles, put them on the floor, and go through them that way for time sequences and repetition of key thoughts, because I was using paper, not cards.

INT: What proportion of time would you have spent on the planning, compared to the time spent writing?

DI: I'd say, at a guess, that the proportion of time spent ordering the cards would usually be around 10 per cent. It does vary a lot, and in this case, the process wasn't as cut and dried as it was with other books. As I worked through it from the notes, I would find that I needed other ideas. I would generate them and add them to the manuscript. Again I would find that I needed more, so I would supply more, expand them, write them out and fit them into the book. Some would have to go, but then others would need to be put in. The idea of the book was growing and filling out all the time. Towards the end, any weaker bits were scrapped, and some reordering was done.

David Ireland—A Woman of the Future

INT: The voice and the point of view of the final version of *A Woman of the Future* are already present in many of the notes, as if you were fairly sure from the beginning that you wanted to tell the story from Alethea's point of view. Were you?

DI: Yes, the story had to be told by the girl. It fitted with her diary notes and observations. First person has its disadvantages, but it's often more immediate. And the startling things in the book have more impact.

INT: Did you ever feel ill-at-ease with a female point of view?

DI: No, because Alethea was as I made her. I wasn't drawing from life, I made her up or, rather, put her together. If I'd been writing about a different sort of person I'd have had to tread far more warily, and spend—waste—a lot of time on hesitations, doubts, uncertainties and gaps in confidence. This would have taken me far from what I wanted to show. Alethea is confident, strong, and trusts herself. She's also cheerful, which saved me time.

At first I was going to take her into her 20s, but there was far too much material already, so I cut her off at eighteen.

INT: Was it hard to speak in her voice?

DI: No. It was easy, given her confidence in herself. In addition, I admire her sort of strength when I see it in women, and I take a lot of notice of it. I do try to get inside any characters I spend a lot of time and words on.

INT: Once you were at your writing stage with *A Woman of the Future*, what was your daily way of working?

DI: Every day, the next sheet of notes would be there on the pile, so I'd work on it. I didn't think of the next bit ahead of time. The tone or flavour or feeling of the whole constantly floated in my head. Like a gas. So I was never without it.

INT: The final book is still in the form of very short pieces. Did you always imagine that the form would be like that, or was there a stage when you tried other ways of putting the material together?

DI: No. This form suited, I *think*, the kind of book it is. Besides, this form is a kind of trade-mark of mine. Everything I've written, except *Burn*, which was adapted from a play, is a variation on this idea of short, lively pieces. It's what I imagined I'd do, in the years before I wrote anything at all.

I have a private quarrel with the old style of narrative, both in how it's written and the way it's set out, in great slabs that go on and on. In 1948 and 1949 and 1950 when I was thinking about shapes of books, I thought: I don't like 50 pages of prose. It's all very well for D.H. Lawrence to come along and there's a paragraph of five lines and a paragraph of three lines, and then, with no further interruption or break, he might say: 'Three weeks later...' I don't like that! It's most unreasonable of me, but if I'm going to be a writer, I'm going to be unreasonable. Rather than go on and on, I would like another section, and put something, perhaps in the heading of the section, that would lift the whole thing, that would catch your eye, and make you think of something else.

I thought I'd do it differently, and I have.

INT: Did you always feel that impatience with the conventional narrative, or was it when you started to write?

DI: I felt it from the moment I had to go to work. My Dad had been gassed in the War and it caught up with him in 1946, and I had to go to work at the end of third year. I was very conscious of the other kids forging ahead: I did the Leaving Certificate about four years later, by private study. They were all going to university, and I thought: Now what can you do, where your experience, you yourself, not your formal education, makes the difference? The answer was writing.

As soon as work was finished, I'd make my way to town, and at least several times a week I'd go to the Public Library. That's where I was influenced by Goethe.

INT: Can you tell us more about that?

DI: I had Goethe's *Faust*, Part 1. That's where I realised—I could write a book in that way! Do you remember the part on the Brocken? It's written in different voices. I'd never seen anything like that. Although I haven't yet written a book with menus and directives and PA announcements and poems and things like that, I still thought you could have things broken up beautifully like that, so that students are saying this, and someone else is coming in and saying that. That's where I got the idea from, of breaking a book up.

I thought: If I'm going to be allowed to leave school at fifteen, and if I'm going to be a writer, eventually, or if I live to 94 and I'm still trying, I'm going to do the job in the way I think best. Breaking the book up into short pieces is what I'll do, with headings to take the eye because to me it makes the page more lively and interesting. Engaging. And of course, that's being most unfair to lots of very good writers.

There's something wrong with narrative, and if I could work that out, I might be an Einstein of the novel. There's something wrong there—I can see it sometimes, and at other times it just glides away and I can't grab it. It's something about the way the writer is seducing you, turning your attention away from what must be going on *there*, on the rest of the page you've just read in the space between the incidents and speeches—and diverting your attention to *this*.

I feel there must be some way of putting words down so you're getting more of what's in the scene, or the conversation, instead of feeling as a reader that you're wrenched from one gear—where you want to find out what *that* was—and you're wrenched away to *here*.

INT: We've been asking everyone whether, when they're working on their novels, they have a sense that they're inventing, or discovering.

DI: Once I get the idea for a novel, that is, have this shape for a book in my head, I get a piece of paper and write down things that I know about it. It's a dreaming time. I'm inventing it. And then, in the planning, I'm discovering what it is I've invented.

INT: We've also been asking everyone whether they have doubts about a book when they're writing it. Do you?

DI: My feelings about work in progress come and go in waves. On some days the work looks okay, then next day it seems like a heap of waste material. A few days later it seems okay again. The point is never to tear up. Moods constantly change. The work is allowed to survive if it stands up to dozens of revisions. In that time I'd have gone through all the different moods I have.

With my method of working, I don't get stuck. If there's some difficulty with one section I go round it and do the next, coming back later when the difficulty may have disappeared or I think of a way to overcome it. Work doesn't need to stop. Blockages can be cleared, preferably outside prime working time.

Before ever I wrote, I came across the phrase 'writer's block' in magazine articles. I was determined that wouldn't happen to me. The obvious thing to do was to have plenty of work ready in advance so a block could be bypassed. This became an essential part of the way I work.

I don't have many doubts. I think if I do a good enough job, some section of people will like it, will see that this is a good phrase, and that's a good sentence. And if it's dug out of *me*, and particularly *me*, then it may be so much different from another writer's experience that it'll be interesting.

Making Stories

Extract 1 from an early manuscript

These are extracts from early notes for *A Woman of the Future*. We have reproduced them in the order in which they are filed in the Mitchell Library.
*
A Woman of/for the Future
*
A Woman of/for the Future
Imitatio Christi
Manual
Aria, Theorem, speech
Jewel,
Alexis Grossman
Don Manuel Grossman
Joy Caldwell

In order by 3.7.74
Writing started 3.9.74
Aim for Oct 74 to finish.
Glass Canoe now start Dec 74
*
My unreal existence
—Writing may be ~~an instr~~ a needed way of fixing experience in permanent form so that I have a past.
There is nothing that gives reality to a person's identity so much as a past.
Now that I am dying,—long after I died,
Assurance, continuity necessary bec. I hardly ever believe I existed.
Some have trouble believing others exist. I doubt my self.
THE WAS
Each moment is a future to the moment past: Each/past/ moment ~~assures my past~~, remembered, assures me that I am I.
*
God is a state of being populated by those who have arrived; having arrived, continue to exist. Some arrive at God, but drop ~~out~~ back.
Most don't arrive.

David Ireland—A Woman of the Future

```
*
Early:
My sp. survived the flames.
Delight—in objects, in eluding other people.
         in being
Stone flowers.
Wonder—molten metal, burnt pressure cooker, electric
cooking coil, aluminium dripping,
Mystery round life—origins, preservation, end,
pity              dream            illusion
beauty            joy              hope
pain              sorrow           fear
brothership       aspire

memory
dead
living
unborn
the spring of life

*
Hadn't a life of misery there, ~~but~~ I'm always missing
it.
Perhaps the ~~misery~~ loneliness frustrations limitations
of the foetus ~~are~~ regretted after birth.
I miss being alive.
*
Each ~~is~~ was alone, in birth & death.
Everyone for self
Community was a word
THE WAS
~~I write for~~
*
THE HISTORY OF MAN—W
The parents. He reluctant.
Written as if by a singer of great deeds who ~~knows he~~ is
a past to thousands of years
for faroff generations who may survive to read it.
I always knew they wd, but it was unfash to say so
Change of tense
Fire & meat
Those who ate cooked, lived.
CUP
```

Making Stories

<u>WHEEL</u>
<u>TROY</u>
Golgotha
Genghis Khan
in adventures, parts named(?)
I, Alexis Grossman, write this. It is my story. I died a lonely death in the 20th century, reckoned after the man called Christ by those in the Christian faith.
*
These days ~~we~~ you are too used to thinking of ourselves as the future, the future of an unfortunate past.
~~We~~ You are not humble. We do not see ~~we~~ you are just/another/unfortunate past.
If no one reads it, as seems likely from present day reading habits, there is no way in the world I'm going to care. All I want is that my story should survive.
*
narrowness of traditional personal history as related synthesised in novels.
Alex the Innocent, the Sad, the Brave—less & less.
And the ocean of Women more & more.
Narrated by a Boswell/Kretschmar?
Total history had to narrow down to v. short time.
Manual?
*
What our forebears called fiction, is known now as history written by the actors ~~of events~~ at the time. And all who wish can add to the history of the moment.
This means none of us writes for the present.
All our histories are preserved for the future.
The land called —— was first used as world library. Now has been converted. All is underground, of course.
The day has been foreseen when the entire land surface of the earth will be used as library—or tomb—for personal histories.
memories of father's sperm—prev. life, depressingly like ours
*
Nothingness:
Creating characters thru' whom one may have a little life.
nothing is lost.
memory.

2 memories. one from /father's/ sperm, one from /Mother's/ egg.
fict. chars. more life than flesh & blood   life is symbolic.
*[Fragment cut from a desk calendar]
Feel assured <u>there is no such thing as</u> ultimate <u>forgetting</u>: traces once impressed upon the memory are indestructible.
       —Thomas de Quincey.
—complete recall 'method'
how recall?
*
One page a section
Due to difficulties in writing from where I am.
desire of the dead to commune, to leave imprint ⟶
invention of writing.
*
THE AFTER-LIFE OF ~~ALEX GROSSMAN~~.
*
Wave motion
Successive developments
       changes

returning always
hopeless   life
   "   "   + heaven
no heaven—make this better.
Still hopeless, since humans are.
   + Hesse—s/thing after life
Soul to God = 0
Successive waves of History
chapter
Circles? spots before the eyes.
*
wave of ideas, reason prevails for a while, until balanced by the wave of injustice unreason, violence, disorder & lies,
until
a new wave of 'truth' prevails for a while.
Hoops. Hopscotch, dancing, fighting.
*
The /long-distance/ lecturer on the end of the world.
—Going for the record.
From her childhood ⟶ to the end.

Making Stories

Shop window
in machine—respected.
Communicated with him by means of written signs.
No Sinack
2 ~~MENTIONS~~ REPEATS
*
THE JOKES.
Pedro the bad Mex
Man's Mustache—just like my Mummy's got down there
*
A child infant sickness.
(used to take his other kids home.)
sleep.
*
Mother told her how diff she was
How clever,
  good
  pretty
The diff was, I believed her.
*
WHAT YOU ARE
WHAT I AM
Cowardly debased corrupt
greedy, generous, petty, large,
*
    CHILD
Sick, as a perf. natural result of thinking pressures?
The more treatment she got, the more child was revealed.
Until...
Child:
open
generous
humble
laughing, skipping,
young play,
easily excited
easily hurt
childlike attitudes— ✝ —

prayer, talking to God (!)
*
2½′yrs of age Hand in father's
Everything is joined to ev/thing else.

*
All things go with each other
       connect
Good & evil together, so they co-exist.
Where's the diff? All acts—.
*
Not exactly lying. I'd say some of it, (acceptable). &
finish the rest in my head.
*
love all round, lying warm in bed./light thru cracks/
naive, childlike, trusting
Then suddenly, distrust, accusing, anger
     Rehearsing?   Dream
change—
+ child thrashed for hours, days, years, 8 hrs a day.
Thick skin. (no him inside)
~~Sniffing Sammy~~, Crying Clive
+ They cldn't stop me crying.
+ The texture of JC, Nails thrashing, thorns
     Fainting—which bones between—
Now, often wants to be WITH—ppl. Anyone, to keep death
(~~loneliness~~ aloneness) away.
(like Davie.) Fight at Tank. Friends fighting in car
*
Hunting rabbits, hares, kangaroos.
Execution at a stake. Coup de Grace.
Absalom, by hair.
~~Man cleavered down.~~
My money based on Sufferings of others
insisted ⟶ Went to factories where <u>all</u> my clothes,
gadgets were made
Gave all money away. Talked to the poor.
Gave me all his change each day
Bigger tins, all time, cldn't move it

Cruelty viol. Boy next door

*
As in WS
Man is food for worms.
Hamlet—she cries for Yorick
Yet man seems greater than other animals
But was any man greater than Creep? or Boof, my faithful
mongrel

Making Stories

*
Conditions — one needs to look,
Price rises & pay rises — all expenses, costs sd/be taken into account.
Bus = greedy
Employees = enemy
pollution? = PR job
Waste
Profit & theft—shops, work
Cruelty, unkindness, absence of love, killing.
PUNISHMENT
Fyodorov's message.
Copyright.
~~Cruelty violence~~
Echoes of the Boy next door
*
The Blonde girl with no Bottom
Between them they proved he didn't do it—then they found the crime committed
didn't like the way he looked when he went.
Businesslike woman walks strt to Gap & jumps over. (have you ever heard of a...?)
Have you ever noticed how so/one always stops the suicide at the Gap instead of being amused & saying Oh, go ahead.
*
The value of writing = recording.
The ash-pickers may find out where we went wrong.
*
Hark I hear the pistol shots
hark I hear the Shostal pits
        Shistol pots
        Postal shits.
Ah fuck it. L & G this is my last performance.
*
HMS Pitiful
    de Fatigable
    Vulnerable
    Movable
    Vincible
    Domitable
Contemptibles
Pertinent, not imp
Tigers of the sea.
Under, then flying.

*
Tokyo, Alabama.
Istanbul, California
Budapest, Illinois
Calvary, Calgary
Rome, Cornwall
London, ~~Victoria~~ Tierra del Fuego
Berlin, Saskatchewan
Munich, Galilee

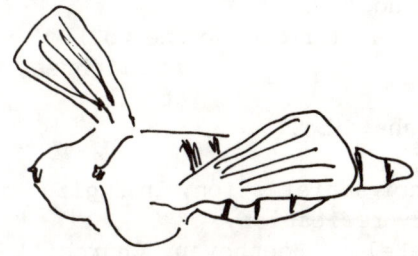

GREAT BANDED BOSOM-FLY

*
GREAT BANDED BOSOM-FLY.
[on reverse]
Jack Ketch
~~Pierrepoint~~
Rockefeller
Rothschild's Wine Cellar
~~Fred~~ Albert Lear
Alfred Hamlet
Bob Othello
URDU
GIBB
~~JERD~~ JURD OR JERD GERD
(none escaped the rhyme)
ICHOR

CANDIDE	CUNEGONDE
PANGLOSS	CUNNIBLONDE
POLONIUS	CUNNILINCTUS
OPHELIA	
HORATIO	
R.Stolz 90s	

Making Stories

*
I took an apple.
So proud of my successful theft that I showed f & m.
I was object of admiration all day.
Forgot abt it, put it on drawers.
Then in cupboard.
Means to Temptation
*
Schoolfriend.   Marie-Louise Fienberg.
Good at one thing only.
Nothing to do with school.
Teaches herself to orgas (or orgase the vb?)
                              at slightest touch
                              at will.
on sport day, there she'd be...
in class.
Finally does it, to her satisfaction, in English class.
Gerunds ~~During poetry recitation~~.
Collects busts: Ned Kelly, Beethoven, Churchill ~~lips,~~
~~cigar~~ Stalin... ~~Dr Spock~~, Einstein, ~~Tolstoi Turgen~~
~~Dostoi~~ where's Dost? Can't understand Raskolnikoff.
Kisses them all good morning & g.night—
*
This is not an affluent society.
cheap building, (less space for rooms
              (same cost, only just strong enough)
Goods can't be produced cheaply & in plenty.
Mortgage of 20 yrs common.
Schools have to help kids with bugs, flowers—tree houses
instead of kids getting them in bush, parks.
*
Kids enter afternoon buses, hanging out the windows,
making hell noise for the driver. Yelling at pple in the
street, walking, and laughing. Silent in envy at a long
red car, a blonde boy & girl.
Sky glow, b/pressure
  crystallised
  Rain, like sweat. Salty
  Coughed thunder, nose ran.

Road—arteries clogged
  Blood
(We were an organ of soc).

David Ireland—A Woman of the Future

We too, embedded in walls of soc.
The wind was picking at the locks, trying the doors for weakness. The roof ~~groaned~~ stays groaned.
*
Fat Lady in Parra.   Mthrs All-Liebe
paddles, fatly approaching, ~~aknow~~ flapping
legs all of a piece with stubby feet. Black
coat, white fatshoes, balding. To gave less
hairy covering. On the head. Head to foot,
...ding shortly, receding feet, lips, hair,
...ngy, breath, all receding. Baptist church
...ds as it always did, Gestetner fiercens in the
..., fine textured bricks heating towards the north.
...s northens, lady southens in a shallow curve.
...you or I or anyone know what makes the
...southward go?
*
3rd pers.
<u>Spoken of</u> between decision to have baby, & the conception.

5 mins not acc'td for: perhaps she was the pregnancy of Ralph Hart, who called & spoke to her outside.
Alexis
[on reverse]
GROSSMAN
GROSSMANN
*
Nothing is lost.
Who father?
Memory of nutty smell of urine
Was he getting a slight sickness that day?
He was my f. after all.
Also: Had been in a cool-~~room~~ place. Refrig place s/where, then hot bath. The egg remembered nutty ~~smell~~ taste & sweet beer-influenced ~~smell~~ taste When I was conc? Was it slippery, easy to get in. Yes, I tht she'd just been rooted.

Making Stories

*
As for how I knew ~~thi~~ it, I
Don't know, any more than I knew how ants gossip, joke abt
their queens, & ~~how they~~ dodge work.
*
didn't become a criminal, because of lack of suitable
companions
*
A Young Girl in my F's house?
Castrucchio Castricani.
*
To say she was happy is perhaps too strong, She was
cheerful. Lively.
Vigorous.

(Reproduced courtesy Mitchell Library, State Library of New South Wales.)

Extract 2 from the published version

A Woman of the Future, pp 180–8

Pistol Shots

Marie-Louise Fienberg was her full name. Like the rest, we were sometimes whispering together, friends for a day, and sometimes talking about each other, apart in different groups: enemies for a day. She cared for nobody and nothing, and I admired her.

In our school play, *The Duel*, she had to pause, listen, and say "Hark, I hear the pistol shots." She rehearsed unwillingly and always in a dead voice, but Plumpton, the teacher, said that would have to do.

On the night, Marie-Louise struck a pose, listened, and declaimed loudly, "Hark, I hear the shostal pits." That was wrong. Her mouth formed "shit." Her face screwed up, remembering. She remembered all right: she was acting. Spoiling the play.

"Hark, I hear the shistal pots."

Audibly she said, "Oh Christ."

She gave it a third try, and roared, "Hark, I hear the postal shits!"

Laughter filled the hall.

The failed actress waited for a break in the noise and said clearly, "Oh fuck it," and paused dramatically. "Ladies and gentlemen, this is my exit, and the end of my stage career." And walked off stage and down to where her parents sat. They tried to get her to go away, out of sight, but she wouldn't. She beamed and pointed at her Mum and Dad as if to say "I'm with them." Nothing embarrassed Marie-Louise.

Her Dad, Ezra Fienberg the newsagent, had the wound of a bullet below his right shoulder, a bullet wound that didn't heal. The sign of its going in was plain, but there was no place to show where it came out. No X-ray plate showed the bullet, though he'd had more than half a dozen done.

Was it made of plastic? people said. They knew from recent wars that plastic fragments don't show on X-rays.

No, there was no plastic bullet in there, just an inward-lipped hole that didn't bleed.

He was proud of it, and it brought business his way. He had a double reason for pleasure. I daresay it was one of the peculiarities of our suburb that he didn't say how the hole was made, and no one asked. Everyone was different, everyone was separate; there was no community shoulder to cry on.

The Great Banded Bosom-Fly

Outside our classroom the hill sloped down toward Hunter's Creek. Slim trees stood straight, birds sang loudly. We watched out the windows when we could. Some birds were bullies, some sneak thieves, some tried to boss the others, but couldn't get them to obey.

Playtime, lunchtime, and sometimes for lessons we sat outside. Delivery men came into the school in their handy, well-used and often grimy vehicles. We—around eight of us in our gang—used to wonder aloud about the equipment they carried under the zips of their trousers. Were they just as handy, well-used and grimy as their vehicles?

For most of us it wasn't till a year or two later that we realized what care they took with their personal equipment; just how clean, pink, scrubbed and shiny—on the horn—they really were. Well-used, too. *And* handy.

Let us return to our lessons in the lovely shade of the smooth-barked erect eucalypts that mostly had only a small crown of foliage above all that length of smooth pale trunk.

Marie-Louise is drawing. I am beginning the set essay, "Tigers of the Sea."

I glanced across at her work. She drew two large breasts that sprouted wings and trailed a thick body crossed laterally with stripes,

Making Stories

like a hornet. Underneath she wrote, "The Great Banded Bosom-Fly."

"What about 'Tigers of the Sea'?" I said. She was supposed to do the essay too. "You pick *your* fucking nose, I'll pick mine," she said rudely.... *fucking* nose?

Plumpton cheered up when she saw my essay. She put it aside to read to the class. Leafing though the pile she passed the bosom-fly, unsigned, and came to Marie-Louise's "Tigers of the Sea." We were reading something while the teacher looked through the essays. As I watched her face I knew ML had done it again. We called her ML to save time.

"Do you really think, Fienberg, that any body of sailors that ever inhabited the globe and sailed the seven seas could possibly fight—never mind fight well, but fight at all—with names on the bows of their boats—"

"Ships," corrected Fienberg.

"Ships, then, and on their lifeboats and equipment—"

"Get to the point, Plumpton."

"Respect, Fienberg. *Mrs.* Plumpton."

"Never mind the self-pity. Call me *Miss* Fienberg."

"All right, Marie-Louise. All right. You tell me how men could fight for their country in ships with names like Vulnerable, Movable, Vincible, Domitable, Fatigable? And this? The frigate Pitiful!"

"Frigate, yes," repeated ML.

"Frigate indeed," added Plumpton. "Well, Miss Admiral Fienberg?"

"Think back a bit, my dear respected Mrs. Plumpton. I wouldn't lay this on you without good historical backing. Remember the Old Contemptibles?"

She remembered. The class waited, yawning delicately on the brink of sleep.

"Their enemies christened them that. And they wore it. Insisted on it. Did they fight lousy?"

"Lousily. It's an adverb."

"Same thing. So why shouldn't sailors have a sense of humor?"

"Don't be impertinent."

"I think it's pertinent," said ML. Plumpton was pleased she knew the word.

Plumpton looked back at ML's essay.

"You have imagination, Fienberg. Ships that move on the sea, over it, under it. You can't have things like that."

"The creatives put imagination into words; scientists then know what to invent. Buck Rogers ... Leonardo."

Plumpton screwed her nose. "Straight off the sci-fi shows, Fienberg. But these places: Tokyo, Alabama; Budapest, Illinois; Berlin, Saskatchewan. Are you making fun of the Americans again? And I suppose this is yours too?" She held up the bosom-fly. "May I ask what this is?"

"The great banded bosom fly," orated ML. Plumpton showed it round.

"Go on, Fienberg. Explain. We'll wait."

Marie-Louise began to sing:

> *"Jesu lover of my soul,
> Let me to thy bosom-fly."*

"That'll do, Fienberg. We get the idea."

She liked Marie-Louise. Liked her a lot. Often we noticed her looking at ML in the playground, if you can imagine a wistfully predatory look.

I can.

One Good Feature

None of the rest of us thought it was much of a poem, but the English master, Mister Jagarnath, had a very high opinion of it, and put it in the school magazine.

Here it is:

> *I am the sister of a motor mechanic.
> I am the daughter of a bush carpenter.
> Maybe I will marry a plumber
> And be the mother of a civil engineer.*

When the magazine came out, with the poem proudly at the bottom of a page on the basketball team, she bore her poem proudly home and showed it to the Lutherburrow family, several of whom could read.

The poems *we* wrote were far more inwardly directed.

Lil had one good feature. Her fingers, from where they joined her hand, down to the nails, were a milky color tinged with pink. But already the dark hairs were hinting on the backs of the third joints, as they were apparent on her forearms and shouting on her shanks, between ankle and calf. I hoped she would keep one good feature when she was grown-up and hairy.

Making Stories

The Thoughts of Mukami

Zekia Mukami played soccer in one of the school teams, and cricket in summer, and had no fights in the playground; he was aloof, self-possessed and looked superior.

One day his superior expression cracked, and his aloofness was abandoned and the anger in him came out with a rush. It was after the social science class; we had been discussing antidiscrimination laws of the past.

"You can't see you are insulting the people you make laws to protect!" he shouted in the playground at a group of us, as if history were in the present tense.

"You are saying they're helpless! But I tell you this: the black races have no intention of passing antidiscrimination laws to protect whites when they get in front of the whites! There are no gentlemanly feelings then! When the black races hold the whip firmly, they will give it to the inferior whites, I can tell you. One day, my father says, the white man will be the colored world's Jew! Whites are animals, they are degenerate, my father says!"

We didn't know what to say. I'd heard father talk of the recurring speculation about the white races being overwhelmed by the colored, and the colored having no love for the white, and when I mentioned it to him that evening, he said, "The world's Jew, eh?" And nodded his head, but didn't say any more. I guess he was getting his opinions in order, or thinking about it.

Zekia Mukami hated us. For him, history wasn't past at all: the hundreds of years of crimes against blacks were against him, and they were now. The rage of history was on our doorstep.

Zekia was a very good boxer. I was one of four girls who were allowed to box at school, but although we sometimes fought boys, we didn't box with Zekia.

Nipple-Napping

It wasn't a special game like the one tit crunch or the tit clash—anyone did it, including much bigger girls; especially the gang-girls of year eleven and year twelve, big-thighed bruisers who intimidated shopkeepers and received warnings from the police not to go round in large groups on late-shopping nights.

Anyone could be a nipple-napper. You simply made a sudden grab for the edge of the breast, and since the fashions made the nipple conspicuous, it was rarely that you grabbed the wrong place. The best method of escape was movement. If you saw a female walking along and suddenly making a waltz step sideways, you could bet she'd evaded a nipple-napper.

It wasn't completely one-sided: we did the same to boys. Theirs were harder to grab hold of.

One of the boys that gave the best reaction to nipple-napping was Anthony Yuen.

His nipple was hard to find for the first two terms of high school, but it grew with constant attention, and became as big and outstanding as most of the girls'. He squawked every time, and went round clutching it, swollen and painful.

Anthony had deer-like features. A few meters away, he would turn his head, and stay still, not so much watching you, as regarding. His thin shanks narrowed to fine ankles. He would stand still, for a long time perfectly still, then canter off, gently, lightly, a few meters, then if any threat or alarm disturbed him he was off like a shot, lightly, on his toes, his legs twinkling as if they had no weight. Or he would stop, and turn again, twitch his ears together, and sometimes one at a time, then if any nipple-napper appeared, he broke into an immediate gallop. He would dash right on into the playing field until he was nearly a hundred meters away, then partly turn, watching, perfectly still again, ready for flight.

If he'd been nipple-napped, he would be holding his chest with one narrow hand that was as close to the fine bones of a paw as you'd want to see.

Always the one nipple, the left one. The big one.

I could make him run just by looking at it hard.

Buck was our name for him. His parents thought of him as Anthony, which was absurd.

Once I saw him backed against a wall. His eyes were stark, but something looked out. Something; and I had thought that place was empty.

Coming Ready or Not

Fulvia Strickland had an older sister and knew more than we did about boys. We gathered round in the playground, eager to learn.

"When they're about to blow," Fulvia told us, "that's when you've got the power. They know if you wriggle free or pull away they get nothing. But that's when you're liable to get hurt. They hang on real tight so you can't dislodge 'em. Animal reflex."

"How can you tell when it's happening?"

Making Stories

"They start to get very sincere—facial expression, hard muscles, more powerful thrusts—"

"What sort of thrusts?"

"Back and forward. They're not going anywhere, but they go back nearly to take it out, then jam it in as far as it will go."

"But their bones must stop it—"

"Naturally. There's nowhere to go, but they take it very seriously. Ever seen dogs?"

"Yes, horses too," I said. "But it never seems to take long."

"Listen, kid." She was forgetting we were the same age. "Some of the older ones, they know how to hold it, they'll stay in all day. The only way to get round it is to relax, but even then your skin gets so tired of being jammed between their bone and yours that you wish you had a gun to put 'em out of their misery. Say, that *would* be an experience!' She was lost briefly in her own dreams, and we looked at each other, and away.

We all knew of Stuart Regan after school beating the other boys in a race to get it to come, and I looked at the faces of the other girls. Were they scared? Were they thinking privately that if they got part of a boy in they could control the rest of him, and wondering if it was true? And were they wondering if it was true that some could shoot it so hard that you could feel it hit the sides, or bounce off the back wall?

The Social Science Class

"Australia has an empty belly," said jolly Mister Chandrager. "Look at the map and you will see that the ocean and the coastal strip contain emptiness. That is the first impression Australia makes. When you get to know it, it is strange how that motif repeats itself. No ghosts, all is plain and above-board, you see. Not even a bunyip...."

He began to laugh.

"Supposed to be a bunyip!" he spluttered over a pile of our exercise books. "A bunyip."

"And what happens?" he asked rhetorically.

"No blooming bunyip!" he squealed. For some minutes he was out of action.

We didn't understand why he laughed but we knew he was laughing at us. Whatever emptiness the land had, we were born to: we shared it.

It was soon the end of the period, and when the siren went we rushed for the door, and he gathered up his papers and things, but couldn't resist shouting after us, "Not even a blooming haunted house! No jolly bunyip! No jolly ghosts! Jolly nothing!"

The next time we had Mister Chandragar he was more serious. He was still on his favorite topic, though, and we had to wear it.

"Australia does as the world does, it sits on the comfortable coast of life, where its settled nature is steeped in the past. The future is the greatest problem. The future is at the center of Australia's problems."

It made a big impression on me, for of all things the future was the most mysterious, the most inviting. And the idea of a useless existence, dragging on till I was old and worn out, repugnant as it was to me, seemed to apply to my country as well. What a future it would be for the land of my birth if Frees and Servants of Society could both be living their lives so that no day is futile and no hour bored!

The Apple Time Bomb

On the way home from school my case was light, and I felt like running. As I passed the shops at a run I lifted an apple from a stand outside the greengrocer's shop and kept going. A few dogs came out to bark at me when I went past their houses, but these encounters came to nothing.

I showed it to my father.

"Why a Democrat?" he said. "You'll have a mouth full of skin—in your teeth, everywhere. They're only good for transporting. They're good travelers, they're so tough."

I put it in a drawer where some of my winter things were kept. The thing about winter clothes is that a lot of them never get worn. You always think you're going to need warm things in the cold weather, but you never do. There might be a few cold days, but that's about it.

I put the apple at the back of the drawer and forgot it. As I got into bed it occurred to me that no one even saw me take it. But lying there waiting for sleep to come I thought: some people are ordinary and have ordinary desires and ordinary rights, but the extraordinary have a right to transgress with impunity.

That wiped the apple off my conscience as if it had never been.

Elizabeth Jolley
Mr Scobie's Riddle

You can't help having a message in your book if you're writing about human beings...messages creep in.

Elizabeth Jolley

Here listen to this, Frankie said

Flop me Drop me
Turn me on
Huh! Huh! Huh!   Yeah Yeah Yeah
Flop me Top me   Report about Thompson's death
I'm turned on   Wait you haven't read the
                   newspaper misprint Food memories
                   Jeeze Squeeze

Something about Hartley here.
                              Look back to
                              Privett's life
                              and death for to
                              put in flesh & gristle

Question
Why are we having the carol services so
early?

Hartley
Oh let's shake paws Hyacinth and call it
quits!

Price
No christian names in the office how often
do I have to remind you Miss Price replies
                              distance any

Frankie and Robyn
singing & dancing for Scobie
                 small wonky peal,   Mr. Scobie can you
To carry on letter from Scobie & Benka   put us on their
to Hartley — brief explanation of   (wanting their voices and
    the walk along the railway track   their song recorded
    and was picked up could not   after Hartley's rest
    remember the name of the nursing home. Vint
         Flash to dialogue   Robyn chased by Miss
                                          Hartley, Robyn leaves
Put in letter reference to John not knowing where he
                                 was going was Scobie why
                                          has the little bird
                                          flown?

Making Stories

Mr Scobie's Riddle was first published in 1983, but early in our research we discovered that Elizabeth Jolley had been working on various forms of it for some twenty years before that.

When we looked through the early writings of *Mr Scobie's Riddle* in the Mitchell Library, we were surprised to find, as well as rough notes, three short stories and a radio play which later became embedded within the novel.

The manuscript extract we chose is from the stage when *Mr Scobie's Riddle* was a short novel, and the outline of two of the short stories can still be seen in it. Elizabeth Jolley calls this version 'the lament'. Since we could see that the basic material had not altered, we wondered how Elizabeth Jolley had gone about creating its re-vision.

Our interview with Elizabeth Jolley took place in Sydney in September 1991.

INT: *Mr Scobie's Riddle* evolved over a very long time—around twenty years. Can you tell us how that came about?

EJ: I came to understand that I couldn't offer a lament, that it was too painful to read. And I wasn't altogether happy with the length, it was a long, long short story in a way, not a novel. I did try sending it off and had one or two rather unkind remarks about it from publishers' readers, which made me realise even more that it wouldn't do. Then as I began my teaching of classes, and I did lots of reading with the students, I began to learn how other writers injected something into a theme that they had—the humour, for example, or more to do with landscape, or more to do with making the character more full. So that was what I was trying to do with *Scobie*.

In the first writing, Miss Hailey was simply a person who stood in the hall—she was Mrs Hailey—and all she said was: 'Will nobody come and fix this blind?' That's all she was in the lament. Because I was brooding, I suppose, and doing little bits, I actually saw Miss Hailey standing by the side of the road when I was driving home one day. She was wearing a hat, a straw hat with a chinstrap, a bit like a Canadian Mounted Policeman's, and she was talking to a group of rather miserable-looking people. She looked as though she was telling them the way, and she looked as though she was really enjoying doing this—tall, thin, and all these people clustered about her.

When I got home I wrote down that picture and realised it was

Miss Hailey, then I wrote the passage with Miss Hailey in conversation with the Matron, when Matron asks her how to spell archipelago. I built on her, I began to explore her a bit more. I discovered that her sponge bag had a whisky bottle in it, and then I found out that she had written a poem for the Shire Clerk on his waterworks, and Matron was irritated by this. Then I discovered that she's really held prisoner by Matron, in the hospital, but I hadn't discovered exactly why or how. Obviously they'd been together since they were schoolgirls, but I didn't know that. The strange thing is that this excitement of discovery in the exploration and the invention—it's a stepping off into the imagination. I'm not one of these people who says that the characters are in control of me. I always like to feel that I am controlling the characters, I am making the character, exploring the character. I can't be starry-eyed and say the characters have taken me over, and they're going their own way. They don't do that for me. I really have to wait till I explore and find out something.

Writing is a mixture of exploring and inventing. You're inventing a character, and once you get the character a little bit on paper, you're exploring them and discovering more about them. With *The Well*, I started off with Hester and Kathy, two women brushing each other's hair, and I just wrote that out. Then I wrote another paragraph a few days later and they were still brushing each other's hair but one was much older than the other. And there was a little window a bit high up looking out into a wheat paddock where the moon was on the stubble, so I put that in. Bit by bit I wrote another paragraph and then they would be still brushing each other's hair, and it would turn out that the older one had adopted the younger one.

After I'd seen Miss Hailey standing on the street she became more of a character in the novel. That was the beginning—the continuation, rather—of a rewriting that I was starting, and she became quite a forceful and full character in the book. She hadn't been before. That kind of thing is very exciting and very surprising and it just came about from seeing her like that. I didn't know her in the first writing of the book. I had to find her.

INT: Is that the sort of thing you mean by 'making a complication for myself', which you mention in another interview?

EJ: Yes, you do make complications for yourself, because you bring in another character and then you have to do another whole rewriting. In 1980, I went to Albany to do a Creative Writing Summer School. I took down the typed copy of what I thought was the finished book to correct it. I took a walk the first afternoon after the first class, up Mount Clarence, and discovered without realising it that Hailey and Matron had been at school together, and that Matron's first name was Hyacinth—it occurred to me that anyone who could call a boy Iris would call their daughter Hyacinth—and that Hailey had called Matron Tin-Tin as a school nickname. Then I discovered that Rawlings had been at school too, the three of them had all been at school together. It was almost as though somebody came up behind me and tapped me on the shoulder and said, 'You know, we were at school together.'

There and then I started rewriting the whole book. You can't just make an alteration in one place when you're brooding on something, so I began a whole rewriting, and got quite excited again—the same excitement as discovering Hailey. But you cannot alter something in one place in a manuscript—although it may be only half a sentence somewhere, you can't just open the book somewhere else and put a bit in there and open the book and put a bit in there. You've really got to do a comprehensive over-writing or rewriting. I was quite prepared to do it and I was quite excited about doing it.

I'm glad I did it because I gave Mr Scobie the hill—he did not have the hill at that stage. That was Mount Clarence, with the rain drifting across it every morning. I never saw the other side of Mount Clarence—I went up from the hotel, walked to the top and came down the same side—I never knew what was round that other side, and I gave that not-knowing to Mr Scobie.

It shows how autobiographical, without being autobiographical, a novel is. I have recently thought about these bits of autobiographical material in novels—I have always denied them, but because people ask me, I find I must tell them the truth when I answer. Yes, I did see a hill there and I did give that hill to Mr Scobie.

INT: As if it doesn't belong to you, though it happened to you?

EJ: I suppose the awareness, and the seeing the rain drift across is autobiographical—it's something you've seen yourself, so you give it to the character. But it doesn't make me Mr Scobie. This is the great difference, that people who are not writers don't understand. You may give a character an experience, and you haven't actually had the experience, you've only had a bit of it.

INT: You could probably walk up that hill at another time or in another frame of mind, and not have any sort of discoveries—do you think so?

EJ: Well, you have to be brooding, although very often you don't realise that you are brooding. You think you're wasting time and not writing, you get in a panic. The fact is that you can go shopping, and at the same time you have your character with you, and you're giving little bits of things to the character. Strangely enough when my husband would say things—he wouldn't even know what I was writing, I could never talk about something while I was working on it because it would kill the brooding, I'd become self-conscious about it—but Leonard would sometimes say something to me while we were in the car driving somewhere, and what he said would fit so exactly—because I was, as it were, stripped ready to receive anything that was coming in that might feed the character.

If you're writing you'll know that feeling where somebody says something and they'd be really shocked if they knew what you had done with what they said. I can't explain why this is. I don't understand it, really. I said something about this once to a group of women and one of them said to me, I can't understand how you can do anything at all while you are brooding and carrying the character with you, and your whole mind is full of this. Well, the whole mind is full, but it's also splitting into the different things you have to do.

When I'm teaching I'm not thinking about my work, but sometimes a student will utter something in their own idiom, something like, 'I'll spread his nose over his face.' That is something that I would never say or think but I'll just scribble it down in my notebook, and then I'll remember to look later and see what I've got there, and put it into a folder.

INT: And are you thinking, 'oh, that will do for so-and-so,' or are you just thinking 'that's a wonderful idiom'?

EJ: 'That's a wonderful idiom.' If I've actually got the character—Scobie for example—he would never say that, but somebody else might, and he might overhear it and be a bit shocked.

INT: So you're really picking up things all the time, almost as if unconsciously you've got a map in your mind where things might go.

EJ: Or a heap of manila folders. I don't write in fixed pages. I used to when I was young, but you need to be able to move pages about. When the children were little I used to just take out the notebook and go on writing where I left off and I didn't do any rewriting. I just was writing things that came into my head for the character in that story.

I realised later on that if I really wanted to write a story seriously I'd have to have separate sheets of paper. It seems a really naive thought, but it did come to me as a kind of profound thing, that you needed separate sheets of paper and folders. In fact it was my husband who said: 'Don't try to cram everything on one bit of paper'. I'd start right up here and I'd fill up the whole page and there was nowhere to write in. He would say: 'Spread your work out,'—he just said that once, having glanced across—'Spread it out so you can write in between lines.' I did start to do that, and would often write in between with different coloured pens so that I could keep the original thing, and then pick up what I had written in, and decide later on, in the rewriting, what I was going to use. That was his idea. It seems very stupid that I didn't think of simplifying things a bit in that way.

INT: Making the notes was part of the business of your life?

EJ: Yes. I'd developed the habit of making the quick note while I was in the kitchen doing things. I think I have annoyed feminist people by saying publicly that I couldn't work until the beds were made and the house tidy. I must have my mind clear. If you do some writing in the afternoon, and you come out to a kitchen where the breakfast things still are, and the washing isn't done, and you've got nothing in the house to cook, it is quite painful and tedious to do the household things, isn't it? But if you do them swiftly and in a way where you're in charge of them, it's not so bad.

INT: You said *Mr Scobie's Riddle* was impossible to fit together. When the moment came to fit the notes together, how did you go about it?

EJ: Oh, that was terrible. I even tried bits of different coloured paper for each segment and for each character, but you can't do that. The characters would all be together in the narrative at some stages, so that didn't work.

But that's why I made that little 'Guide for the Perplexed' at the beginning of the book. I made the 'Guide' with numbers for pages in a particular manuscript, so that I could then find roughly where I wanted to go. They were key bits in the novel, so I'd find that bit, and then I'd know what was around there. I was such a long time writing it, and I was doing other things as well. But when the 'Guide' went to the typist she typed it and collated it with the page numbers in the typescript, so when it came back from her I sent the whole thing to Penguin, and they quite liked the 'Guide' and it stayed in.

But some people have been really put off by it, they've phoned me to ask what the reason is for it. I did pick key bits for my own benefit, but they are bits that are rather ridiculous, aren't they? Well, the whole novel is full of ridiculous things about human living, really.

INT: The lament is heartbreaking, and in the finished book those layers of outrage and anguish are still there, but there's also the humour and the irony...

EJ: I wrote the lament in the early 1960s, when I was doing C-class nursing—that is, nursing-home nursing. The lament belongs to the actual time of nursing. I was able to put in the black comedy and the ridiculous when I was no longer nursing. Little things I could make up, about the Matron and the night report, were much easier to do.

INT: So it was time distance.

EJ: Yes, time distance, and also perhaps as I was older I was able to see more the ridiculous side of living. Perhaps as you get older you see the tragic, but you also manage to see a bit more the ridiculous, especially if your home life isn't all that easy.

People have sometimes thought that because of a difficult home life a writer might escape into fiction. That wasn't true at all, because I always regarded my fiction as an art. It's like making a pot or a dress or a really beautiful cake; it isn't something you're just doing in order to get better from something. People will always say: 'Oh, you must have been glad to get that off your chest.' Well, it's never been on my chest!

INT: You said in the beginning that teaching your students was one of the things that got you back into *Mr Scobie's Riddle*.

EJ: In the 1970s I was asked to do Creative Writing classes at Fremantle Arts Centre, then I had country workshops, then I had a couple of classes at Western Australian Institute of Technology, which is part of a degree course, so I had very different groups. I firmly believe that students must read if they're going to write. They've got to read and see what writers have done that makes something successful. When you read a short story with one group, then with another group and another, and the students all say things about the story, then you see things that you didn't see yourself, because a whole lot of fresh minds are coming forward.

When you have leisure classes you have all kinds of people—

from builders and plumbers to doctors and lawyers, housewives, teachers, childless people, children, women who've grown up and left school at thirteen and had to look after younger brothers and sisters—so you get a very varied look at the writing. That taught me such a lot, and helped me with my own writing.

INT: You did say that teaching helped bring you to the irony and the black humour.

EJ: Yes, it did. In order to help people feel at ease I found myself seeing the ridiculous side of things. In those classes I could get people who would get hysterics over something and scream, a release of pent-up emotion. The first time it happened I didn't know what to do. I sat quietly for a minute and thought, I'll leave her and we'll just go on, and this particular person resolved it for herself, she got up and danced around and then sat down, and then afterwards came and said she felt marvellous. I had a builder who burst into tears. He had written a passage about something from his childhood, and it was to do with a dead child, and it was obviously his own little brother, and he'd never ever thought of writing about this or facing it even, and he cried. When something like that happens, you have to keep the class going, perhaps break the mood with a ridiculous remark, or a comforting remark together with something that points to—I can't quite explain it—the ridiculous side that there is to everything. So I began to see how important humour was.

Even more important, I read a book called *Alien Son*, by Judah Waten. In that book Judah Waten's character speaks about the settlement of his family in Midland, which is just outside Perth. The Jewish community had put on a play, and Judah Waten's father tells the main actor that there's something missing in the play, it needed a wedding scene or a dance.

I already knew about this injection of something to lift the message—this little dance, that I teach my students about. I knew about that before I wrote the lament, in a way, because I read *Alien Son* as soon as I arrived here. That was 1959, and I resolved to try and lift things. But even making that resolve, I wrote that lament, knowing it wouldn't do. I tried description, and flashback—the exquisite memory, as it were, the special memory. But it also needed the black comedy, which I think is very hard to do. But I think I managed it in *Scobie*.

INT: You wrote about five other books between when you started and when you finished *Mr Scobie's Riddle*.

Elizabeth Jolley—Mr Scobie's Riddle

EJ: *Palomino* and *Milk and Honey* were being written at the same time, and in the early 1970s I wrote the stories that are in *Five-Acre Virgin* and *The Travelling Entertainer*. 'Night Report', which is now part of *Mr Scobie's Riddle*, was published in an anthology called *Frictions*[1]—it was done on radio like a little play—it doesn't stop you putting it into a novel if you want to.

INT: *Mr Scobie's Riddle* has three short stories and a radio play in it. What is that urge to re-use material?

EJ: It's hard to explain. You write something, a novel, and then if you're taking a long time writing it, you may craft something out of it into a short story and try it somewhere, because you're trying to get your name known. I thought, you see, in my ignorance, that you couldn't send a novel to a publisher without you being known in the literary journals or by radio. Also, the craft of the short story fascinates me, and if I saw a short story forming, or wanted to create one, I would do that, while at the same time it was part of a novel.

INT: Did those other things you wrote between beginning and finishing *Mr Scobie's Riddle* teach you something about the journey of Mr Scobie?

EJ: Yes they did. *Milk and Honey* was written in the first person, and it borders on a lament, it has hardly any humour in it at all. I find the first person narration of *Milk and Honey* tiresome. It and *Palomino* are very slow moving, whereas in the writing of *Scobie* it's swifter, and that is something I learned alongside those slower things. The fragments in *Scobie*—I felt they were an improvement.

INT: What about the shift from first person in the lament to third person in the final version?

EJ: I think it distances you a bit, and makes it easier for it not to be a lament. I like writing in the first person, I very often will start something in first person and change to third.

I always find it hard to approach the writing, especially if I've been away from it for a while. I would often write a bit to my father—we had a great correspondence—I would often write to my father what I was writing about, then I would leave his letter and start writing. That was a great help. The letter form is a way to get the language easily, it is the most colloquial and free-running form.

1 Edited by A. Gibbs and A. Tilson, Sybylla, 1983.

INT: What is the thing you like about first person—why would you start off in that?

EJ: It's very often present tense too. Just to capture a mood, or a scene—the immediate—and then to place it somewhere else.

INT: Do you feel you live more intensely in the character if you write it in first person?

EJ: No, because even when it's in third person I'm still brooding and I'm still intensely in that character. I think also if you keep a writer's journal, which I do, you will often write a passage in the journal, and it's 'I'. It will have the date on it, and I'll have also perhaps the weather conditions, if it's hot or if it's wet. It's very useful to write that in first person. It gives you an environment. You can pick from that what you need with some kind of authenticity. It's no good writing about a scene and you want it to be on a very, very, hot, dry day with the East wind really tearing at everything, if in fact it's quite cold and it's early in the morning and the electric fire is on and you're wearing about three dressing gowns.

INT: The hospital in *Mr Scobie's Riddle* is so clearly visualised that a reader could draw a map of it: where the bucket is, and so on.

EJ: Well you see I have the actual authentic picture of the passage in that hospital—the front steps that are broken, where the kitchen is, where the things growing outside the kitchen are and where Room Three is. But I don't have the whole of it, only a bit of it.

INT: In your head?

EJ: In my head. I've drawn it from a real place, and people have tried to drag out of me where the place is. It actually doesn't matter, because I worked in more than one place, and I joined bits —there wasn't a caravan in the garden at one place, but there was at another place.

With *Scobie* I've got unfinished ragged edges on the map. I've decided that doesn't matter, but you need when you're writing not to do something that would make it impossible for a reader to build their own landscape. Obviously people put their own picture to the landscape, because with *Foxybaby*, which is so definitely set in one of the most isolated places in the wheat belt, I had a most lovely letter from a woman in East Anglia, in England. She said she'd just read *Foxybaby* and it was lovely for the first time in her life to have a book set in East Anglia!

Elizabeth Jolley—Mr Scobie's Riddle

INT: In another interview you mention that Brahms's *German Requiem* underlies *Mr Scobie's Riddle* in some way—can you talk about that?

EJ: The different passages of the Requiem that Brahms used underlie the novel, because I wanted the novel to be a celebration of life and not just a thesis on nursing homes and on death. I haven't been clever enough to actually divide the book into the divisions that the *Requiem* is in.

The music itself is important because Mr Scobie has tapes of it, and can no longer play them and enjoy the music. If you remember, Mrs Rawlings says at one point: 'Why don't you listen to your music?' But he's lost heart. I used the not-playing as a sign that he's not able to console himself with the music any longer. Similarly, I also show him as not being able to use the stored memories of life, to console him and comfort him in the loneliness of his old age.

I use music of another kind to show something about Scobie, and the great gap between him and Frankie and Robyn. Do you remember—to please them he lets one of them put something on tape, and all he can think about is that her hair needs a good wash!

INT: So the *Requiem* inspired not only Mr Scobie, but also you?

EJ: I was writing the lament. I listened to the *Requiem*, and I didn't like it at the start, but Leonard had put it on a cassette, and he said: I want you to listen, and I listened...and then I listened to it again, and it began to really mean something to me, and I got the German words. Then I found the passages in the English Bible [see Extract 1, page 167].

INT: Do you get anxious about the work, the book that you're writing?

EJ: Oh yes, and this year I've been anxious that I wasn't working at a novel, and then it occurred to me that I've been like that before. In fact I said to Leonard: 'I'm really upset about my character, I'm not getting anything written,' and he said: 'Can I remind you that you're always like that at the beginning of a work, only you forget.' That made me feel better.

INT: Do you cope with that just by keeping on going?

EJ: I think so. Doggedly persisting I think is the thing. It was very depressing to be rejected for so long, and rather cruelly rejected, partly I think because one lived in the West.

Making Stories

INT: So what kept you going?

EJ: Just because I wanted to write. That is why there are so many repetitions in my work. I thought: this is a lovely image, I'll use this, like a piece of music. I thought: they're not going to be published, what does it matter, this fits in very nicely here. I don't see any harm in the repetitions. I rewrote some of them because my editors said: You don't want to be considered the person who recycles images. But some do repeat.

INT: Cezanne painted the same dish of apples over and over.

EJ: Exactly, and you can recognise a Beethoven piece without knowing what it is, simply because of a phrase that has recurred. And I don't think that matters.

INT: Have responses from editors been helpful?

EJ: Some rejections were helpful. I knew without being told that *Mr Scobie's Riddle* was a lament and somebody added that nobody on earth would want to read it. That really hit home. I actually knew that, but it was good that somebody said it.

INT: They weren't ever constructive?

EJ: No, I never had any constructive remark. Over *Palomino* I got some terrible remarks: that nowhere in Australia would there be an audience for a book like this—when books 'like this' were being read and written all over the world, but not in Australia. Oh, it was the work of a 'sick mind'. 'This person is neurotic and needs to see a doctor.' 'This is not US,' capital U capital S.

INT: So there was no one you could turn to in those moments of doubt?

EJ: No. I was really hurt, and I felt that I must be mad. The thing that comforted me was to write a reply to those things but never send it.

INT: A lot of people would get rejections and not recover...

EJ: Well, I think I'm an optimist. Also I really did want to write. The art of the small novel and short fiction really does attract me. I can't help making a note in my journal about something that I see. When we travelled across to Australia by ship, other people were taking photographs. I had a camera but I never used it, and would just sit somewhere and just write something in my diary about the journey. To put down your emotions about landfall, for example, to me is the thing that matters, more than a photograph of it.

INT: Is there a particular thing you're saying in your work?

EJ: You can't help having a message in your book if you're writing about human beings, because everything touches on different social things—messages creep in. But I don't sit down and say, I'm now going to write a story about the hardships experienced by old people in old people's homes. I'm not writing a historical paper or a learned paper, I'm just writing a novel.

Extract 1 from Elizabeth Jolley's notes

In her interview, Elizabeth Jolley mentions Brahms's *A German Requiem*. She sent us these notes, dated 1981, with her handwritten comments added for us.

Psalm 39
Verse 4: Lord, make me to know mine end, and the measure of my days, what it is: that I may know how frail I am.
(*This part in particular underlies* Scobie, *the death of Scobie/Privett and Hughes—is he called Hughes? And the idea of continual resurrection i.e. 3 new old men as new patients.*)
Verse 5: Behold, thou hast made my days as an handbreadth; and mine age is as nothing before thee: verily every man at his best is altogether vanity. (*the span of the hand over the skull*)

Psalm 84
Verse 1: How amiable are thy tabernacles, O Lord of Hosts!
(*Miss Hailey's tabernacles*)

St John 16
Verse 22: And ye now therefore have sorrow: but I will see you again, and your heart shall rejoice, and your joy no man taketh from you.
(*the celebration of life in the novel and it not being a 'thesis on nursing homes'!*)

Making Stories

Epistle to the Hebrews ch.13
Verse 14: For here have we no continuing city, but we seek one to come.
(*The continuation of 'life'.*)

Extract 2 from an early manuscript

In her interview, Elizabeth Jolley refers to this as a 'lament'.

They have put away my clothes in a suitcase on a shelf behind the bathroom door. So now in the mornings I do not get dressed but stay in my pyjamas and put on this new dressing gown which Matron rushed into town ~~for~~ to buy for me.

'I'll put it on the Account Dear,' she says very pleased with herself, she comes straight in with the parcel and makes me wear it at once. 'Joan, your niece, remember Joan Dear? She was going to get one for you, remember Dear? When you first came? Well she must have forgotten. And when I saw the advertisement I said to myself "Just the thing for Dear old Uncle Martin," so I rushed off, it seemed such a wonderful Bargain Dear!' Matron and Mrs Rawlings both say I look very nice in the dressing gown and I ~~haven't the heart to~~ don't want to spoil their pleasure by saying I would rather wear my ordinary clothes.

So now I sit. Mrs Rawlings comes to fetch me for my shower late in the mornings. They do the ladies first.

'I'm quite clean,' I say to her. 'Once a week would be plenty. Too much water takes all the natural oils out of the skin,' I say. But she says there's nothing like plenty of soap and water to put everything to rights.

I think this daily shower is weakening me and I have a head cold, something I suffer from rarely as a rule. I think this daily shower, sometimes the water is only tepid and I am left shivering, is the cause of this cold I have.

'Why don't you play your music these days?' Mrs Rawlings says one morning. I never thought Mrs Rawlings liked the music. I always thought she just put up with it.

'Do you like music Mrs Rawlings?' I ask.

'Well it helps to pass the time if it's not too loud,' she says pulling the Tape Recorder from under the bed where it has been all these weeks.

'My Word,' she says. 'Just look at all that dust.'

But I haven't the heart for Chopin or Bach or Mendelssohn. How could I listen to some tender phrase from the past and not break down. ~~Among the tapes there is a whole reel of songs are several songs.~~ I always loved the intimate bond between the singer and the pianist. There is this same bond between and within the music, matching phrases, questioning and answering, leading and sustaining, explaining and comforting, all the time the notes of the piano running towards or /following/after the singing voice. This bond between the music and those performing it I loved. If I listened now and heard them as I used to hear them sustaining each other in this way it would only enhance the loneliness that has come upon me more than ever.

'No I won't have the music just now thank you,' I say.

'Well what about the Bible then?' Mrs Rawlings says. It is raining outside and too cold for the verandah. 'Or what about another book? What's this. "Songs of Innocence" by William Blake. That sounds all right. You couldn't go wrong with a title like that.' She opens the little book and puts it in my lap.

'There,' she says. 'Have a nice quiet little read till dinner time.'

It is a poem about the night. I read because Mrs Rawlings tells me to.

'The sun descending in the west,
The evening star does shine;
The birds are silent in their nest,
and I must seek for mine.
The moon like a flower,
In Heaven's high bower,
With silent delight—
Sits and smiles on the night.'
Agnes gives me this book /when/ she is the Sunday School teacher at Home.
'Farewell green fields and happy groves,'
But my tears begin to come and I can only half read, the

page is all blurred so I turn over and the words are there but I don't read their meaning, my heart seems to be crumbling with sadness.
—'Saying Wrath, by his meekness
And, by his health, sickness
Is driven away
From our immortal day.'

Dinner is all over by twelve noon as they want to be finished early and the kitchen girl, Betty this one is called, is fetching ~~in the trays~~ the trays in as fast as she can.

There is some kind of argument going on. I can hear the raised voices, the Cook and Matron and the men from 'The Fish'. They seem to be hammering at the refrigerator, all of them together. It seems something is stuck in there.

'What is wrong?' I ask Betty.

'Oh,' she says. 'They can't agree about the price of the fish he brought last week, and they want to show it to him but it's gone and froze into the fridge and they can't get it out to let him see it.'

So that is what all the noise is.

And then there is another noise, one of the women is screaming out, an appalling noise of pain, and the bell is ringing and one of the other women is calling out

'Are you there?'

'Are you there?' it sounds like old Mrs Hailey. I can hear her voice all down the passage.

There is a tremendous commotion. It seems that Mrs Nunne has slipped and fallen while trying to seat herself on the bedside commode.

'She shouldn't try to walk in those bedsocks,' I can hear Matron as she rushes up to Room Three. 'Who ever put those socks on her!' she is angry and worried, her life is like that.

'Whatever did you try by yourself for Aunty?' Matron is shouting. 'Why ever didn't you ring the bell? It's here, Dear, look! Pinned to your Nighty!'

And Mrs Nunne is moaning dreadfully. I suppose the poor woman has broken her hip or something equally bad like that. What a terrible thing, I am upset and need to go to the toilet, so I walk out across the passage.

'Nurse take Mr Scobie to the toilet!' the Cook shouts.

Elizabeth Jolley—Mr Scobie's Riddle

'We don't want him to fall on his arse and break something too.'

'It's all right,' I say to the Nurse, I have not seen her before, possibly she is new here, 'I can manage,' I tell her. She seems a nice enough woman.

'Sure now?' she asks, and she goes off to Room Three where all the trouble is.

When I have finished in the toilet I go into the bathroom and there behind the door with all the other suitcases is the one with all my clothes in it. At least I hope they are there.

The man from 'the Fish' is helping them lift poor Mrs Nunne, she must be a good fourteen stone or more. Poor Woman I can hear her moaning, one of the others is sobbing I can hear her and the Nurse is trying to soothe her. The whole place is full of women and the noise of them in trouble. I am making no noise at all. None whatever.

With some difficulty I drag my case down and take out my clothes and it is with difficulty that I dress myself as I have not dressed all these weeks. I am not sure now how long it is since I wore these clothes, they are very much the worse for being bundled in the case. Very crumpled, and they seem damp too, but everything is here even my cap. And the ticket to ~~Parkerville~~ Roseville is in my jacket pocket too, just as I hoped it would be.

I daresay I shall be longer than I used to be walking up the Terrace to the station, I shall have the case to carry too. I pack my Bible and my pyjamas and other small things. The tape recorder will have to be sent on after me. I have only a pencil and a scrap of paper but it serves.

'<u>Please</u>, Deliver to Mr M. Scobie, ~~Parkerville~~ Roseville. (at your convenience).'

I am excited and yet calm. I must leave soon, at once in fact, otherwise it might be too late. Outside it is raining, but it is not much. The sky is overcast and dark and chalked all over with almond blossom. I have never minded getting wet and once I am home I can soon get a good fire going in the stove and, in no time, I'll be dry and warm. But listen!

The train hooter sounds and resounds triumphant like a

trumpet ~~followe~~ and it is followed by the dull rolling drumming of the following wheels, steady and monotonous on and on and on into the far distance. Soon I shall be part of that. Oh, very soon.

When Mrs Rawlings comes in I tell her.

'When Father died, that was many years ago of course, he cried. I remember him crying, like a child, he wanted to feel the soft rain on his face and he knew he wouldn't ever be out there in the rain or the sun again. He knew he was dying and he kept telling us and of course he was an old man by then. He left home and left us in our poverty, he couldn't help himself you know and years later, when I was a grown man he returned, old before his time and with a fatal illness. Mother was devoted to him in spite of what he had done, and Agnes too. Though by this time she was broken down by what her own life had done to her.

He wanted, he said, to see raindrops on the leaves and bushes and he wanted to smell the blossom of the orange and the grapefuit when it was wet.' Mrs Rawlings waits till I ~~hav~~ finish.

'That was very naughty of you Mr Scobie to go and get dressed up and everything while we were all busy with An Emergency,' Mrs Rawlings sounds hurt. I don't want her to be offended so I explain.

'Oh but I'm going home today, Mrs Rawlings,' I tell her. 'When this rain goes off a bit I'm going up the Terrace to the station. See I've even packed my case,' I show her all my things neatly packed in. I feel really pleased with the way everything has fitted in the case so well.

'So you have,' Mrs Rawlings says 'But I'm sorry to have to be the one to tell you that you are not going out today. Home or anywhere else. So just you unpack and get back into your nice warm pyjamas. I'll be along to help you in just a minute. You Old Folk, you're all the same. A Great Trial to yourselves and to others!' poor Mrs Rawlings sounds so out of breath and tired. She is always going for her life with never a moment for herself, always on the go, morning, noon and night.

But why is it people always talk about Old Folk as if we were something different from them? It is only that we are a bit more advanced in years, we are all the same thing really.

So I must sit here. I suppose Mrs Rawlings was wise. The rain is really coming down. I would have had to sit all this time waiting for the train and then in the train, in my wet clothes.

Of course the best thing would be if Hartley or Joan, Hartley would be better, were to come now and I could be driven in the car all the way to ~~Parkerville~~ Roseville and there would be no problem about my tape recorder. I could take it with me.

I do hope Hartley comes, oh come Hartley. Please.

Mrs Rawlings is in a hurry pulling off my clothes and in a very short time she has me in bed.

'I suppose Hartley ~~may~~ might come today,' I say to her.

'Whatever makes you think that Mr Scobie?' Mrs Rawlings says.

'You mean because he hasn't been all this long time,' I say.

'No,' says Mrs Rawlings, 'Though there's something in that. I meant not on a day like this,' she says. 'Just look at that Rain! The roads will be terrible. I shouldn't think he'll come today.'

And I can hear her and the kitchen girl, Betty, busy in the kitchen getting the trays ready for tea. Betty is a noisy girl.

Of course I know Hartley won't come. He has forgotten me. He is somewhere wrapped up in his affairs and with the Divorced Woman. They are getting older, though they are not thinking that they are. Joan too is growing older. I wonder if Joan will come today.

She has forgotten me too.

And the rain is too heavy for either of them to come. They have sent me in a chop for tea, it is long and greasy /and so tough/ and there is only about one and a half inches of meat on it.

I can't cut the chop and it is impossible to chew, and it will not be easy to swallow.

Perhaps they will send in a steak knife.

'Why are you in the dark Mr Scobie? Why are you sitting in the dark Dear? Why haven't you put your light on Mr Scobie?' Mrs Rawlings is calling for Matron.

'Are you there? Can you come? Come quick!' she calls.

It seems they want me to write. They want me to sign my name on a paper.

'Here Dear,' Matron's voice. 'Along this line here Dear, just write your funny old name Dear.'

It seems dark to me and we would all be better with the light on. Perhaps it is on and not making any difference. How can I know.

'Why ever didn't he cut it up with the steak knife?'

I can hear them wondering about the terrible chop.

'Your name Dear. Please! Try and write your name!' They are exasperated already. I am a tiresome old man. To tell the truth I feel only half alive, no pain, just this darkness and weakness and my breath short though that has eased. But it's no use to try to tell them any of this.

'What was Job's question,' I ask them. 'Oh that I knew where I might find Him.'

'Never mind about Naughty old Job now Dear, come along Dear, let me try and sit you up. /Forget about Job he was a naughty old man.'/

'~~Job's~~ The answer.' I want to tell them. 'The answer to Job.'

'If I take the wings of the morning, and dwell in the uttermost parts of the sea, even there shall Thy Hand lead me, and Thy right Hand shall hold me.' I want to tell them it is Psalm 139, so beautiful, it is like music but I want to cry in my weakness at the beauty of it. Beautiful things always make me cry.

'I'll bet that Niece of his, whatsaname Joan or whatever she calls herself, will be here first thing in the morning, after not being here all this long while, with a Dirty Big Taxi Truck to get all his things.'

I can hear Matron hushing the Cook.

'Help me hold him up,' she says and I /can/ feel Mrs Rawlings helping me to sit up ~~with~~. They are all here in my room.

~~'That's two today,' she says. 'You never can tell,' she says.~~

And I try to write for them where they want me to write.

'Where Mercy Love and Pity dwell,
 There God is dwelling too.'

I expect I have gone off the line. Never mind.

'That's very nice,' Matron says. 'But it's your name I want. Put your name Dear, come along "Martin Scobie" that's all you need to put. I only want you to write your Name!'

But I can't hold the pen any longer, the pen is slipping all the time, I am not able to hold the pen,

[ENDS]

(Reproduced courtesy Mitchell Library, State Library of New South Wales.)

Extract 3 from the published version

Mr Scobie's Riddle, pp 184–95

The meal was all over by twelve noon as the cook and the new girl, Betty, wanted to be finished early. Betty was racing on long noisy legs to bring the trays in as quickly as possible.

There was some kind of argument going on. Mr Scobie could hear voices raised in anger from the kitchen. It sounded as if, as well as shouting, someone was hammering.

'What is wrong?' Mr Scobie asked Betty.

'Aw!' she said, 'it's one hell of a row over the fish. It's Matron and Mrs Rawlings and the man from the fish. Can't agree about the price and Matron's saying he's gotta take it back if he won't look at it and bring his price down. She'll not be robbed by a fish she says and he's saying he'll have it back even if he has to smash the fridge to get it. It's froze in there, see, he brought it last week and Matron's never paid. Just hark at them! Going for each other. It's my half day. My first one. Looks as if I'll miss my bus.'

There was another crash from the kitchen and, from the other direction, the sound of an old woman screaming. It seemed, to Mr Scobie, to be an appalling noise of pain. The bell in Room Three was ringing and he heard Miss Hailey's deep voice calling.

'Are you there Hyacinth? Hyacinth! are you there?' Other voices called and cried. The noise in the kitchen moved swiftly, passing the door of Room One, in the direction of Room Three.

'Damn and Blast this bucket! Who ever left this mop and bucket here!' Mr Scobie heard the bucket kicked aside. The sound was so familiar that he did not pay much attention.

'She should never have walked in those bed socks!' He heard Matron Price; her loud voice seemed to fill St Christopher and St Jude. 'Who the hell put those socks on her! No patient is to walk about in bed socks. No socks!'

In a softer voice, Matron asked, 'Whatever did you try by yourself for; by yourself – Miss Nunne? Whyever didn't you ring the bell?' she said. 'It's here, dear, the bell, pinned to your nighty. Now stop moaning if you can, dear, we'll get you off to the District right away. It's all right dear, I expect you've broken your hip or something. There! There then There! Miss Nunne, Aunty Dear, don't cry like that. You'll soon be all right. Mrs Rawlings has phoned for a lovely ambulance. There! There!'

Mr Scobie, hearing Matron's voice and Miss Nunne moaning, felt upset. He needed to go the toilet. He walked out into the passage.

'Betty!' screamed the cook. 'Take Mr Scobie to the dunny willya. We don't want him falling around on his arse and breaking whatever he's got there to break.'

'It's all right,' Mr Scobie said to Betty who, eyes full of fear, a result of the initiation to the unaccustomed sights of Room Three, came rushing to him. 'I can manage perfectly well on my own,' he said. 'Thank you very much all the same.'

'Sure now?' she asked and, without a backward glance, she fled, her cart-horse legs kicking out as she ran.

Mr Scobie peered round the bathroom door and found the case which, he was sure, contained his clothes. He heard them calling the fish man to come to Room Three to help lift the stout old woman. She must be, Mr Scobie reflected, a good fourteen or fifteen stone in weight and very bulky to handle. It seemed as if the whole place was filled with crying or shouting women. The Lt Col., posting himself by the front door, called out from time to time, 'Are you receiving me. Roger. Roger. Am on recce. Hyacinth. No sighting of relief vehicle yet. Over and out.'

With difficulty, Mr Scobie dragged the case to Room One. He took out his folded crumpled clothes. He was not sure how long it was since he had worn them. They seemed the worse for being kept in the case, damp and shabbier than he remembered. Everything was there, even his cap. Quickly he searched his pockets. The ticket to Rosewood East was still there and a few coins.

With difficulty Mr Scobie dressed himself. He hovered over the open case packing his loosely folded pyjamas, the Blake poems, his cassettes and his Bible. The dressing gown seemed too big and the cassette player would have to be sent on. He found his writing pad and pencil. Tearing off a sheet of paper he wrote,

'Please deliver to Mr M. Scobie care of
P. O. Rosewood East'
(at your convenience).

He was excited and yet calm. He placed the paper on the cassette player. He thought he should leave at once. The sky was darker with the storm. He could hear the wind rushing. Outside the window, the leaves and branches tossed as if being torn at by the fury of the wind.

He never minded getting wet so what did it matter if, on the way to the station, he was caught in a squall of rain. Once home it would be a simple matter to dry clothes by the wood stove.

He thought he could hear the train and the accompanying long drawn-out sound of mourning and of triumph. Distant and near, followed by the dull rumbling drumming of the wheels steady and monotonous on and on with the matching rhythm of travel and hoped-for arrival.

It would not be long before he was part of that rhythm.

He thought he could smell his own home here in St Christopher and St Jude. It was the storm bringing a fragrance as if from wet, sun-scorched grass, from dripping pines and from the soaked pathless scrub of the hill.

It was disturbing to find among his few possessions something which he did not immediately recognize. A floppy cardboard book tied together with pieces of different coloured tape. Quickly he put his hand, palm down, over the extraordinary picture on the outside of the cover. He turned it over and placed it next to the cassette player on the bed. Of course, he remembered, it was that Miss, whatever was her name, the lady writer, it was her manuscript. It had never been returned to her. He wondered what to write on another piece of paper to put with the manuscript. He wrote,

> I am sorry I do not read works of fiction.
> signed M. Scobie

and spent some time wondering whether it was suitable. Tearing up that page, he wrote on another page, 'Please return to Miss...' whatever was her name? '...her name eludes me' he wrote and carefully placed this paper on the cardboard novel.

Outside, the wind was more boisterous. The little wellbred leaf faces on the vines scraped and banged on the window. They seemed to rush towards one another and then to rush away trembling and shaking. A sudden shower of hail-stones hit the glass. The sound was frightening. Mr Scobie sat on the side of his bed. He was ready to leave. He looked out at the darkening afternoon. He would wait, he thought, for a few minutes till this fierce little storm blew over.

'When Father died, that was many years ago, he wept, – many years ago of course,' Mr Scobie told Mrs Rawlings when she came hurrying later into Room One. 'I remember him crying. He had his hands over his face but he cried like a child,' he said. 'He wanted to feel the soft rain on his face. He knew, you see, that he wouldn't ever be out in the rain or in the sun again. I know there's nothing new in this, but that's how it is with people and how it was with him. He knew he was dying. He kept telling us, "I'm dying", he kept saying it, Of course he was an old man by then. He left home, you see, in spite of kneeling with mother to witness before the Lord. He left us, in poverty, at that time. He couldn't help himself, you know, and years later, when I was a grown man, he returned, old before his time and very ill. An illness for which there was no cure. Mother was an angel. She devoted herself to him in spite of what he had done. My sister, Agnes too, though by this time she was broken down by what her own life had done to her.' Mr Scobie smiled, 'You know Mrs Rawlings, Hartley, that's my nephew, Agnes' son, was a dear little boy. Very loveable. My Father said he wanted to see rain drops falling through green leaves. He wanted to smell the blossom of the orange and the grapefruit when it was wet...'

'That was very wrong of you Mr Scobie.' Mrs Rawlings stood in the doorway of Room One, her big arms folded round her bosom. 'That was very wrong of you Mr Scobie,' she said, 'to go and get dressed up and everything while we were so busy with an emergency.' Mrs Rawlings sounded offended.

Mr Scobie, having no wish to hurt her, hastened to explain. 'Oh. But I am going home today, Mrs Rawlings. When this rain goes off a bit I'm going up to the station. See, I've even packed my case. Everything has fitted in so nicely. There's even room for the player, but it makes the case far too heavy. I have packed and arranged everything.'

'So you have Mr Scobie,' Mrs Rawlings said, 'but I am sorry to have to be the one to tell you that you are not going out today. Home or anywhere else. So just you unpack and get back into your nice pyjamas and dressing gown. I'll be along to help you in just a minute. You old folk, you're all the same. A great trial to yourselves and to others! Now just you start getting ready for bed while I hot up the water for the teas.'

'Oh Badders! Bad show there!' Miss Hailey paused by the door on her way to the bathroom, her sponge bag dangling from her wrist. 'Rawlings always going for her life, always out of breath, I couldn't help overhearing what she said. I feel sort of, well you know, sort of sorry for Rawlings,' Miss Hailey paused, 'but she's like everyone else. Why do they talk about, inverted commas, Old Folk, close inverted commas, as if we're something different. Actually,' she gave a shy laugh. 'Ectually I'm the same age as she is though you wouldn't believe it because of fate, call it what you will, the shape of destiny, *Weltschmerz* and the ability to feel it, *toute la tristesse du monde*, I am the same age as those two – Felicity Rawlings, Simmonds she was then, and Hyacinth Price. Used to sit together in class, I think I've told you this. Form IV was an absolute riot I can tell you. Felicity lived up to her name then. Remind me to tell you some time of how we ragged the ass. dep. princip. and the ass. mat. all thought up, I might add, by one, Felicity Simmonds.' Miss Hailey loosened the string of her twirling sponge bag. She laughed.

'But to be perfectly honest old chap,' she said, lowering her voice, 'it's one hell of a night out there. You simply cannot venture forth in this. Why, the rain is simply streaming down, you can see for yourself. You'd have to be in soaking wet clothes for *hours*.' She paused and said, with a self-conscious tremble in her voice, 'and you know, old bean, I really do care what happens to you.'

Mr Scobie and Miss Hailey were rescued from the moment by the unmusical voice of the cook, 'Miss Hailey! MISS HAILEY! Where the hell does that woman get to! MISS HAILEY your bloody tea's goin' stiff on the plate. MISS HAILEY TEA!'

'Coming! Coming!' Miss Hailey sang in her best cadence. 'Chin up!' she said softly over her shoulder to where the bowed figure of Mr Scobie sat. 'I suppose,' she added, still in as gentle a voice as possible, 'I suppose we, safely inside St Christopher and St Jude, should be noble for a few minutes and put our minds to the people who are, at this very moment, bearing the full brunt of this cyclone or whatever it is and wherever it is.'

'Of course the best thing would be if Hartley or Joan were to come and I could be driven home by car,' Mr Scobie said to Mrs Rawlings when she returned. 'That way, there would be no problem about my cassette player. I could take it with me.' Mrs Rawlings began to pull off Mr Scobie's shoes and socks.

'I suppose Hartley might come today,' Mr Scobie said.

'Whatever makes you think that Mr Scobie?' Mrs Rawlings attacked his trousers with both hands.

'You mean because he hasn't been to see me this long time?' Mr Scobie said, he was shivering.

'No,' Mrs Rawlings said, 'though there's something in that. I meant not on a day like this,' she said. 'Just you take a look at the rain. After a freak storm like this, the roads'll be terrible. I shouldn't think he'll come today.'

'No,' Mr Scobie agreed, 'though Hartley is very unpredictable,' he said letting Mrs Rawlings help him into his pyjamas. 'He was a lovely child. I loved him very much. Joan too, but something seems to have gone wrong, I can't understand how or why both of them live the way they do. I mean take Hartley...'

'Oh, your trouble is,' Mrs Rawlings told him, 'your trouble is that you're not able to move with the times.' She pulled back the white counterpane. 'Now, into bed with you. You'll soon warm up in bed.'

'I wish Hartley would come,' Mr Scobie said, 'though of course, with this weather, I wouldn't want any harm to come to him.'

'No of course not,' Mrs Rawlings said, hurrying out of the room.

Thinking of Hartley's previous visits, there was always the chance that he might come, though, as he sat in bed shivering, Mr Scobie felt sure that Hartley would not come. He thought he would not see him again, though he did not want to think this. Certainly he would never say it. He heard Betty, whose half day had been cancelled, galloping down the hall and back to the kitchen, gathering in the trays.

When Lina walked, he remembered, she made no sound, she seemed to move softly over the carpet to take her place at the piano, ready for her lesson.

'Ready Lina? one two and one...' he listened for her first notes...

'Mrs Rawlings done this chop for you,' Betty brought him a tray, 'tea's done but she says to tell you she done this for you and there's bread and butter and a jelly...'

'You don't happen to know my niece Joan, by any chance, do you?' Mr Scobie, still shivering, let her place the tray on his knees.

'No I don't. What's she like? Nice?' Betty pulled her hair straight using her faint reflection in the window pane as a mirror. Mr Scobie smiled up at her.

'Well yes, I suppose she is, in her own way. Though the last time I saw her, I'm not sure if it was the last time, I was speaking to her about her mother, my sister Agnes, and I said something like if Agnes hadn't married she and I could still be living together...'

'Wow!' Betty said, polishing the toe caps of her shoes on the corner of Mr Scobie's bed quilt.

'I could never understand Joan,' Mr Scobie said, he shook his head. 'I said to her once that it was a pity her mother, that's my sister, Agnes, had died. And d'you know what? Joan rounded on me. I'll never forget her words...'

'Betty! Where the hell is that girl!' the cook's raucous scream interrupted the conversation. 'Betty! I can't stand here all night waitin' for you to decide whether to wash up or not. Betty!'

Mr Scobie looked at the chop. It was long and greasy. There was perhaps one mouthful of meat on it if he could get it off.

He remembered Joan's voice, '"Uncle! You are impossible. How could you wish for Mother to go on living. I know she's your sister and I'm sorry. How d'you think we feel? Hartley and me? Of course she's ill and she can't eat that bread and butter you've made for her. She's too ill to eat. She's in pain. Can't you understand Uncle! Look at her all yellow like that. How can you wish for her to go on living. Uncle! Leave her in peace. Please Uncle!"'

He remembered Joan crying. Once you had seen someone cry you always felt differently about them. Sadly he thought he had learned, in his life, that it seemed necessary to see and feel real grief before being able to feel real compassion. Joan, when she cried, was red and swollen about the face and eyes for quite some time afterwards.

He had cried too.

He thought he could hear someone crying in the hall, somewhere down the passage. There was always someone calling or crying, always someone hurrying falling over that bucket in the hall, kicking the bucket, he laughed softly, wasn't that what people said, 'kicked the bucket', he could make a fine riddle from that too.

Perhaps someone would bring a steak knife for the chop. While he tried to cut the meat, the tray kept sliding from his knees.

'Why are you in the dark Mr Scobie? Why haven't you got your light on? Have you eaten your tea? What? Well! I never! Aw!' Mrs Rawlings, tray in hands, reached the hall.

'Matron! Matron! Are you there. Come quick! It's Mr Scobie he's . . .'

'Why is it so dark?' Mr Scobie tried to ask them. He blinked, 'Oh, you have put the light on.'

'It's all right Mr Scobie, you've had a funny old turn. Now, just let Mrs Rawlings and me prop you up. Here, let me put in these pillows. There, that's better.'

'Why ever didn't he cut it up with the steak knife?'

He wondered why they were worrying so much about the chop.

'Here, Dear,' Matron was saying to him, 'along this line, here, Dear, just your funny old name, here's the pen, no, not there, here.'

Mr Scobie fumbled with the pen and the paper, letting both slip from his hands.

'Your name, Dear! Please! Try and write your name.' Matron Price, bending over the old man, sounded exasperated.

'I am a tiresome old man,' Mr Scobie smiled weakly. 'I'm sorry I'm such a tiresome old man,' he said. 'To tell the truth I feel only half alive, no pain, just this shivering and the darkness and my breath so short though that has eased. I am thankful for that.' He paused. 'Now what was Job's question?' he asked. '*Oh that I knew where I might find Him.*'

'Never mind about naughty old Job now Mr Scobie, Dear. Come along, try and hold the pen. Mrs Rawlings will help you. Guide his hand Rawlings.'

'Oh, I couldn't do that Matron.'

'Oh! Go on Rawlings. Of course you can. You've never refused before. You've always done it before. You can do it this time. Help him to write. Now!'

'The answer,' Mr Scobie said, 'the answer to Job.'

'Forget about Job Mr Scobie, dear, he was a naughty old man.' Matron Price glared at Mrs Rawlings.

'Go on Rawlings, help him to sign, or else...'

'The answer to Job,' Mr Scobie had a fit of coughing which sent the pen and paper to the floor. He lay back gasping and smiling. 'The answer to Job,' he said,

> *If I take the wings of the morning,*
> *and dwell in the uttermost parts of the sea;*
> *Even there shall thy hand lead me,*
> *and thy right hand shall hold me.*

'It's Psalm one hundred and thirty-nine,' he said, and he wept. 'It's so beautiful,' he said, 'it always makes me cry in my weakness. Before such beauty I have to weep.' Mr Scobie smiling and weeping turned his white head to look first at Matron Price and then at Mrs Rawlings.

'I'll bet that niece of his,' the cook's voice came from the doorway of Room One, 'whatsaname Joan or Jean Frost, whatever she calls herself, will be here first off in the morning with a dirty big taxi truck to get all his stuff away. She'll take everything though Lord knows there's not much.' She gave a series of disapproving grunts.

'Here! help me to sit him up again Rawlings,' Matron Price arranged the pillows. Mr Scobie began to write.

Where Mercy Love and Pity dwell,
There God is dwelling too.

'I expect I have gone off the lines,' he said. 'I'm sorry, but I think you can just about read my terrible handwriting.'

'That's very nice, thank you Mr Scobie,' Matron Price was trying not to be impatient. 'But it's your signature, your name, I want on this very important piece of paper. Put your name in your lovely handwriting, Martin Scobie, that's all you need to write. I only want you to sign your name, dear, Your Name!'

Mr Scobie could no longer hold the pen. It slipped from between his fingers. He was not able to hold the pen.

Thomas Keneally
The Chant of Jimmie Blacksmith

I have an image of the novel as a vortex of turbulent forces, and of myself at the material's mercy. I learn to swim by about the second or third draft...

Thomas Keneally

In April 1900, Jimmie Blacksmith's maternal uncle, carried Jimmie's initiation through all the grades
Tabidgi, Jackie Smolders to the white world, was disturbed
by the news that Jimmie had married a white girl in
the Methodist church at Wallah. Jackie Smolders was of full-blooded
the Tullam section of the Wondilli tribe. Tullam Jackie as was Jimmie
was old-fashioned, to his mind, people still married by the
married Mungara, Mungara married
old tribal pattern. Tullam married Mungara, Mungara
married Garri, Garri married Wilbera, Wilbera took
Tullam's women. It afflicted Jackie that his nephew
had the simple fact was married the white girl and
not a Mungara. These tribal arrangements were
still be made, even if Tullam was on a mission station, a hundred
miles from Mungara.
   It dispirited Jimmie's mother, Dulcie Blacksmith, a full-blooded native who had conceived
Jimmie when some white fellow had visited Brentwood
blacks' camp in 1878. The missionaries, who had never been
told perhaps heard of Tullam, Mungara, Garri or Wilbera, had made it
clear that if you had pale children it was because you
had slept been rolled by white men. They did not know
any thing of the Crow and the Emu-Wren people, that
Crow girls women to Emu wren, that Emu wren quickens
the womb. Mrs. Dulcie Blacksmith believed the
They took such a low view of living in other people that they were unlikely the
missionaries. Christ, she'd been rolled by white fellows.
It helped, of a hot night, of a cold night. Christ, she'd been
rolled. but the higher truth
rolled. What disturbed her was that Emu-Wren quickened
Jimmie Blacksmith, pale or not, and Mungara owed him
a woman.

Thomas Keneally achieves what seems the impossible for a writer: he writes books quickly (to date he's written eighteen novels), but the speed with which he works doesn't result in any loss of quality.

We assumed that because he writes so quickly, he must sketch out each book with a master plan before he writes, and that he must always be in sure and conscious control of exactly where the book is heading. It was most unlikely, we reasoned, for a novelist who works at such speed to allow his story or his characters to be wayward, or to allow himself to be surprised by them.

We examined the earliest draft of *The Chant of Jimmie Blacksmith* available to us, the one in the Mitchell Library. Comparing this draft with the published text, Keneally can be seen rearranging the material, and adding the detail and specificity which give the book its richness of texture. The changes, though, were more an elaboration than a rethinking.

Before we spoke to Keneally we had no way of knowing what had preceded this draft, but it seemed to confirm our assumptions about the controlled way he worked. Then we talked to him, and found how wrong we'd been.

Our interview with Thomas Keneally took place at Sydney University in February 1992.

INT: Can you tell us about your writing process, from its genesis to its conclusion?

TK: It begins, as everyone says, with something that's befallen you. You start to write nearly anywhere. You intuit where to begin and this may not be where you begin it in the end—you may change the order later on. I begin without much specific planning, I tend to be an instinctive writer. I intuit the beginning and then start writing about the people and the action as a means to getting to know about it. I try to write absolutely perfect prose in the first draft and that never works—you know, I'm lucky if it's competent after five drafts.

But I tend *not* to take short cuts in the first draft, I tend *not* to postpone problems of the development of the novel. I tend *not* to be able to postpone, say, the big crucial question at the heart of the book, such as the motivation of someone, or some mystery which impacts very strongly upon the central character...I try to work out the full subtlety of the relationships in the first draft. I tend not to say: Well, we'll go later on into the symbolic and psychic impact of all this. You know: In the second draft we'll work it up into something fancy—a bit of Freudian jargon, say—but for now I'll get on with the plot. I tend not to be able to do that and so I tend not to write the first draft quickly. The first draft is the hardest part for me.

I don't rewrite every day what I have already written. I don't produce a novel cumulatively, but in strata. I envy people who can write 500 words a day, revise it the next morning and that's basically what's in the book. Graham Greene could write like that. But I can't. That first draft is very much finding the tale and finding the dynamics of the thing.

INT: You say you write in 'strata'—can you explain that?

TK: Well, the first layer is the first draft. From start to finish. I never start to rewrite till the first draft's done. The second draft adds another sedimentary layer on top of the first. It's often a complete rewrite.

In the old days before the coming of word processors, I would write the entire first draft in the way that *The Chant of Jimmie Blacksmith* is written here—in longhand. I would get that typed up, and then stick bits of the typing onto completely new material—so the second draft was very much a new text, with little saved bits of the first draft stuck on with glue. I would end up with long scroll-like documents made up of material rewritten in longhand, and the few salvageable segments from the first draft. That's what I mean by stratification. Likewise with the third draft. It's only with the fourth draft that I begin to make small amendments to the text. At least three strata, at least three writings, from beginning to end.

With this manuscript of *Jimmie Blacksmith*, you're at a late long-hand version, rather than an early long-hand version. I would imagine there was another earlier longhand version. I remember that some of the book was written on much smaller format paper. So this is probably not as primitive as the very earliest draft would've been. This would've then been typed up by a typist, and I would've made some more amendments to that before sending it off.

INT: Would that very earliest draft have been in the form of rough jottings?

TK: This isn't the way everyone should operate—the biggest rule is, if a writer starts telling you that there's a particular way to write a book, that's not the truth. But I don't begin with jottings. I've rarely even written down a set of notes to myself. Occasionally I've written down lists of problems to be solved—such as, perhaps, what happens to a character in the second half of the book, how they're to be connected to the rest. But not often, and I don't do many pre-writing notes. But they're very valuable to a lot of people who use that method.

My only salvation is to throw myself in. I have an image of the novel as a vortex of turbulent forces, and of myself at the material's mercy. I learn to swim by about the second or third draft. I'm rather disoriented, bewildered and groping in the first. Nonetheless, as I said earlier, I still try to solve the basic problems of the book. I stress, *try* to.

INT: So you might, to begin with, plunge straight to the difficult part of the book?

TK: No. I tend to write it serially, I tend not to write part of the book out of order, even though later it might become apparent that material should be shifted around. I need the illusion, even in the first draft—even when I'm bewildered and really know in my water that the stuff is no good—I need the illusion that I'm working in a publishable form. I would find the idea of having to do any preparation other than research (for the books I've done research on) just too hard and intimidating, and I'd be stopped writing.

INT: A 'disoriented, bewildered and groping' process sounds like a very anxious process.

TK: Yes, it is. In that first draft, not everything works evenly. For example, I'm working on a book now in which one element—the sort of graphic stuff—is sounding too much like a cop show. I'm finding it hard to give quality and individuality to that part. At the same time, another element of the book is working beautifully. I rewrite the first draft if I feel that the elements are there for ultimate redemption. If I feel that the essence is there, even if it's not working, then I press on and deal with it in the second draft.

My problem is if I feel that the elements aren't there at all. Then I get this internal itch, this sense of being baulked, this desire for a resolution—which generally comes unconsciously when you are not sitting there straining to make it happen.

INT: Do you write against that for a while, hoping...?

TK: I do write against it for a while, hoping it will be resolved. You know, you're very depressed at those times. One of the worst, most dangerous aspects of writing is the inevitable depression that comes from that curiously pervasive failure that you suffer in fiction. It's pervasive because it affects other areas of your life.

Thomas Keneally—The Chant of Jimmie Blacksmith

I used to rewrite the second draft in longhand on a typed script, and then I began to use the word processor. And I've taken to using a tape-recorder, either to straighten out the second draft, to edit straight onto tape from the page, or even to get the first draft written—that great crisis, where I'm most bewildered and depressed because I'm far more at the mercy of the elements of the book, and naturally one doesn't know if it's going to work.

INT: What started *Jimmie Blacksmith*? Was it a mood, for example, or an idea, or a character?

TK: It was the idea—the neatness of events as they existed in history. That's why, for a period, I wrote a lot of stuff that was based in history.

When I was writing *Jimmie Blacksmith* our troops were in Vietnam, there was a lot of debate about that. At the time of the Blacksmith murders—the Governor brothers' murders in real life—we were in the Boer War; there was a lot of emotion about that. And there was a surge of nationalism which the New South Wales Crimes Act of 1900 was instituted to prevent: it says that whoever promotes the idea that there will come a time when the Monarch is not the sovereign of Australia is guilty of High Treason. Basically, without being whimsical, there are parallels between Australia in the late 1960s and Australia in 1900—a sense that the question hadn't gone very far in that time, in those 60 years, and a sense that these events were extremely dramatic. In 1901 the indigenous people of Australia had no place in the Constitution, and just before I wrote the book they were given a place, in so far as the Federal Government was given the power to legislate for them—all these parallels seemed too good to be true.

It was also the form—the neat, the nifty ways the historic tale encompassed Australian problems. I liked that because I'm probably a bit of a didacticist by temperament. (There had to be some reason why I wanted to become a clergyman at one stage in my life!) The lessons from the tale were obvious.

I do remember that I began at the beginning with the missing child, the child who was away being initiated. By and large I do begin first drafts with what turns out to be the beginning.

INT: As you went through that anxious first draft, would you have often returned to the feeling you had when you came across the historical event—returned to it to keep you going?

TK: Oh yes. I find that, often, people will ask you what you're writing, and I'm one of those writers who have no inhibitions about saying what I'm working on. A lot of writers can't, I know, but I'm hard to shut up about it. So you start to tell people what the book is about and they get enthusiastic, and you get what is sadly lacking in the writing process—that is, human feedback, you're getting this human feedback. With a few experiences like that, you begin to think positively and without desperation about the book, and it's often then that the breakthroughs come.

INT: Tell us about the historical research you did for *Jimmie Blacksmith*. Did you do it before you started writing?

TK: Yes. I really enjoy that part because you come across piquant material. You think: This is wonderful, what wonderfully strange events! And we are helped by the fact that there is a pattern to human life. Because every human life is patterned by the same dominant forces—dominant strengths and dominant weaknesses. There's actually an almost literary shape to a life. We can't see it in our own lives, but we can see it in our friends'. We say: She is always attracted to the same kind of man—that's her plot. And the reason she's always attracted to that kind of man was that her father was an embezzler and he ran away when she was five, so she's always going to go for men who are potential embezzlers and likely to leave her. So we see other people in terms of a plot, and that is of great asistance to the novel. The fact that we see our parents, or our siblings, always falling for the same old tricks, and demonstrating the same old sets of courages and strengths, enables us to see their lives as a sort of artistic unity.

So reality can turn up these patterns, particularly reality that's been digested by newspapers or historians or documentary-makers. Newspapers I find are always good research materials because they are not accurate, not always accurate, but they do show you infallibly what the aspirations and civil and cultural habits of the people of that time were. For example in 1900 the *Daily Mail* considered babies should be fattened up because in those pre-antibiotic days the theory was: fatten the child up, it'll soon be thinned down by fevers. I enjoy that research period, and I got it done for *The Chant of Jimmie Blacksmith* before going to England in 1970—I was writing another book, and I was going to write *Jimmie Blacksmith* back in Australia, but the earlier contract fell through and I thought: This one's going to be worth writing and it's going to be relatively easy because it's got a great shape to it.

INT: So you could see that at the start?

TK: Yes, you can see the shape, that you're not going to have the technical problems with this tale that you might have with others.

Thomas Keneally—The Chant of Jimmie Blacksmith

You know how the plot of a novel can sound very clever in an anecdote, but you can't make it work in practice, because characters will not react in the novel the way they react in the anecdote. But I felt that this was one where the motivations were clear and above all, the shape was clear.

I did the research in bulk, and I read also Frank Clune's book on the Governor brothers—that's what started it all. I thought: Wow! I didn't agree with the book but I was sparked by it. There was a pattern there that Clune wasn't concentrating on—he was concentrating on police and pursuit aspects purely.

INT: More recently, with your novel, *Flying Hero Class*, you've again written about Aboriginal people, although with a very different perspective.

TK: Yes, I'd always wanted to write about Aboriginal people on tour, not in the arrogant way of *The Chant of Jimmie Blacksmith*, by writing from within, but by writing from the point of an observed travelling companion and tour manager. Aboriginals are always perceived as being in Australia, but of course increasing numbers of them are travelling around the world having exhibitions, acting in movies, etc. And I wanted to look at that and perhaps even raise—without being didactic about it—the possibility that we are fairly lucky to have got away with our plunder so easily.

INT: You have a mastery of inserting past information in the flow of present narrative. When you revise, is it apparent to you from early on where those pieces from the past should be fed in? Or is there a lot of shuffling around?

TK: Sometimes those pieces from the past are shuffled round and put elsewhere. I don't do it with absolute infallibility the first time. But often the first instincts are valid ones. Often what I come up with from the unconscious in the early drafts, particularly about the arrangement of the material, can be very valid because I find out that if I try to move stuff around, it generates all manner of problems. Past material is not a discrete organ of the book; it has nerve endings stretching out through the whole corpus. If you move it, it's like putting someone's heart on their knee.

INT: Does a book ever become a real obsession to you, so that it stays with you when you're doing other things?

TK: Yes. I don't look upon travel books, screenplays or journalism as real writing, for some reason. I wish I did. I look upon fiction writing as the only work and it does stay with me obsessively during the writing of other material. Even when I'm out promoting the Australian Republic in the media and so on, I'm thinking of that book. Because to a fiction writer, rightly or wrongly, fiction is the most important thing. Most of us, sadly, would sacrifice everything for it, and find out too late it's really not worth it, I mean not worth it emotionally, and not worth the cost it implies to yourself and other people. Yes, I'm an absolute obsessive.

Another thing that motivates me is that very often I can see a book in the future that I want to write, and it looks like a perfectly easy project. It's like someone else's spouse—you could really get on with *that* book. That gets to me too, that desire to get a book done, so that I can get on to the new relationship with the next book.

INT: So there's no sense of loss when you've finished a book?

TK: No sense of loss, except that in some books there's a kind of magic that you do miss. Now, there was a kind of magic for me in this new book of mine, *Woman of the Inner Sea*, about a woman in her 30s, early 30s. I thought that I'd have to go out and interview youngish women. But it turned out that I felt that I knew this woman intimately, as intimately as myself. I knew everything about her, I knew every shift of her soul, I understood the nature of her bereavement, I felt I understood exactly what she was doing, the loss of her two children—I understood that she was trying to make herself into a woman who wasn't culpable, a woman who hadn't lost her children. She gets this obsession with cellular change; from a background of eating langouste and angel-hair pasta she attacks the cuisine of the bush—white bread with lots of salted butter, steak for breakfast. She tries to change herself in a cellular sort of way. I think I really knew all that stuff. Mind you, I've changed myself in cellular ways too. So I have experience of that. But the magic of that relationship with her, I miss.

There are some books that you craft, and some books which seem to be—I don't want to sound mystical—but seem to be given, and which have a quality of enchantment. There's enchantment to the intimacy you feel with the character. I miss that. It's not in the present novel, even though the present novel may very well be more readable, and more laudable.

I don't like going back to my books, I don't even particularly like giving readings from them. If I have to read, I would go to a lot of trouble to find the two or three paragraphs which are least offensive to me in some old work—even though I get offended when critics are offended by it, it's okay for me to feel offended by it—and I generally read from new work.

Thomas Keneally—The Chant of Jimmie Blacksmith

The great thing, if you're a writer, is that you're eternally presented with the fresh no matter how old you get, that's one of the payoffs. You are perpetually taken by a concept which you believe the world needs—against all the evidence!

INT: Earlier in this interview, you mentioned the presence of the unconscious in your work process. Can you tell us more about that?

TK: I think that there are all sorts of options we take which are dictated by the unconscious. They are connected to the swamp of mythology and imagery that lies there down in the unconscious. They're options we take by the feel of it—we often make wrong instinctual decisions, but they're the only decisions we could possibly have made at the time.

I remember a computer expert talking about betting by computer. He said: 'I think that gambling by computer—horse racing—is more an analogue than a digital problem.' That is, you can put in all the numbers you want, but you still won't get the full mystery of the event. Similarly I think, in novel writing, it's an analogue rather than a digital business, the whole is greater than the sum of its parts, in that characters and events don't go in the way we've consciously proposed that they should—they don't in *my* novels, they take directions which are often very creative directions, which appear to us to come from no one, not from ourselves.

So that we're all used to the writer saying to an agog audience of lay folk: 'The book seemed to write itself! The characters had a will of their own!' That's not true. The characters have the will of the unconscious solely because you don't quite know what you're doing—but you are doing it. It's only because you don't quite have a conscious grasp of what you're doing that you feel as if the characters have self-government and that the direction of the novel, the impetus of the novel, has a kind of self-government.

INT: In fact, it's a question we've been asking other writers—when they're deep in the novel, do they have a sense that they're discovering rather than fabricating. . .

TK: Yes, absolutely. Our unconscious is putting up an agenda for us that we're not conscious of. We discover that agenda rather than consciously participate in it. That's right—it's an uncovering process in terms of all aspects of the book, even in terms of imagery. The discovery of the crucial images of the book. . .that's done, in many cases, without deliberate plan. Of course, there are some great writers of whom that's not true, who deliberately, perhaps for the sake of literary orthodoxy or doctrine, have chosen the leitmotiv of their work. But I can't do that consciously and I can't set myself conscious agendas except for the broadest ones.

I think there's this feeling in human beings that something descends upon a person when they're writing well. It's there in the idea that the Bible is inspired by God. I believe that we have experience sometimes of the finished work being greater than the sum of our conscious efforts. And therefore we feel that the product is daemonic, in the sense that it comes from outside ourselves. I don't believe that it does, but that's what it feels like.

In the same way, people who claim to have died say that they've gone down a long tunnel: I believe that that tunnel has no physical or external existence. It's in their head.

It's like the belief in the very concept of inspiration. The layperson asks: 'Do you write every morning, or do you only write when you're inspired?' So they absolutely believe in the concept of some infusion from on high. There isn't an infusion from on high, but it feels like it. It feels like it when we know we're bringing the sum of the parts to something quite excessive. Because the subconcious is so powerfully at work in our books, it feels sometimes as if the influence is external.

As I get further into a book, the control does become more self-conscious, and more technical. I am more technically confident, because I know the direction of the thing now. But still I can get surprises—daemonic surprises—out of the material. Of course, this is the charm of fiction, this is why writers themselves are charmed by the process. You might as well construct dental bridges as write fiction, if fiction didn't have this unconscious and daemonic side.

Associated with its daemonic side is some of the depression and some of the exaltation. The exaltation is what we write for, I think. There's an audience implied in that exaltation—it might only be three people—who will be as exalted as the writer is by the experience of running this material through their brains. But the exaltation is, I think, a primary motivation. I mean, fiction writing can be like alcoholism, an addiction to a long misery and an occasional divine exaltation. Booze itself in the deserts in tribal societies used to be drunk only at certain times, because it was associated with either a divinely awarded licence or a divine right to make your brain go crazy. The same idea of booze as coming from the gods is there with fiction. Fiction can be just as compulsive an experience.

That's how books get written: through the fiction becoming a compulsive experience. Every book is written from the basis of a delusion about its value, its competence, and the forces that are operating. And if it were not so, there wouldn't be any motivation.

INT: Helen Garner told us that in the writing of *Cosmo Cosmolino*, there was a moment when writing was just 'wonderful play'.

TK: Yes, that's right. I do have that feeling when the writing's going well. What I've noticed over a long career is that writers' assessment of what's working and what isn't working is abysmal; it's very subjective and quite unreliable. The exaltation can attach itself as easily to a weed as to a rose. Nonetheless, you do have the sense that you're at play in the fields of the Lord, and you're dancing with angels. It's a great feeling. I wish I had it more regularly.

INT: Is there some part of the writing process that's more important to you than anything we have asked you about?

TK: No. The only thing I'd say is that I like word processors although I don't understand them, and sometimes they're annoying. But one of the great practical problems of writing is to have a little ritual which eases you into your daily work. It's like jumping from a 30 metre board into a six foot pool: you need something to ease you into it. A computer, with its little rituals of entry and its little squeaks of approval and disapprobation, gives a kind of response that you don't get from a mere pen and paper, and it is a ritual that leads you into it. There you've got the stuff up on screen and it's in part fluorescent—lit from within. It has a certain authority to keep you going. It gives some feedback, however minimal, that the pen and the pencil never did.

Extract 1 from a manuscript

This is from a handwritten draft of *The Chant of Jimmie Blacksmith*.

In May April of 1900 1899, Jimmie Blacksmith's maternal uncle Tabadgi, Jackie Smolders to the white world, /carried Jimmie's initiation tooth all the way from Brentwood Mission to Wallah./ was disturbed by the news that Jimmie had married a white girl in the Methodist church at Wallah. Jackie Smolders was /full-blooded and/ of the Tullam moiety section of the Wondilli tribe /as was Jimmie/. Tullam married Mungara, Mungara married

Jackie was old-fashioned; to his mind, people still married by the old tribal pattern. Tullam married Mungara, Mungara married Garri, Garri married ~~Gubbari~~ Wibbera, ~~Gubbari~~ Wibbera took Tullam's women. It ~~filled~~ dispirited Jackie that his nephew had ~~The simple fact was~~ married the white girl and not a Mungara. These tribal arrangements ~~could~~ were still ~~be~~ made. /even if Tullam was on a mission station a hundred miles from Mungara./

It dispirited Jimmie's mother, Dulcie Blacksmith, a full-blooded native who had conceived Jimmie when some white fellow had visited Brentwood blacks' camp in ~~1878~~ 1877. The missionaries, who ~~knew nothing~~ had never been told the higher things of Tullam, Mungara, Garri or Wibbera, had made it clear that if you had pale children it was because you had ~~slept~~ been rolled by white men. They did not know any thing of the Crow /people/ and the Emu-Wren people, that Crow ~~must marry~~ gives women to Emu-Wren, that Emu-Wren quickens the womb. Mrs Dulcie Blacksmith believed the missionaries. /They took such a low view of lying in other people that they were unlikely to lie themselves./ Christ, she'd been rolled by white ~~men~~ fellows. It helped, of a hot night, of a cold night. /It helped at any time/. Christ, she'd been rolled. ~~What~~ But the higher truth that disturbed her was that Emu-Wren quickened Jimmie Blacksmith, pale or not, and Mungara owed him a woman. Yet here he was marrying a white girl off a farm at Wallah.

So her brother Tabadgi Jackie Smolders brought Jimmie's initiation tooth all the way from Brentwood to ~~the farm in~~ Wallah ~~where~~ to give it to him and remind him of Tullam and the Emu-Wren people. The tooth was wrapped in clean flourcloth and carried in Jackie Smolders' left pocket, away from the sevenpence that belonged in the right pocket and might be infected with malchance. It had been knocked from Jimmie Blacksmith's mouth/by Wondilli elders/ when he was thirteen, in 1891. So too he had been circumcised with stone, the incision poulticed over with chalk-clay and similarly the eyes. As far as Dulcie Blacksmith knew, the great ~~spirit~~ lizard had swallowed him and he would ~~be reborn~~ give birth ~~to him~~ as a full Wondilli man. He was gone for weeks and the Rev. H.J. Neville, B.A., kept asking where he was but was not incommoded with the truth.

Thomas Keneally—The Chant of Jimmie Blacksmith

Not that the lizard story was the /full/ truth. Grown men who had been through initiation themselves knew that

[page cut off here]

~~In the spring of 1893, Rev. Neville was awarded the Methodist church in Muswellbrook. Immediately he asked Jimmie Blacksmith if he would go with his wife and himself as a houseboy. He'd given Jimmy ideas, the family said of Mr Neville. 'If I watch me manners,' said Jimmy, 'and try to marry the right kind of white girl, me my kids'd be quarter-caste, me my grandkids eighth-caste. Hardly noticeable at all.~~

Jimmy was not a white snob at that time, but the Rev. Neville was to make him one. Don't wander away from any job you take on. As far as whites are concerned, that's what blacks always do. They're unreliable. You be reliable!
In the spring of 1893, Rev. Neville was awarded the Methodist church in Muswellbrook and asked if Jimmy could come with him as some kind of houseboy.
'You gotta better yerself, Jimmy,' Dulcie said.
The cart jolted away towards the railhead, Mr Neville waving in his sober way. Perhaps he understood how soon his memory would vanish /from this air and wanted to impress it on it plastically with his hand/.
Dulcie sang,
  'Tall is my son who goes away.
  He ~~will not will stumble trip~~ will stub his feet on the mountains
  And ~~snare~~ catch his hair in the stars.'
She would not see him again.
They crossed mountains ~~they~~ he had never crossed before, and came to a town on river-flats, a green town such as /greener than/ he had never before seen.
One day, during the unpacking of Mr Neville's books, Mrs Neville said, 'It's as if you never were black, Jimmy. Maybe we could find you a nice girl off a farm to marry. Your children would be quarter-caste then, scarcely black at all.'
Muswellbrook had a broad, still river and weatherboard homes on the curve of the high street and all the way down to the river flats.

Making Stories

'Maybe we could find you a nice girl off a farm to marry...'

[page ends]

white /branches/ of dawn

On your brow put pride as firm as ~~the Dubra~~ the berry tree
Out of the chrysalis and out of the lizard's mouth your son comes man.

Every now and then he swung the bull-roarer lest the women from ~~B~~rentwood mission came near. You were hexed beyond all knowing if you were seen by a woman during your isolation. It You were finished for good.
It was autumn. There was very little rain and the winds ran warm beneath a high Easter sun. The Rev. H.J. Neville could have used a good boy like Jimmie for the Easter hymns.
'Deuced blacks!' he told his wife. 'The best of them are likely to vanish at any time.'
He had reached for the butter /at table/ and found the flies about it as thick almost as at high summer.
'If a person could be certain that he had imbued one of them with decent ambitions.'
Until recently, he had thought he had managed it with Jimmie Blacksmith. It wasn't as if Jimmie were full-blood, so there was half a chance. And Jimmie was eager. Jimmie was eager and polite.
H.J. Neville was a man with a true Evangelical vocation. If he had been a student of anthropology he might have been more statistically successful / and less baffled before his fly-blown butter-dish/, but anthropology was a two-way subject, if it was a subject at all in 1891, in Australia, in Brentwood blacks' camp. It is two-way because it requires white sympathy and talkative natives. ~~It would not~~ How would it have occurred to Jimmie Blacksmith to be talkative about initiation? /It was a forbidden topic, and if not that,/ it might have offended Mr Neville, who had been so nice to him.
Since Jimmie Blacksmith's recent disappearance, Mr Neville had taken to cutting notifications of vacant pastorates out of the Methodist Church Times. All over the ~~house~~ little weatherboard pastorage were mislaid

Thomas Keneally—The Chant of Jimmie Blacksmith

little squares of newsprint ~~announcing~~ promising Hay in the Riverina, Walcha in New England, Lismore, Eden, Wilcannia. They yellowed in the high autumn sun, in Jimmie Blacksmith's /lasting/ absence. And Rev H.J. Neville continued faithful to his dull wife amidst so much cheap and wantonly attractive black flesh.
~~Ten days~~ Meanwhile, Jimmie Blacksmith had all the comforts. For some days his penis itched almost beyond bearing. He ~~used~~ would sing:

> In the sting of ~~their~~ our manhood
> Mungara's daughters being few ~~like the~~
> ~~Like the~~ As hills behind Marooka ~~the~~ river
> snake—scant hills
> Mungara's daughters scant,
> Over Marooka we went singing,
> ~~Followed the~~ Stalking Widjarra ~~beneath three~~ under
>   dusty suns.
> Came roaring at them ~~out of the~~ from moon
> ~~Painting~~ Painted blood upon Widjarra-men with
>   strokes of warclubs
> Took the shrilling pee-wit women for
> daughters to Mungara,
> Wives unto the men of Emu-Wren.

He sang it hard, accentuating every corner the monotone turned. It was a good song. /the raid had been carried out ~~three~~ six hundred years before./ But apart from the itch, he had all the comforts. A blanket. His shirt and trousers. Ten days after Easter, Jimmie reappeared at Brentwood. His half-sister, Bibra Dottie Blacksmith, was the first to spot him, then other women and his young half brother Morton.
Dottie ran before him ululating in her high fifteen-year-old voice.
  Born from the lizard comes my shining brother Tullam man.
Morton woke Jimmie's presumptive father, Wilf, who ~~had two years~~ would die of alcoholism and pneumonia in a year or so and was damn hard to wake. Dulcie dropped Wilf's shirt, from which she was washing sick on the warm side of their hovel. /For/ With Jimmie's manhood, the ~~hot~~ cold weather had set in.
She could see her son coming amongst the huts /spread

Making Stories

through the loose thicket of Brentwood/, the sun emphasising his funny pale hair. Men hooted his passage in a comradely way, small children ran across his path. Piercing the day, Bibra Dottie's voice sang the news.

Out of the monster's mouth, ~~shaking~~ sealed in manhood comes my Tullam brother.

How Dulcie laughed. 'Where ~~you~~ yer bin, ~~you~~ yer pale bastard?' she screamed /in English/. Wilf stood squinting, grinning stupidly. ~~Dot~~ Still holding Wilf's irrelevant stained shirt she took a note from Dottie.
'Out of the lizard's belly come my sons returning in manhood who were sucklings born to Emu-Wren of me.'
Mr Neville had watched ~~Jimmie's~~ /from his verandah/ the return of young Jimmie Blacksmith. 'Excitable people,' he murmured. 'Excitable people.' He smiled. God must love people who greet mere absentees ~~so enthus~~ with such ardour. It was as if the boy had come back from the dead.
The Rev. Neville considered if, this once, he might get a sensible, explicit answer from a black. He walked down the path and out onto the ~~dust baked clay~~ dusty grass of the mission station.
'Jimmie Backsmith,' he called. His voice cut the shrilling off. Thank God. Jimmie came up to him.
In the new silence his feet could be heard padding the earth in their ~~soft~~ light economic way.
'Where have you been, Mister Blacksmith?'
'~~Catching~~ Catchin possums,' Jimmie said.
/Mr Neville flinched./
'Did it occur to you that I might have wanted your presence for the Easter Choir?'
'Wot, Mister Nev'll?'
'You've missed a lot of school, Blacksmith.'
'Yair, Mister Nev'll.'
'Very well. Come into my study, please.'
In the study /a front sitting-room with ~~three~~ a desk and three shelves of standard evangelical works, a bowl of asters topping them/, Jimmy was caned for truancy. No one resented it—it seemed no unseemly thing for a /new/ Wondilli buck./No one had stopped Wondilli elders from gathering to make Jimmy's initiation, although some of

them had walked a hundred miles to initiates, it seemed no unseemly thing that the new buck they had made should now be lashed on the arse./ For the truth of Mr Neville and the truth of Emu-Wren and lizard ran parallel. Mr Neville had his place as did the poor-buggar-white-fella-~~got~~ son-of-God-got-nailed.
'Cane ~~taught~~ teach you ~~to~~ t'be ~~good~~ goo'boy /now/ ~~even Dottie said~~ Wilf muttered '~~Not that you~~ Don' let that ~~stand~~ stan' in yer light.'

(Reprinted courtesy Mitchell Library, State Library of New South Wales.)

Extract 2 from the published version

The Chant of Jimmie Blacksmith, pp 1–6.

IN JUNE of 1900 Jimmie Blacksmith's maternal uncle Tabidgi—Jackie Smolders to the white world—was disturbed to get news that Jimmie had married a white girl in the Methodist church at Wallah.

Therefore he set out with Jimmie's initiation tooth to walk a hundred miles to Wallah. The tooth would be a remonstration and lay a tribal claim on Jimmie. For Tabidgi Jackie Smolders was full-blooded and of the Tullam section of the Mungindi tribe. To his mind people should continue to wed according to the tribal pattern.

Which was: that Tullam should marry Mungara, Mungara should wed Garri, Garri should wed Wibbera, Wibbera take Tullam's women. But here was Jimmie, a Tullam, married in church to a white girl.

Jackie felt distressed, a spiritual unease over Jimmie Blacksmith's wedding. These tribal arrangements should still be made, Tabidgi Jackie Smolders thought. The elders kept the tribal pattern in their heads and could arrange a tribal wedding even if the Tullam buck was on a mission station eighty miles, two hundred miles, from Mungara woman.

Jackie Smolders was therefore dispirited—so too even his flippant sister, a full-blooded lady called Dulcie Blacksmith. Half-breed Jimmie had resulted from a visit some white man had made to Brentwood blacks' camp in 1878. The missionaries—who had never been told the higher things of Wibbera—had made it clear that if you had pale children it was because you'd been rolled by white men. They had not been told that it was Emu-Wren, the tribal totem, who quickened the womb.

Making Stories

Mrs Dulcie Blacksmith believed the missionaries more or less. They took such a low view of lying in other people that they were unlikely to lie themselves. And certainly, Mrs Blacksmith had been rolled by white men. For warmth in winter, she once said. For warmth in winter and for comfort in summer. But the deep truth was that Emu-Wren had quickened Jimmie Blacksmith (pale or not) in the womb and that Mungara owed him a woman.

Yet here he was marrying a white girl off a farm.

Therefore off went Jackie Smolders carrying Jimmie's initiation tooth wrapped in clean flour-cloth and carried in the left pocket, away from the sevenpence that belonged to the right pocket and might be infected with malchance.

It must be said that although Jackie Smolders was alcoholic and knew that Jimmie Blacksmith was earning wages which Jackie, as maternal uncle, could claim for liquor, his chief reason for setting out towards Wallah was tribal and centred in the magical tooth.

The tooth had been knocked out of Jimmie's mouth by Mungindi elders when the boy was thirteen, in 1891. So too he had been circumcised with stone, the incision poulticed over with chalk-clay and likewise the eyes. It is necessary to take cognizance of Jimmie Blacksmith's experience from the day of this initiation to the time in 1900 that Jackie Smolders went to Wallah.

When Jimmie was taken from camp for his initiation, Dulcie Blacksmith presumed him dead for the time being. The epoch-old agenda of ceremonies was kept a secret from all the women. As far as Dulcie knew, the great Lizard had mashed and swallowed him and would now give birth to him as a completed Mungindi man.

He was gone for weeks. The mission superintendent, Rev. H. J. Neville, B.A., kept asking where Jimmie was but was not incommoded with any part of the truth.

Grown Mungindi men—Jackie Smolders for example—knew that Jimmie was hiding in the scrub close to an anabranch of the Macquarie River. Here he waited for the wound to heal and lived on possum meat. He was full of the exhilaration of tribal manhood and the relief of finding that the lizard story was not true to the extent of his being actually chewed or swallowed. He sang:

Dash surprise from your eyes, my mother,
As crested parrots are dashed from the white branches of dawn.
On your brow put pride as proud as Dubra the berry tree.
Out of the chrysalis and out of the lizard's mouth your son comes
    man.

Sometimes he swung the bull-roarer lest any woman from Brentwood mission come near. If seen by a woman during your isolation, you were hexed beyond knowing. Women in their turn were raised to fear the voice of the bull-roarer. If you twirled it now and again, you were more or less safe.

Jimmie Blacksmith's initiation took place in autumn. There had been very little rain, and no frosts yet. The winds shifted, casual and warm, under a high Easter sun.

Back at Brentwood, the Rev. H. J. Neville could have used a good boy like Jimmie for the Easter hymns.

"Blasted blacks!" he told his wife. "The best of them are likely to vanish at any time."

He felt that Jimmie was a protégé and had a sobriety none of his half-siblings possessed. The European who had impregnated giddy Dulcie Blacksmith must have been of a pensive nature; a man who perhaps hated the vice of sleeping with black women yet could not master it. Mr Neville himself had often felt the distinctive pull of some slant-grinned black face.

Townspeople spoke of this sin as if it were a distinctive form of immorality, substantially different from fornicating with a white woman. It was an accredited old wives' tale that by lying with blacks a white man was gradually reduced to impotence with white women.

Good Mr Neville now reached for the butter at table and found the flies about it as thick almost as at high summer.

"If a person could be certain," he said, a little peevishly, "that he had imbued *one* of them with decent ambitions!"

Until Jimmie Blacksmith vanished, Mr Neville had thought that he had a chance of bringing off the trick with eager, sober, polite Jimmie Blacksmith.

The Rev. Mr Neville had a true evangelical vocation. If he had been a student of anthropology he would have been less baffled before his fly-blown butter dish at Easter, 1891. Anthropology was a word he had never heard. It was, as well, a two-way traffic, demanding a specialized white awareness and talkative natives. Jimmie felt it would have been bad-mannered to upset Mr Neville by being talkative about initiation.

Since the boy's disappearance, Mr Neville had taken to cutting even more notifications of vacant ministries out of the *Methodist Church Times*. All over the little weatherboard manse were mislaid small squares of newsprint proposing pastorages, anchorages, from the Riverina to the Darling Downs. They yellowed in the high autumn sun, in Jimmie Blacksmith's lasting absence; while H. J. Neville continued faithful to his dull wife amidst such cheap, such wantonly appealing black flesh.

For some days Jimmie's incised genitals stung beyond bearing. He would sing:

In the sting of our manhood,
Mungara's daughters being few
As hills beyond Marooka, river snake—scant hills,
Mungara's daughters scant,
Over Marooka we went singing,
Stalking Widgarra under under dusty suns,
Came roaring at them from the moon
Painting blood on Widgarra men with strokes of warclubs,
Taking to us all the shrilling pee-wit women,
                              daughters to Mungara,
Wives unto the men of Emu-Wren.

He sang it in monotone and with dissonances Mr Neville would have found strange. It was a fine song about an ancient raid. The woman-stealing it recounted had taken place during the English civil war, two and a half centuries previously.

Apart from the itch, he had all the comforts. A blanket. His mission clothes. Fresh-water crayfish and slightly muddy perch, left land-locked when the river took a new course, were plentiful. Possums came out at night. He flung his club at their phosphorescent eyes.

Ten days after Easter, Jimmie reappeared at Brentwood.

His half-sister, Bibra Dottie Blacksmith, was the first to notice his quiet entry. Then some other women and his half-brother Morton.

Dottie ran before him ululating in her high fifteen-year-old voice:

"Born from the Lizard comes my shining brother Tullam man."

Morton woke Jimmie's presumptive father, Wilf Blacksmith, who was well on the way to death, only a few years away, by pneumonia and alcohol. Dulcie dropped a shirt of Wilf's that she had been washing in a basin in the sun. She shivered, for—with Jimmie's manhood accomplished—the cold weather had already set in.

Dulcie could see her son coming through the loose thicket where the hovels of Brentwood stood. The sun emphasized his funny pale hair. Men hooted his passage in a comradely way. Small children ran across his path. Piercing the day, Bibra Dottie's voice sang the news:

"Out of the monster's mouth, sealed in manhood, comes my Tullam brother."

How Dulcie laughed! She and Morton laughed wildly on solemn occasions and Mr Neville therefore thought them dense. It was not the truth.

"Where yer bin, yer paley bastard?" Dulcie screamed in the crisp, Cockneyfied version of English that natives spoke. Still holding Wilf's irrelevant stained shirt she picked up the song from Dottie.

"Out of the Lizard's belly come my sons, crushing frost, making large marks on the earth, sons returning in manhood who were sucklings from my belly, born to Emu-Wren by me."

Mr Neville had watched from his veranda the return of young Jimmie Blacksmith.

"Excitable people," he murmured. "Excitable people."

It made him happy to see them. God must love those who greet mere absentees with so much ardour. It was as if the boy had come back from the dead.

Mr Neville wondered if, this once, he might get a sensible, explicit answer from a black. He walked down the path and out onto the dusty grass of the mission station.

"Jimmie Blacksmith!" he called. His voice cut the shrilling off. When Jimmie broke off his path and came towards the missioner, his brother Morton staggered about with the hilarity of it. But there was silence. Jimmie's feet could be heard padding the earth in their light economic way.

"Where have you been, Master Blacksmith?"

"Catchin' possums."

Mr Neville flinched. "I can't understand you. Didn't it occur to you you might be needed for higher things? The Easter choir perhaps?"

"How d'yer mean, Mr Neville?"

"You've missed a lot of school."

"Yair, Mr Neville."

"Very well. You must come to my study, please."

In the study, a front sitting-room dignified by desk, an *orbis terrarum*, three shelves of standard evangelical works, Jimmie was caned for truancy. No one resented it. No one had hindered Mungindi elders from gathering to make Jimmie a man. Though they had come from places spread over more than two thousand squares miles to initiate him, it would have seemed no unworthy usage that their new buck should now be lashed on the arse by a Methodist minister. For the truth of Mr Neville and the truth of Emu-Wren ran parallel. Mr Neville had his place, as did the poor-bugger-white-fella-son-of-God-got-nailed.

'Cane teach yer to be good feller now," Wilf stated. "Don' let that stand in yer light."

Finola Moorhead
Remember the Tarantella

I wanted to write something that was feminist in aesthetic...I chose twelve women readers, of different star signs, to read [the manuscript], and that took years...The process of having those women readers involved for those three years is part of what [Remember the Tarantella] is.

Finola Moorhead

without a word. Beatrix, knowing Etama's shrewdness,
sharing the same European addresses and aware that she would
not much longer than travelling time on her own, deduced
more accurately than Etama had told her, her whereabouts,
however.

* * *

The Moon Weakly Pictorial Review Centre-fold Tease

Pics and pleas from the past! Test for literate ladies.
Pictures and captions set out in eye-catching assymetry.
Single initial and date of quotation provided. Consult
your subconscious general knowledge or whatever you have
at your mental finger-tips. Don't be afraid, ladies.
Above all, don't feel alone. Remember some things never
die and never change. But what?
It could be you.
Now: who?

                    Top Left illustration: a photograph.
                    Light catches the profile front on; the
                    face is long, the nose aquiline. The eye
                    we see is musing on the source of light;
                    morning sun through a window? Caught in
                    a beautiful swirl are ribbons of smoke
                    issuing from a long thin cigarette between
                    two narrow fingers of the right hand, the
                    elbow rests on the desk. The other arm
                    hangs loosely beside the chair. It draws
                    attention to the lower half of the portrait.
                    We see she is knee-deep in a sea of
                    crumpled paper.
"Shall I continue this soliloquy, or shall I imagine an
audience, which will make me describe? This sentence is
due to a book on fiction which I am now writing -- once
more, O once more. It is a hand to mouth book. I scribble
down whatever I can think of about Romance, Dickens etc.
must hastily gorge on Jane Austen and dish up something
tomorrow."   V. August 12, 1928.

                    Left: a lithograph. We have an entire room.
                    Elegant Regency; to the right a bay window,
                    to the left a firepalce, in between an
                    occupied armchair. The bodice of the lady's
                    dress is striped. The hair is dark, parted
                    in the centre and drawn tightly back. The
                    head is tilted up, the eyes stare straight
                    at the lithographer and they are the black-
                    est thing in the picture, piercing. The
                    hands are on the lap where an embroidery
                    frame has fallen to one side revealing an
                    open exercise book. Peeping out from the
                    skirts of the chair's upholstery are a
                    little inkpot and a pen.
"I begin already to weigh my words and sentences more than
I did, and am looking about for a sentiment, an illustra-
tion or a metaphor in every corner of the room. Could my
ideas flow as fast as the rain in the Store Closet it
would be charming."   J. January 24, 1809

Making Stories

The writing of Finola Moorhead's *Remember the Tarantella* was a vast work that spanned many years. This book has a revision history unlike any other book we know. It did not begin life as a plot, or a character, but as diagrams. As Moorhead writes in the book's preface: 'The first draft was a series of diagrams, and nouns...the second draft was flow-prose.' Through its early gestation Moorhead shaped the book according to patterns suggested by the Tarot, astrology, the double helix, and mathematics.

Remember the Tarantella was, as the author put it, written in the 'plural of women'; Moorhead showed the book at various stages to a large number of other women: 'Throughout the many drafts, I had readers, arguers, encouragers, critics, and researchers.' The changes she made are in part the result of the responses she got from these women.

In the extracts we've selected, we've tried to give a linear sense of how the writing of the novel progressed. There were about eight drafts altogether: we've chosen extracts from three different stages. The first consists of some of the diagrams that made up the first draft. Extract 1 is the first prose draft, and Extract 2 is a later prose draft. The extract from the final book, Extract 3, is transformed, but all the earlier processes are visible within it.

Woolfe's interview with Finola Moorhead took place in Sydney in July 1991.

INT: We've read that you began writing *Remember the Tarantella* with diagrams. Can you tell us how that process worked?

FM: I'd written a novel which was called *Lots of Potential*. Most first novels are pretty awful, so I thought, I'll make all the mistakes I can. And the book was totally chaotic. I sat down and wrote whatever I felt like when I felt like writing, regardless of plot or anything like that, figuring this was a first novel. I gave it to Christina Stead to read, and she said: 'You're really mathematical.' It was really chaotic but it was really mathematical.

That's why the first draft here is mathematical—diagrams. Consider the diagrams a draft, which I do, because it was the first work on it. I started *Tarantella* just purely from diagrams and nouns. No sentences because sentences bind you to themselves.

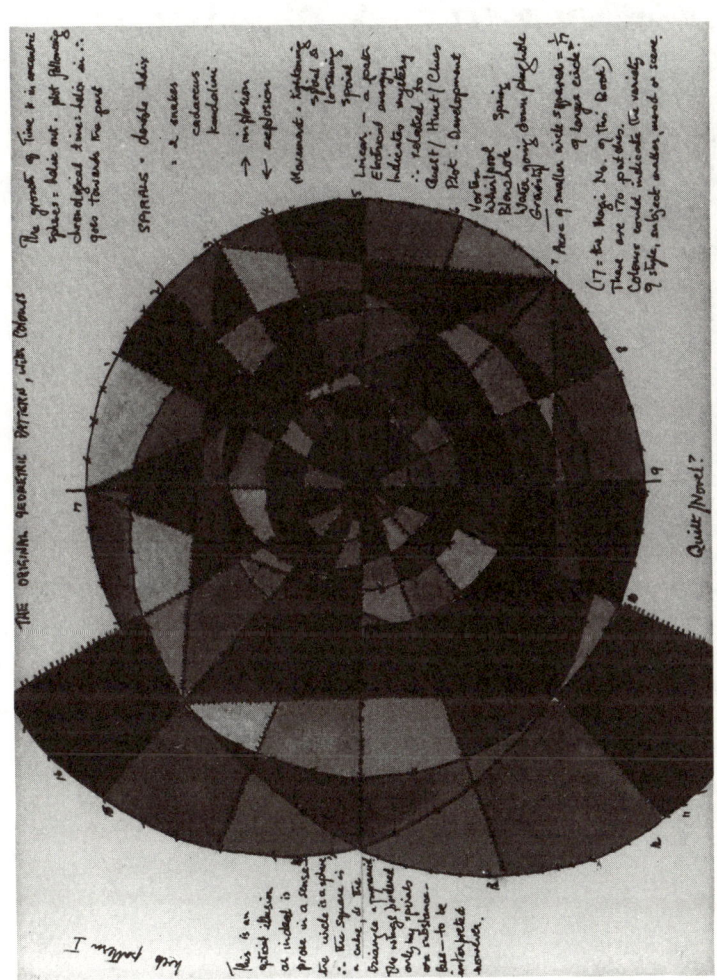

That was the first, that was done on big blotting paper when I was a writer-in-residence, and that was children's coloured playpaper stuck on a photocopy of it. I keep that winged circle going throughout.

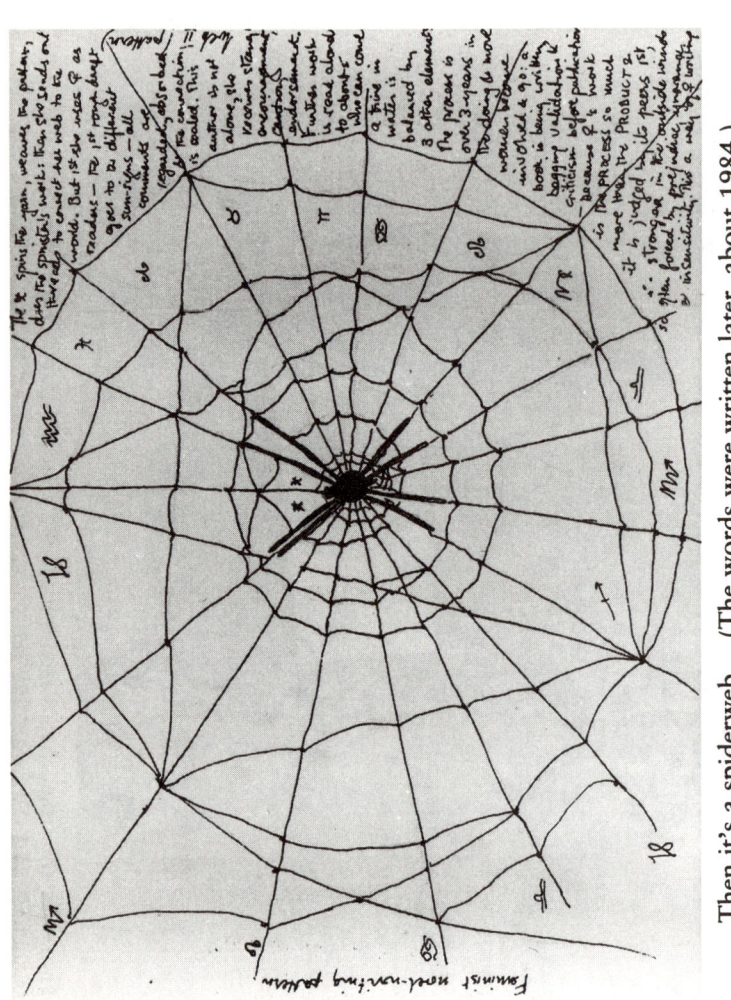

Then it's a spiderweb...(The words were written later, about 1984.)
The female aesthetic was my main thing.

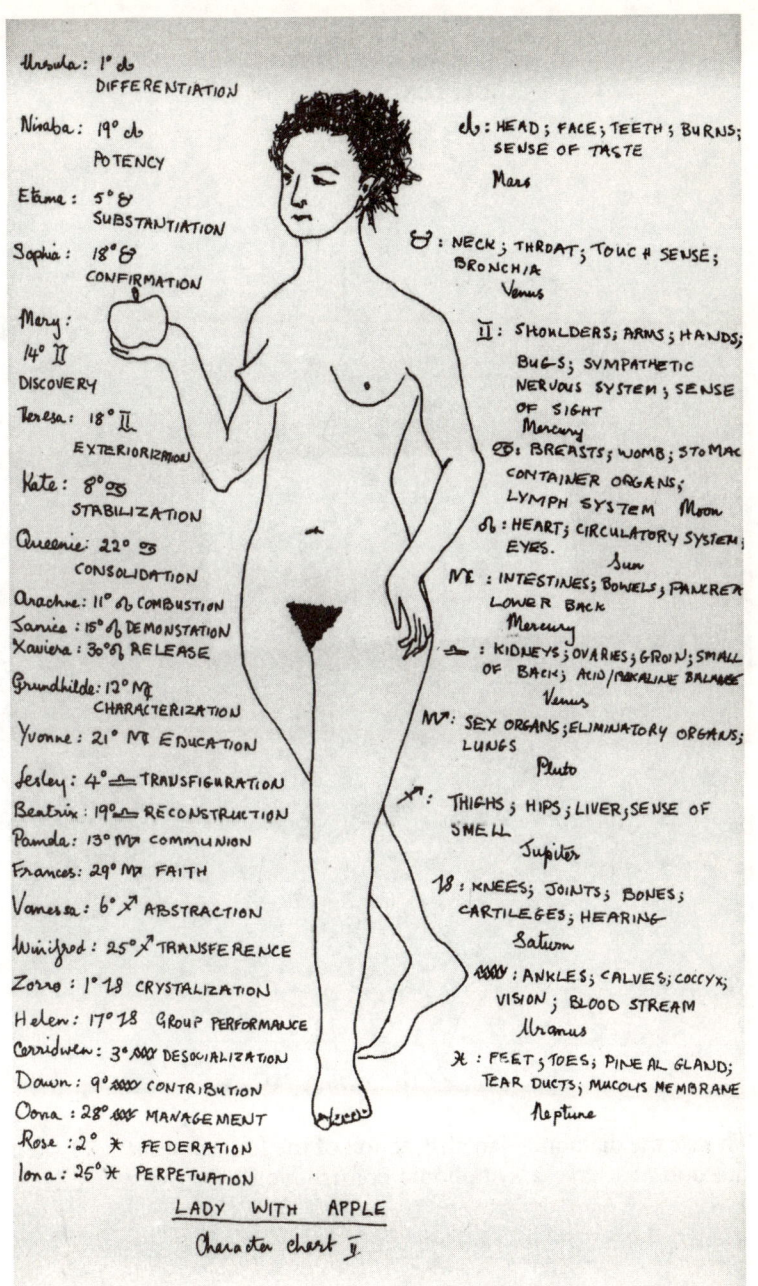

And that's the woman—sun signs and Sabian symbols for each character.

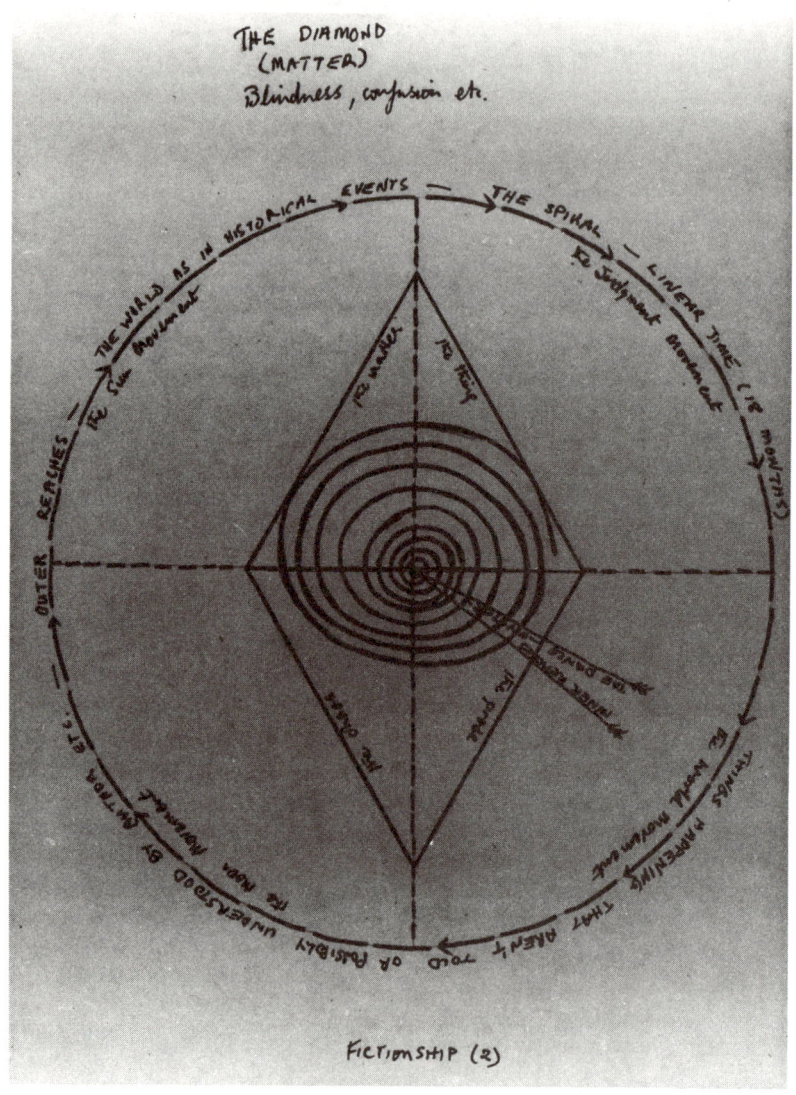

There's the diamond—an abstraction of the four movements. I wanted the book to have a symphonic construction.

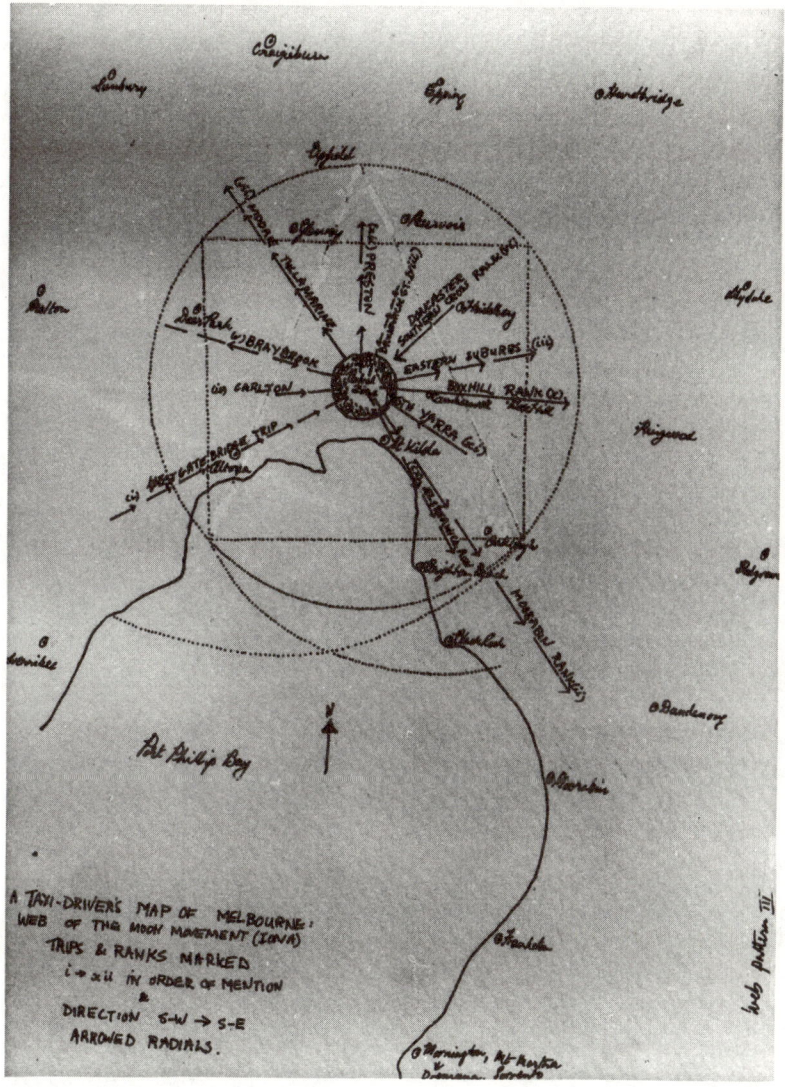

That's the spiral going through—the taxi-driving map—you get Iona going to Auburn and round about, spirals again. (Couldn't have that particular map in, say, Sydney. Melbourne, with its main radial arterial roads, works.)

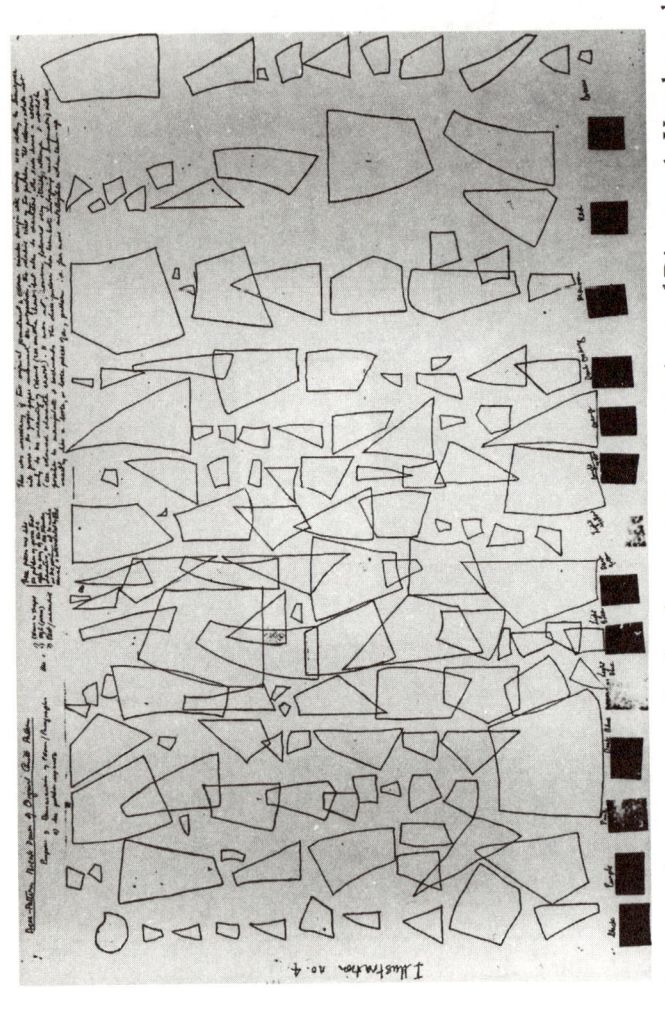

Here it is as a dress pattern—they're the separate pattern pieces of Diagram 1. You know how the Tarantella's got spots of one character, then another character: that was this one.

INT: Why a dress pattern?

FM: Because it's another female thing.

Finola Moorhead—Remember the Tarantella

INT: What came after the diagrams?

FM: The movements. Prose and poetry. Four poems. There are about eight drafts. I was using so many arcane images. I was using the Tarot for characters up to seventeen, then I had the Moon, the Sun, the World and Judgment, and they became movements because you couldn't make those particular Tarot cards into characters. What I used Tarot cards for was to give the characters an essential moral of their own, the basis which they go back to. Like my moral might be freedom, or someone else's might be justice.

INT: So the Tarot cards stand for different...

FM: How I interpret them. How I use them. Because I couldn't be seventeen different characters, you know, they'd all sound like me. So I had to look at, say, Queenie, as the Tower. The Tarot informed me about how she would be in the world: solid, then sudden change. You remember Queenie, she's the one that shot her father, got rid of the old order. So seventeen of the Tarot cards worked for me like that, to give me something to go back to when I was not talking about me, but talking about the plural of women.

INT: So, when Queenie is represented by the Tower, which itself represents sudden change, that would make you think about the incidents that were important in her life?

FM: There's other things that inform Queenie too. Like being Cancer, she's the one that gets pregnant. The diagrams help me get to a deeper level than my life. My life bores me silly. When I'm talking fiction I'm talking something exciting, something that's elsewhere, in the soul.

Also, I wanted to write something that was feminist in aesthetic, not just coming to the climax and that's it. I wanted something like in the diagram, having many knobs. And something like music. I informed myself through the Tarot and also through the star charts and through colour and through number, all those arcane kinds of disciplines. Not that I'm an initiate of any of it, but I just used what came for me.

A friend of mine saw this and gave me coloured kindergarten paper when I was trying to sort out how to go beyond 58 pages, to write something big.

You start writing a novel, but my interpretation of it is, if you don't have an underlying theme, or spring, you can dry up. And the only reason to write is to be constantly excited by writing—by other than yourself as well.

Making Stories

INT: So the Tarot and the colours took you to another level?

FM: To the level of inspiration. It's the alphabet too, informing it. Queenie is quick, Ursula is ugly, the U sound throughout Ursula's pieces—so that informs me about the adjectives, verbs and so on. She might 'utter' rather than 'talk'.

INT: What did Christina Stead say to you about mathematics that gave you a kick-off point?

FM: She was writer-in-residence at Monash then, and she read *Lots of Potential*. She took me to lunch with a person called Crossley who was a mathematician at Monash. To sit down and have this conversation about absolute abstract purity! She and I knew each other to the tune of about five or six conversations like this, and how it helped was, it said to me: 'Go for it. Be it, be abstract.' That's why I go that way to start.

I can get music that way at the fundamental level of reverberation, and I can get a choral kind of thing going through the book—through the abstract thing. Such a lot of music is similar to maths. I don't have access to music really but I understand it on a mathematical level. Christina Stead wrote to me while I was at Monash—I was sitting up at a desk, not knowing what to do. Will I rewrite *Lots of Potential*? She said: No, forget that, write something else.

I'd been two weeks sitting up there as writer-in-residence myself, thinking about my own life, boring myself. Why should I relive it? What's to relive? Make something else! Create a concerto—which is what the Tarot is—a symphony or a choral work, something that you can read over and over again if you want to, a chorale of characters.

I proved my point about the female aesthetic, I can make a novel that does have very few men in it. I only had cut-out type men in it, without it being considered ugly. I wrote it too damn well for it to be dismissed. They do that a lot with a lot of feminist writing, they say: 'Oh, that's ratbag, that's heavy.' They dismiss a lot of feminist lesbian writing as marginal. I proved to myself the point that I could be central in terms of the literary values—I could take *my* lifestyle as the centre, not society's lifestyle, which is what most people get centred to. You get mainstream, you write mainstream aesthetics. That was my big challenge. It took me eight years.

INT: Eight years?

FM: The diagrams, and that work of research in the arcane, happened in 1980.

Finola Moorhead—Remember the Tarantella

This next draft [Extract 1] is from 1981. I wrote most of that draft down at Mornington with my mother who had cancer, being a spinster daughter with her, and that was a very important time to just be with her, understand her frailty, and do something while I was doing it. I decided not to edit at all, I just went on. I just wrote it, and some of it's sustained right through to the end.

INT: Did you follow that principle all the time, that you'd write a whole draft, then another whole draft?

FM: Oh, they're all unique. The diagrams were followed by a 144-line poem, a quarter of which is the Moon, the Sun, Judgment and the World, and the poem informs me as much as the diagrams do. Then after the fast draft I wrote this 'slow draft'—I call it the slow draft, it's just type type type type—and the poem and the diagrams got thrown out in the very last draft.

INT: Was that a difficult decision, to abandon them?

FM: No. There were many refigurings. The artifice goes, becomes unnecessary—for example, *The Moon Weakly Review, Book the First*—the conscious, self-conscious pointing out the alphabetic position of the character. So does the naked inspiration of the writing. Ursula had to sit alongside other characters and take her place in the plot. So how, my question must have been, can I retain her internal romance cargo—that is, mine—when I'm first imagining Ursula see Dawn surf? And at the same time how to make her physical reality poignant? That's just technique and work and decisions.

But in the first place I set up such a broad blueprint with so many guidelines. Most of it was discarded—not really, it's beneath the surface—in favour of a decent read. Describing the bay, for instance. Hack work.

INT: What were the processes that took you from this extract to the rest of the book?

FM: That's the very first prose draft of the novel. There was no rewriting before that one. There may or there may not have been something written on the beach in the wind.

That first prose draft was written quickly in a fever of enthusiasm and consequently used basically as raw material. You see, I was frightened I would run out of inspiration. I wanted to create a block of marble at which I could chip away, make into a reasonable form and eventually polish. What one is looking for there is the guts, the gems, the jewels, which you can later set in a muted background, which, naturally, makes them shine the brighter.

Then I thought: I can't edit this without help. So I chose twelve women readers, of different star signs, to read it, and that took years. I started with just two readers, a Capricorn reader and a Libra reader; the Capricorn reader's a legal person and the Libra reader's into astrology, so they were informing me from different disciplines quite interestingly. They were reading that as I was writing it.

Then I thought, this is a good idea but as I've got so many broad-based women here, I'll need a broader-based readership to tell me what is actually here. So the next draft was read by twelve women. After getting their comments on that, I had meetings for reading each new chapter as I wrote it.

INT: Did they ever meet all together, to talk to you, or did they come one by one?

FM: As many as I could get together I did, but some were up in the bush, some in Melbourne, some in Sydney, some were overseas.

I cast for traits as well as personality. I didn't ever care if the women liked me or not, I just wanted intelligent women readers. It didn't matter whether they were into literature or not, although a number of them were.

At that point the diagrams had seventeen segments, so there were only seventeen chapters. Big chapters. So they read that, I absorbed their comments, then they came and we read the new chapter aloud, like the old Russians or Dickens or whatever. In a weekend gathering we all read the new bits.

INT: Each reading a character, or taking turns to read a chunk?

FM: Taking turns. At a time there would be eight of them there. It wasn't exclusive—if their lovers were coming along that was fine too. At this stage no men were admitted, except Kris Hemmensley, I showed a bit of the first draft to him.

INT: How did you sift out the comments, the good from the bad, the useful from the useless?

FM: Well, I'm the boss, I'm the writer!

INT: Do you think you could ever be swayed...I'm just thinking how vulnerable I'd feel...

FM: I don't feel vulnerable because I love criticism. It's not me personally that would be hurt, it's that the writing is not adequate. They contributed heaps, they would get excited about the whole prospect of informing me of stuff I didn't know.

Finola Moorhead—Remember the Tarantella

INT: About the characters, the scenes...?

FM: The world. Their brains... Their contribution was unselfish as mine was unselfish, in that I was sharing. You know you get that question: 'What's your book about?' Most of the time you think: I hate this question. But during *The Tarantella*, because I was experimenting, I would answer anybody who asked me: The book is about women, I'm doing da da da da. So by my giving in that way, I received.

INT: It's an extraordinarily open way to work. I meant by 'vulnerable' that if someone makes a comment, I could write in a direction that in the end I wish I hadn't.

FM: Yes, well, I allowed myself to do that. You've got to constantly have your own critical faculty in gear, because you can throw out good stuff. You have to be able to say: 'No, that's a gem.' You can actually be blinded to what is a gem and keep things that are a bit of old rot. But eventually you know, because you just keep rewriting and rewriting and re-seeing, seeing from a different angle.

INT: Were you deep into the book by the time you got back all the responses?

FM: This draft of the women readers is 1982/3/4: those three years it took to make a big draft, which was a real fatty—so big, so amorphous, that I was pinned to the ground by it. I tried it with Jackie Yowell, managing editor of Penguin at the time, she said: 'It's brilliant, Finola, it's absolutely brilliant, but it's too hard for us to take on, it's too much editing.'

INT: How big a book was it at that stage?

FM: Well, when Paul Brennan took it on he said, 'You'll have to cut it by a third.' So it was a lot bigger than the book you've got.

INT: Why were you willing to cut the book?

FM: Because I knew it was too big.

INT: Did you feel the structure had become amorphous?

FM: The structure, yes, was bursting at the seams. Because while I'd had all these structural, blueprint plans—like seventeen chapters, movement of the Sun, Moon and World and all that sort of thing, and I'd been very academic or mathematical about it, there was a chaos within—the neutron within the atom if you like, the chaos within the simplicity.

For six months Paul and I would meet. And we did the final drafts on the computer. Why did I accept so generously his constant criticism? Because criticism is what I needed, flattery you don't need while you're writing a book, criticism you need—but I now had the male viewpoint. I gave my attention entirely to the male viewpoint of this female book that I was writing. I was very well aware that we now had the 'Yang' and I needed that, I needed to cut it, I needed the assertion, the self-assertion that a male presentation does. So what might have been a philosophical treatise, became a statement in the cutting, so five pages could become one paragraph.

It was a helluva job and it was distressing in certain ways. But Paul did not write a word of it. What Paul did was to show me what he understood, just as the women had shown me what they understood—but they also contributed. He didn't contribute, he just showed me ...What he wanted to change, all sorts of things that never got changed, all of those were related to the myth, male myth.

The process of having the women readers so involved for those three years is part of what that book is, part of its multi-energy. And I don't think other writers should write like that. I didn't with *Still Murder*, it's not written in that style. Only *The Tarantella* is written with that sort of openness, because I had to make a great act of faith in women.

INT: Why didn't you want to use that technique in *Still Murder*?

FM: It's too hard. I had a couple of readers for *Still Murder*. I like to have a reader during the drafts because you don't see it like someone else does. I politely ask, 'Will you read it? Say what you like as long as I get some idea what's there.' *Still Murder* is just as long a book and it's just as big a book in terms of as many drafts, and the editing by Jackie Yowell for Penguin was just as intensive, just as much cutting, and my individual process was very similar—write write write write write, put everything down, then cut like crazy.

I really like the rewriting but I won't rewrite unless I'm just as inspired as I was to write the initial thing. I don't consider rewriting unexciting at all, I think it's fabulous, I love it. It's sort of like sculpture, you get closer, and closer and shinier, more detail and shinier, and then you finally finish and you're...it's furbished.

INT: As you write, do you have a feeling of discovery, uncovering something, or are you inventing?

FM: Yeah... Both. But within both is the mystery too, isn't it? You will get as much as your tiny mind can do, and then you trust... I personally think there's quite a strong moral thing in writing, that you're doing the right thing in terms of your own morals. You're trying so hard to express something well, and the words keep evading you, and then: Zoom! out of the blue a whole new thing you'd never have invented or discovered happens—not when you're actually writing but when you're reading through it. There it is! There!

So there's that mystery element that, personally, I think is related to your good intentions and your respect—respect for your characters, respect for the world, the earth, respect for the mystery of the human mind. You sit down at your desk with a certain level of humility, but arrogance at the same time because you're daring to do it. There are times when you think, look what I'm doing! But there are other times where you're humble in relation to it. It's 99 per cent hard yakka and one per cent... but that one per cent is so important.

INT: Do you despair at times?

FM: Not I!

INT: In all those years, you didn't have any doubts?

FM: Yeah, I went through that, a terrible down period in this at the end of 1984. The enormous fat draft was finished, and I had no ability and nothing to do—I just had this enormous manuscript, and an enormous lot of my life had gone into it.

INT: By then it was about three years?

FM: About four or four-and-a-half. There were other little short stories and things but I couldn't get into them because my mind was constantly trying to feed this one. I just ran down like a battery, and I didn't know whether it was a load of bullshit or whether it was a great book. I really didn't know. But I knew whatever it was, it was alive. I didn't like those years. The emotional journey to there was to the South Pole and back. A wiser woman...

INT: So part of what you're saying is that after writing like that you come out a different person.

FM: You become more of what you may have been. A gum tree doesn't ever become a wattle.

Making Stories

INT: So it's a sort of transformation?

FM: I think any art is. It's a sort of mining of the self, and if you're going to write anything that's different from what anyone else is going to write, you don't copy, you have to go into your own uniqueness.

I become a relatively sick person when I'm writing, because I smoke a lot and drink black coffee, and wring, there's this wringing of the essential self. There's all that constant questioning, the 'Who am I?' of it. I am a writer because I write, therefore if I feel bad I'd better go to the computer and start work!

I don't have a work ethic in relation to writing. I work extremely hard out of respect for what I'm capable of, and what I've been capable of. I feel I've been initiated into something, in the sense of being given insights that I would otherwise not have, because of that work. It's not because you're published or because you're in the scene, something so artificial, I call that selling your soul.

But I feel that I've got the right now not to write. But I didn't feel that before *The Tarantella* was finished. The right not to write! Think about it! It is like I had been so trapped in the idea that I had to write—because I'd decided I was going to be an Australian writer, and an Australian writer with all the laurels that come, being recognised and so on. From 1972 to 1988 I constantly had this duty in relation to writing.

So the good reviews of *The Tarantella* and the acceptance of it finished my need to write. But then I got three grants in a row, which is the reason I could finish *Still Murder*. It's a good book too, just a different process, a different book. *The Tarantella* is written out of the pronoun 'we' and *Still Murder*'s written out of the pronoun 'they'. The 'I' book hasn't come yet. The 'I' book's the hardest of them all, but the 'I' book is what most first novels are. Me me me.

My mother was a very intelligent woman and a very good writer in her own right. She said: 'I'm sick of this first person in all these new writers, they're all "I".' That's why I've got an alphabet in *Tarantella*, it was she who gave me the idea. I thought: well, the 'I' has to go! If it's not an 'I' then which letter is it? So I'll use the alphabet.

INT: Your mother said that?

FM: My mother said she was sick of the 'I' in the new writing.

Finola Moorhead—Remember the Tarantella

Extract 1 from a manuscript

This is an early prose draft of *Remember the Tarantella*.

A Constable Day & An Old Overcoat's Burden

No one could be a saint who dreams as Ursula does. For dreams are quite out of the reach of morals, ethics and charity; as Oscar has put it: 'Art is out of the reach of morals, for her eyes are fixed upon things beautiful and immortal and ever-changing.' As to morals and ethics and charity, what choice does Ursula have? The prison of her facial scar assured all three. Is sincerity a virtue? The Great Maligned, the signed-sealed worshipper of all nine Muses and priest of Plato crooks his finger to the horrendous virgin and brings his lips close to her ear: 'A little sincerity is a dangerous thing, and a great deal of it is absolutely fatal.' To give the Last Vowel her due, she has never indulged in sincerity, hence, has no pedestal for Blame in her heart. Her heart broke away from the Promethean chains of her visage long ago, fidelity to the daily facts of life took flight on the same date, truth became as fickle as beauty—as fickle as her married sister?—in that the Beholder's eye is the salient factor.

On an ugly winter's day ten used Roman calendars away, Ursula witnessed a scene that threatened to crack open the separate spheres of her life, and release passion into her daily round—a force antipathetical to its equilibrium—in such a case, a great deal of sincerity might have been fatal. For her married sister? For her mother? The wind was howling and the waves were rising high and cracking down on the shallow beach and the sky was a pack of ferocious grey bears, the temperature was bitter. No Scottish coast filmed for an introduction to Macbeth could have boded more evil. As the gods were angry, Ursula rubbed her purple hands into each other with glee and leaned her little body into the gale hoping to gain the headland to meet the worst of it. But her arduous steps were arrested. Divine Madness decreed, a moment from the depths of Art! In dark Victorian oils! Dramatic aloneness suddenly punctured!

Making Stories

Against the thunderous sky a figure on a surf board.

There were two: the watcher and the watched. The watcher watched, and was moved, so moved to stand stock still! Clad in black rubber, such a slight thing was flashing across the battling great waves through the spitting wind. The surfer seemed to dance. Dance in a Japanese stance. Speeding, then disappearing into the mess-mad whiteness and for goodness sake! The undertow, and the board leaping up like a shark on its tail. If ever such a light thing, it could still crash down on a skull. No. And lo, paddling out again to the treacherous deep where the waves were long giant ripples.

Never before, for Ursula, had /the/ Beauty of the living human being leapt out of Art and Dream into the Real World; she was so shocked she was afraid she might behave uncharacteristically. This was a moment of soul to soul, in /a/ region beyond the limited prejudices of the physical. She put the headland behind and made her way down onto the beach, where she stood feet apart, perpendicular to the graceful antics of the surfer, and waited, spellbound.

A solo ballet on the immensely restless sea-surface; a folly performed entirely for her, for herself alone. She was reverent, she was transfigured. And when it was finished, she clapped her hands and jumped into the air several times to show her appreciation. The surfer squelched back the bonnet of the wet-suit, and a mass of hair, blond as sunshine, tumbled out. The board was heaved onto the hip and the young lanky girl approached her through the receding-encroaching-receding sea. Ursula did not recoil from this blond-haired, red-cheeked, blue-eyed, white-teethed apparition of Aryan health and courage, no, she rushed forward, lightly, as if she were as mystical a being as the Valkyrie coming from the ocean.

'My dear, my dear, aren't you cold?' Unfortunately sounding exactly like a maiden aunt, which part of her was, but not the part that was moved to speak. 'How old are you, you brave girl? O how I have loved watching you!'

Finola Moorhead—Remember the Tarantella

Dawn dropped her eyes shyly, kicked a lump of sand and breathed out, 'I'm thirteen. I'm a bit cold now, but I wasn't when I was out there. At least I didn't notice it, though I suppose I was. You see I'm going to win the Girls' Surfing Championships in January. And to win I've got to train. I'm teaching myself on the Bay beaches. I can do anything if I put my mind to it.'
'I'm sure you will, I'm sure you will. My dear child, where are your clothes?'
'Just over there.'
The two walked up the beach together to where a green towel was hanging on the bushes, behind which was a neat pile of clothes and a childish bag.
'Well, excuse me,' said Dawn, 'And thanks for clapping. I'd better dress now.'
Ursula backed away, shaking her hand in an imitation wave. The girl smiled politely.
'I will see you again in the sporting pages in the summer.' called Ursula.
When Ursula reached the headland and stood with her body facing the weather, the teeth had gone out of the gods' anger and they—wind, sea, clouds and rain—were merely boisterous, matching this pure Beholder's playful mood. She opened her coat to let them get closer.

The coat was one of those made for a man in that honest combination of gabardine and wool to last /out/ long and hard wearing. No planned obsolescence about it, it was made in England during the war. 'My Rolls Royce' to Ursula, and what better model for the chrystalline spinster to wander around the winter cliffs in? She existed within /it/ with warm familiarity, comfortably taking it for granted. But now, this 1970 July day, the mauve fingers detached the large flat buttons from their holes; unused to such freedom the old coat billowed out behind her into a Romantic cloak, and thrashed and dashed as if she were galloping over the solitary moors two centuries back. Deep in an inner pocket something crackled. Curiosity beat the vision of grey turbulence, and old Ursula took herself off to shelter behind some boxthorn; she crouched down and unfolded the yellowed pages of newsprint. The 1949 Editorial of the <u>Moon Weakly Review</u>.

Making Stories

'The Moon is only about a quarter of a million miles away. It is believed that the Earth and Moon were originally one rotating fluid globe, round which the Sun swept a daily tide of molten matter. Eventually the pull became too great, and a huge mass departed, to swing around the Earth as a satellite. It has even been suggested that the great deeps of the Pacific Ocean are the gap left by the Moon's departure. The Moon has no atmosphere. Its gravitational pull is too small to prevent the swift moving molecules of gas from escaping off into Space.
. . .
No other object comes so vividly to life in even a small telescope as this dead world. For an hour or two, sunrise on the mountain tops may be followed, the peaks catching the light long before their surroundings, and showing as tiny glowing islands of light in the dark area. At full Moon, under vertical illumination, mysterious systems of bright lines, called 'rays', appear radiating from certain craters.
Some people suppose that a great shower of projectiles, perhaps meteorites struck and damaged the Moon, leaving scars which do look something like bomb craters, and which also resemble the few meteorite craters on the Earth.'

Extract 2 from a later manuscript

This is a later prose draft.

CHAPTER THREE

The Old Moon in the New Moon's Arms.

Unlike days at any other time of year, or unlike days anywhere else, the wind blows out in fierce, short-lived gusts, licking upon the ~~waters~~ water of the Bay to immediately ~~spit~~ spill it out. One is inside a huge breathing machine—a lung—on these days, an excited lung, panting. Flush, the terrier-dog, scampers on plasmic sand. Ursula, out for her morning walk, endorses ferocity of this sort. The beaches are hers alone, especially as it is Monday. She shrugs, our crow-faced saint, within the rhythm of her stalking along the tideline where the sea must leave its worthless assortment of treasures caught in the black tangles of dead seaweed: the dome half of a tennis ball, bright colours of plastic all torn from toys and soft drink containers, white polystyrene, empty shells and encrustations, fish's bones, unbelievably beautiful sea-frosted glass of green and brown, cans and water-logged citrus fruit, and the smooth-skinned driftwood ~~both of~~ of both milled and natural shape. She stalks along the scalloping lace of the sea in the sand, the hemwork of the Bay. On these days cottonwool clouds gambol, for Ursula, on their way across a blue pasture. She doesn't slacken her pace to gaze: it is all familiar to her.

Some paper suddenly rises up, pirouettes and rushes full-blown towards her. She thinks at first it had fallen out the bag of an errant pupil from the primary school behind the cliff, because it looks just like that. ~~But~~ As it stops close by, she picks it up to check to see what silly questions they ask them these days. Shiny foolscap sheets are stapled together in the centre of the left-hand long side. It is only a few pages thick. The purple copy is fairly faint, some typed, some handwritten; in the middle is printing of a different kind: off-set: with pictures, one of which Ursula promptly recognises. Such accidents please Ursula. A whole corner is sodden with sea-water. She decides to take it home and dry it out.

When you know Ursula better, you will wonder why the author did not say that she was thrilled on having <u>The Moon Weakly Review</u> dance up to her feet: why she was not excited, delighted and hurrying home to hang it over the radiator to have it dry enough to read with her afternoon cup of tea, while Mother snoozes in another room. In an earlier draft of this plot it would have been so. . .but as it is now, I must confess that Ursula felt an inexplicable nausea, a reluctance to continue her rapid 'constitutional'. When she reached the cliff, she sat on a rock and stared at the sea, angrily. You see her face with its horrid puce stain all down the right side, pinching in the skin of her eyelid and permanently spotted with white-headed, pimple-like protuberances was more than simply 'unfortunate', it had closed her off

Making Stories

from the world as effectively as a Carmelite's grille, and she did resent it. So the left side of her face which could have relieved the ugliness through pure force of character wore, habitually, a most ungracious expression—that of deep-seated resentment. Activity must always be snipped in the bud, the instinct to be gregarious ruled off with a frown, the energy to gasbag on philosophy stifled at its inception. Her growth was somehow stunted, twisted, and the ordinary emotion of excitement, recognition, affinity—as that occasioned by the first words of <u>The Weakly</u> (...)—bent savagely into its opposite, antagonism, argument, loneliness.

After forty years, self-sorrow can descend intensely, but it is not indulged, defences against one's own vulnerability are stuck, as it were, on automatic, and set in motion soon after the stimulus is registered. As indeed, Ursula herself is soon in motion, excited, delighted and hurrying home to dry and preserve her new find.

Extract 3 from the published version

Remember the Tarantella, pages 15–19

"On days like these, we are inside the lung of a huge breathing machine. A panting, excited lung."

Ursula would seem to be a conventional old maid, nurse to her invalid mother, a spinster more unfortunate than most because of the right side of her face. The skin of her eyelid is pinched in and stretched through her eyebrow. The cheek is bulbous and pulls down the corner of her mouth. A slight dribble of saliva is always visible. The colour is maroon-purple, permanently spotted with whiteheads. It has closed her off from the world as effectively as a Carmelite's grille. The left side, which could have relieved the unsightliness by pure force of character, habitually wears an ungracious expression.

After forty years, self-sorrow can descend intensely but is not indulged. Defences against one's own vulnerabilities are stuck, as it were, on automatic.

She puts her diary back in her coat pocket and continues along the "plasmic" sand. Her dog, Flush, scampers ahead on the scalloped tideline, where caught in the black tangles of seaweed are treasures: the half-dome of a tennis ball, plastics of toys and soft drink containers, an abandoned set of dentures, waterlogged citrus fruits, white polystyrene, fish bones, shells and encrustations, green sea-frosted glass, smooth driftwood of natural shapes and hairy wood of the milled variety. It is the lace on the hemwork of Port Phillip Bay.

The wind blows out in short fierce gusts, licking up the sea into spitting waves. These equinoctial days suit Ursula's type of angry energy. That mark of Cain, the scar that forces her to be a saint, frustrates her. Growth has been stunted. Activity must always be snipped in the bud, the instinct to be gregarious ruled off with a frown, her desire to gasbag on about the meaning of life stifled. It has twisted in her, bent her character savagely into antagonism, loneliness. She pursues her rapid constitutional every morning at ten, covers miles of the foreshore in a couple of hours, with her diary in her pocket. The scavenging of her irrepressible terrier is a canine projection of her own searching.

"The wind cry, the wave cry, the vast waters of the petrel and porpoise" give Ursula her best communion. T.S. Eliot's words are Ursula's knowledge, for the sea is her great mirror. The sea is as she is inside, behind the shell of appearance, beyond the unopened door of her hymen. Virginity does not describe her state of mind. She dreams all.

For Ursula, waking from sleep is the running aground of a small yacht from a turbulent sea. She is all a-shudder, having to take her bearings while being dumped by breakers.

In a bit of a pickle, panicked and brittle. She is racked with feelings, wave-motions, dismayed and bored by the heaviness of the body. Every night is the same. She's off adventuring on the high seas. Her dreams are crowded with personalities. Flying about the night sky with the fittest of astral bodies, she drops in wherever she is called, whatever the age, place, society, materialising and dematerialising. She is free in her dreams, but on waking, she is as helpless as a beached whale. Consciousness is an arrest of a velocity as could only be described algebraically. It is a slow clearing of smoke, a desolate landscape. Concussion.

During the day, what does Ursula have? She has her walks along the foreshore. And she reads.

With her cups of tea, she reads. When she has a moment, she reads. Apart from her mother, her sister and her sister's sons, Ursula has one friend in the world, Jocelyn, a demented dog-show lady with kennels. None of these give her the intimacy she gets from reading. Fine literature over the centuries has provided some great associates for the price of a book, a stop at the Regional Library. She keeps diaries, dozens of exercise books, each with a colour print stuck on the cover, a habit which started thirty-three years before with a couple of reproductions from *The Ladies Home Journal* of the artwork of Nisaba Diana Kirby. The picture, often cut out of a magazine, names the diary for Ursula, it recalls her mood, the date and the matters inside.

When Ursula goes to her church, to whom does she pray? Jane Austen, Joan of Arc, Cleopatra, Mary Shelley, Leibnitz. In her time, Ursula has talked to all the dead creators she has met. Ursula does not waste her time beating her breast. 'Mea culpa' would be a lie, her conscious life is a purgatory. She has nothing to say 'my fault' about. Neither Lucifer nor God would be interested in her petty sins, nor, if the truth be known, is Ursula. She has not conjured up heavens of purity and bright light and is scared of no hell she can imagine. Somehow salvation must be lived in the life she's got.

"Mimbo settled with tea and crumpet.

The other evening she said my diaries look like a collection of Dickens, an entire shelf of uniform height and spines of dark green canvas. I wonder if all mothers have such cunning ways with small flatteries.

On such a day as this I saw the wave-dancing girl. Oscar Wilde: 'Art is out of the reach of morals, for her eyes are fixed upon things beautiful and immortal and ever-changing.'

My facade puts me out of the reach of immorality. Another one, Oscar: 'A little sincerity is a dangerous thing. And a great deal is absolutely fatal.'

We were inside a Turner seascape on that day. In the winter of 1970, the wind was howling and the waves were cracking down on the shallow beach. I was wearing my gent's gaberdine overcoat, with the huge pockets, and my hat was pulled down at the ears. I was the watcher and she the watched. We were both in a moment of art, immortal and ever-changing. Clad in black rubber, she was such a slight thing battling the surf. Her knees wide apart, her arms weighing this way and that, it was a performance just for me. To show me it could be done, ballet on the sea.

'My dear, aren't you cold?' I said. Her feet and hands were purple but she assured me that the wet suit worked. She was training for some surfing competition. She came from Bells Beach. 'It is not a girls' sport,' I said. But not for this androgynous creature, my shy Valkyrie, she could be better than the boys. 'Indeed, how old are you?' I said. Thirteen, neither man nor woman, boy nor girl, but an embodiment of all human potential, a spirit, a myth. How I managed to talk to her I don't know. The unique. She would not be taken aback by my looks. Or rather, that didn't matter a fig.

'80 − '70 = 10. 10 + 13 = 23.

Now she must be twenty-three.

She instigated a faith I find returns every time the wind blows from the south-west. She brought to me a belief that my wishing life could be the one I live some day. I often trouble myself over how this can happen. Now instead of praying to dead writers, from which communication nothing can come, I have taken up hunting for a live one, listening to the radio and reading the newspapers, looking for the hole through which I might slip to meet the real ... she must be great ... no, I check myself, it is through her work I will know her. Her characters must be able to give me the intimacy that I know from so much reading. I have my rules and they are by no means easy.

The local library sadly lacks Australian work, except that of the most popular and vulgar kind.

Time laps in me like the seasons. My constant round, to the beach, to the shops, attending to Mimbo's every need is monotonous, except for Flush. Every minute is new to him, that way he loves routine. Except for my secret expedition. Will it be an Elizabeth Barrett Browning? An Emily Bronte? I hardly think we'd hit it off. With one of her sisters perhaps. I fancy I'd get along with a George Eliot, actually."

Patrick White
Memoirs of Many in One

Whether archives or memoirs contained the truth it might be difficult to decide. Fossicking through the memoirs was not a job I looked forward to, but I had a sense of duty to this family whose lives were intertwined with mine.

Patrick White, *Memoirs of Many in One*

× I had known Mrs Gray for years. We
  were all the incongruous grandchildren of
  Australian pastoral *Faustian*
                    Introduction
              Mrs Gray's Memoirs
  After her death I was asked by her
  daughter, Hilda Gray, to edit the memoirs Alex
  had kept locked in a Morocco writing case with
  arabesques blazed title, the
  work of some Turkish craftsman,
  "Grand Vizier's *something* it" back from Constantinople.

  Alex preferred not to be known by her married
  name. Gray was too banal, nor her father's:
  having too many syllables, "Papapandelides" became inevitably a boring joke. So she evolved
  the name under which she was registered in
  the *deceased* grave accounts department in the Nile
  Cold Storage at rue de Ramleh Alexandria
  and later at David Jones, Castlereagh + Market
  Streets, Sydney: Mme Alex Xenophon Demirjian
  Gray.

  Alex acquired names as other women encrust
  themselves with *jewels*, + bower birds
  collect fragments of coloured glass. It must be
  remarked that *Alex should become*
  according to mood or period, "Llewellyn" or
  "Diaconos" for instance, even briefly "Bogdaddy"
  It was truly amazing that Alex should
  choose to be labelled "Demirjian" when
  her mother-in-law, one of more, *she hated most*
  had been born a Demirjian. The detested
  Magda could resign herself to Gray - from
  recognising in *her daughter-in-law* the *brows*
  exoticism So each of the women was *now ok*
  less content, while inwardly despising, contentment and each other.

  The Gray family and my own had been
  known to each other for generations as members of the New South Wales squattocracy (so-
  called). Henry was a cuckoo in the *fatty nest*.

There is only one surviving manuscript by Patrick White, that of *Memoirs of Many in One*. All the others were destroyed after his death, according to the instructions in his will.

Some years before, however, Manuscript Appeal, a group whose proceeds go to the British Defence and Aid Fund for Southern Africa and the Canon Collins Educational Trust for Southern Africa, had asked Patrick White to donate a manuscript for auction. In 1988 he sent them a manuscript of *Memoirs of Many in One*, accompanied by this note:

Dear Ethel de Keyser,
I have found this practically unintelligible MS of Memoirs of Many in One published in 1986. Perhaps its messy condition will make it more appealing to the ferrets.
Yours sincerely,
Patrick White.

When the manuscript was auctioned, shortly after his death, the State Library of New South Wales and the National Library of Australia jointly purchased it.

For us, the question of whether to include this was not an easy one to answer. We were conscious that White had more than once expressed such sentiments as 'I pray that enough of you have escaped infection from the writers' disease of talking about ourselves—all that yakker about "how I work". It's more important to get on and *do* in this dangerous age.'[1]

Then there were the alterations he made on the manuscript itself. They are in the nature of finetuning rather than any dramatic rethinking or even re-wording. We conjecture that there was an earlier draft, or drafts, but we have no way of knowing. We also cannot know whether this manuscript represents his normal method of work, or whether this book—his last full-length work of fiction—was written in a different way from earlier ones.

It is also possible that the edits on this manuscript were tailormade by Patrick White for Manuscript Appeal and thereby, indirectly, for 'the ferrets'. If this were so, the manuscript would be highly untrustworthy as a clue to his work processes or his thinking. Paul Brunton, Curator of Manuscripts at the Mitchell Library, State Library of New South Wales, suggests this. He wrote to us that:

---

1 From *Imagining the Real*, edited by D. Green and D. Headon, ABC Enterprises, 1991.

It is the great writer's last, devastating and witty comment on the academic scroungers that he should ensure the survival of a heavily annotated manuscript of the one novel that satirizes this very activity...It is almost as if its 'messy condition' was created precisely for this purpose.

As support for this idea, he points to the subject of the book itself (the conceit of the book is that Patrick White is merely editing the papers of Alex Gray—being a 'ferret', in fact); and internal evidence concerning the manuscript and the various kinds of alterations to it. At a talk given to the Library Society in February 1992, he postulated that the manuscript itself could be in effect, a hoax.

In the end, however, we felt that readers should be given the opportunity to examine part of it for themselves.

We have transcribed the first ten pages of the manuscript. For ease of comparison, we have printed the manuscript and the published version in parallel, on opposite pages. On the manuscript pages we have used two different typefaces to indicate two different layers of changes. `This typeface indicates the earliest writing;` **this typeface indicates later changes, made in red on the manuscript.**

Making Stories

Extract from the manuscript

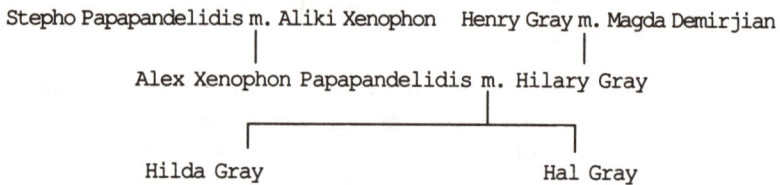

To Barbara the Flying Nun

Dedicated to those it may concern

Check early reference to Carmelite nuns. Gregory should read Benedict.

It is hard to work out how Magda created the impression of a beauty which wasn't. Her fragmented beauty stopped the conversation whenever she chose to appear at some Alexandrian patisserie during the six o'clock brouhaha. It would have stunned the Royal Sydney Golf Club if her breeding had allowed her access.

FORTUNY

Patrick White—Memoirs of Many in One

From *Memoirs of Many in One*, pp 9–16.

Stepho Papapandelidis m. Aliki Xenophon   Henry Gray m. Magda Demirjian
            | |
       Alex Xenophon Papapandelidis m. Hilary Gray
              ┌──────────────────────┴──────────────────────┐
          Hal Gray   Hilda Gray

Making Stories

Introduction

After ~~her mother's death the death of Mrs Gray~~ **Mrs Gray's death** I was asked by her daughter Hilda ~~Gray~~ to edit the memoirs ~~she~~ Alex had kept locked in a Morocco writing case, ~~inside an entanglement of Arabic calligraphy decorated with arabesques~~ behind arabesques in faded gilt, the work of some Turkish craftsman, ~~of an antique age.~~ of another age. (Grandfather Gray brought it back from Constantinople.)
The memoirs had soon overflowed the writing case.
Alex preferred not to be known by her married name—Gray was too banal; nor her father's: having too many syllables, 'Papapandelidis' became inevitably a boring joke. So she evolved the name under which she was registered in the **/account/** books ~~the accounts department~~ of the Nile Cold Storage at the Gare de Ramleh, Alexandria, and later at David Jones, ~~Castlereagh & Market Streets,~~ Sydney: Mme Alex Xenophon Demirjian Grey.
Alex acquired names as other women encrust themselves with ~~exotic~~ jewels and bower-birds collect fragments of coloured glass. It mystified ~~friends, & even relatives, that~~ acquaintances that Mrs Gray should become, according to mood or period, 'Llewellyn' or 'Diacono', for instance, even briefly 'Bogdarly'. It was truly amazing that Alex should ~~cling~~ choose to be labelled 'Demirjian', when her mother-in-law, one of those she hated most, had been born a Demirjian **(we think)**. The detested Magda could resign herself to 'Gray' from recognising in ~~that name~~ it an inverted brand sort (?) of inverted exoticism. So each of the women was more or less content, while inwardly despising contentment and each other. The Gray family and my own had been known to each other for generations as members of the New South Wales squattocracy (so-called.) **I had known the Grays for years. We were all the incongruous descendants of Australian pastoral families.** Henry was a cuckoo in the Gray nest, a scholar who wasted his years drifting ~~through~~ round the Middle East collecting <u>objets d'art</u> and rare manuscripts. He brought them back to Sydney and founded an antique business which his son Hilary, my schoolfriend, developed very profitably in later years, and the grandson, Hal, carried on. ~~Hilary~~ rather fitfully. Hilary, another

Patrick White—Memoirs of Many in One

Editor's Introduction

After Mrs Gray's death I was asked by her daughter Hilda to edit the memoirs Alex had kept locked in a morocco writing case, behind arabesques in faded gilt, the work of some Turkish craftsman, which Grandfather Gray had brought back from Constantinople. (I should say the memoirs had soon overflowed the writing case.)

Alex disliked her married name: too banal. Her father's polysyllabic 'Papapandelidis' inevitably became a boring joke. As her mother Aliki saw it. Aliki preferred her maiden name, 'Xenophon'. Alex could not very well avoid the Gray bit, but evolved the names under which she was registered in the books of the Nile Cold Storage at the Gare de Ramleh, Alexandria, and later, at David Jones, Sydney: Mme Alex Xenophon Demirjian Gray.

Alex acquired names as other women encrust themselves with jewels and bower-birds collect fragments of coloured glass. It mystified acquaintances that Mrs Gray should become, according to mood or period, 'Llewellyn' or 'Diacono' for instance, even briefly 'Bogdarly'. It was truly amazing that she should choose to be labelled 'Demirjian', when her mother-in-law, one of those she hated most, had been born a Demirjian (we think). The detested Magda could resign herself to 'Gray' from recognising in it a kind of inverted exoticism. So each of the women was more or less content, while inwardly despising contentment and each other.

I had known the Grays for years. We were all the incongruous descendants of Australian pastoral families. Henry was a cuckoo in the Gray nest, a scholar who wasted his years drifting through the Middle East collecting *objets d'art* and rare manuscripts. He brought them back to Sydney and founded an antique business which his son Hilary, my schoolfriend, developed profitably later on and the grandson Hal carried on somewhat fitfully.

Hilary, another

of the Gray mavericks, was got on a ~~Franco Levantine~~ Levantine woman, another objet d'art Henry brought back from Asia Minor before the war broke out between Turks & Greeks and most of Smyrna was reduced to ash and rubble. Henry's wife, Hilary's mother, was one of those women who acquire a reputation for beauty through a flair for clothes & jewels, an arresting body, and an aggressive kind of ugliness. She had her voice, too. She had her legs, and her taunting breasts. Most of the men who ran across her hoped they might take over from her husband, or her current lover. But although Magda Demirjian Gray took lovers, there was no indication that she would leave a husband, certainly elderly, but still virile, who kept her in-style, ~~and~~ **Additionally**, their son Hilary, to whom she was not overly attached, (**Magda was attached to no one but herself**), ~~was still~~ acted as a pledge between them ~~which~~ that could not be overlooked.

Hilary ~~turned out~~ had the appearance of a slender green-complexioned Levantine rather than a rowdy extrovert Australian **with pastoralist forebears**. He had moist black eyelids, & curving lashes. **At school**, it got round that he was delicate and allowances must be made for this. He was given milk at break, and was allowed to sit ~~about read~~ in the sun reading books **of his own choosing**, frowning under an eyeshade the colour of milk chocolate.

We saw much of each other as young boys. Hilary was ~~always~~ welcome at ~~the~~ our house, after school, and for weekends. We cut up a frog in the bath to watch its heart movement, we smoked a ~~cigar~~ cheroot under the Buhl table in the hall, and we masturbated together in bed. We were quick to tidy up & and it seemed to me at the time my parents were unaware of /any of/ these activities. They must have been. For the friendship came to an abrupt end. It filtered back to me through the conversation of maids & ~~adults~~ adult **innuendo** /from the masters/ that Hilary was an unhealthy influence: you couldn't expect much from the union of an Australian gentleman with an Armenian? Arab? Jewess? or whatever the woman was. So Hilary & and I ~~avoided~~ **began to** avoid each other at school. His mother had never been much more than a silhouette and a perfume. She did not fit into /the/ acceptable, that is, dull Sydney society, to which my parents belonged, but went down ~~better~~ well with her husband's friends from the art-of the Gray mavericks, was got on a Levantine woman, another *objet d'art* Henry brought back from Asia Minor before the war broke out between Turk and Greek and most of Smyrna was reduced to ash and rubble.

Henry's wife, Hilary's mother, was one of those women who acquire a reputation for beauty through a flair for clothes and jewels, an arresting body, and an aggressive kind of ugliness. She had her voice, too. She had her legs, and her taunting breasts. She stopped the conversation whenever she chose to appear at some Alexandrian *pâtisserie* during the six o'clock brouhaha. She would have stunned the Royal Sydney Golf Club if her breeding had allowed her access.

Most of the men who ran across her hoped they might take over from her husband, or her current lover. But although Magda Demirjian Gray took lovers, there was no indication that she would leave a husband, elderly certainly, but still virile, who kept her in style. In addition, their son Hilary, to whom she was not overly attached (Magda was attached only to herself) acted as a pledge between husband and wife that could not be overlooked.

Hilary had the appearance of a slender, green-complexioned Levantine rather than a rowdy extrovert Australian with pastoralist forebears. He had moist black eyelids and curving lashes. At school it got round that he was delicate and allowances must be made for this. He was given milk at break, and was allowed to sit in the sun reading books of his own choosing (Henry James and Proust) from under an eyeshade the colour of milk chocolate.

We saw a lot of each other as young boys. Hilary was welcome at our house, after school, and for week-ends. We cut up a frog in the bath to watch its heart movement, we smoked a cheroot under the buhl table in the hall, and we masturbated together in bed. We were quick to tidy up and it seemed to me at the time my parents were unaware of any of these activities. They must have been. For the friendship was brought to an abrupt end. It filtered back to me through maids' chatter and innuendo from the masters that my friend was an unhealthy influence: you couldn't expect much from the union of an Australian gentleman with an Armenian? Arab? Jewess? or whatever the woman was. So Hilary and I began to avoid each other at school. His mother had never been much more than a silhouette and a perfume. She did not fit into the acceptable, that is, dull Sydney society to which my parents belonged, but went down well with her husband's friends from the art-

dealing and bohemian worlds. (My mother heard that the Demijohn had once performed a belly-dance on a dinner table at Vaucluse.)
Hilary and I were brought together again in World War II when we went over in uniform to the Middle East. There was no mention ~~, no flicker of an eyelash,~~ of the past, not even the flicker of an eyelash. I forget how Magda turned up in Cairo, but she did, announcing to an entourage of officers that she was there to do war work. Of what kind, nobody dared ask, and Magda merely slapped more orange powder on her cheeks and sucked ~~at~~ on her lipstick. She ~~could give herself the appearance of~~ became a reflection of one of those superb desert sunsets to the west of Mariut. Flaring her nostrils, lowering her eyelids, she suggested an inscrutable camel. But without becoming grotesque. She was a beauty by birth & ~~milieu~~ of her milieu. Even Alex, who grew to hate her, had to admit it. As for Magda, she went her own way. She valued her independence and the respect of those she despised.
Hilary Gray was ~~slightly~~ superficially wounded during the Syrian campaign. While on leave /sick/ leave in Alexandria he met a girl, the daughter of Greeks from Asia Minor who had escaped to Egypt ~~from~~ **during** the sack of Smyrna. I met the parents ~~only once~~, at the time when Hilary was courting Alex. They were very correct, even distinguished /people/, Anglicised by governesses once you got over the name 'Papapandelidis'. They were distressed at the thought of their daughter marrying a man of whom nothing was known except that he came from a barbarous country ~~like Australia~~, his father an antique dealer, his mother practically an untouchable from ~~the~~ 'Frango Levantini' ~~ghetto of~~ Smyrna.
I was standing with Stepho and Aliki Papapandelidis on the Alexandrian Corniche, what had been the Pharos **behind us** in the distance.
'It is too soon, too soon,' Aliki was agonising.
'Too soon,' Stepho echoed in antiphon, /touching ~~at~~ **on** a ragged moustache/.
'People lose their heads in revolutions & wars.'
'They are carried away, into marriage and adultery.' /A wind was ballooning Stepho's trousers./
'Half the children born in war or revolution are unwanted. Can'~~t~~ you **not** do something, ~~Mr White~~ ~~Lieutenant~~

dealing and Bohemian worlds. (My mother heard that the Demijohn had done a belly dance on a dinner table at Vaucluse.)

Hilary and I were brought together again in the Second World War when we went over in uniform to the Middle East. There was no mention of the past, not even the flicker of an eyelash. I forget how Magda turned up in Cairo, but she did, announcing to an entourage of officers that she was there to do war work. Of what kind, nobody dared ask, and Magda merely slapped more orange powder on her cheeks and sucked on her lipstick. She became a reflection of those superb desert sunsets to the west of Mariut. Flaring her nostrils, lowering her eyelids, she suggested an inscrutable camel. But without becoming grotesque. She was a beauty by birth and of her milieu. Even Alex, who grew to hate her, had to admit it. As for Magda, she went her own way. She valued her independence and the respect of those she despised.

Hilary Gray was superficially wounded during the Syrian campaign. While on sick leave in Alexandria he met a girl, the daughter of Greeks from Asia Minor who had escaped to Egypt during the sack of Smyrna. I met the parents at the time Hilary was courting Alex. Once you got over the name 'Papapandelidis', they were very correct, even distinguished people, anglicised by governesses. They were distressed at the thought of their daughter marrying a man of whom nothing was known except that he came from a barbarous country, his father an antique dealer, his mother practically an untouchable from 'Frango Levantini' Smyrna.

I was with Stepho and Aliki Papapandelidis on the Alexandrian Corniche, across the bay the mole where the Pharos is believed to have stood.

'It is too soon, too soon,' Aliki was agonising.

'Too soon,' Stepho echoed in antiphon, his lips dragging on a frayed moustache.

Aliki was too proud to whimper. 'People lose their heads in revolutions and wars.'

'They are carried away into marriage and adultery.' A wind was ballooning Stepho's trousers.

'Half the children born in war or revolution are unwanted. Can you not do something, Lieutenant White, to help us, Lieutenant White?' She was looking at me hopefully, but without ~~conviction~~ expectation.

'How can I alter the course of history?' It was what they expected.

'Exactly,' she said, and her husband echoed, 'Exactly.' These decent people, ~~were to~~ in their dark clothes of another ~~age~~ time, another fashion—I remember his anonymous tie, her carefully blacked lace-up shoes—were enacting a tragedy, nothing major, they /themselves/ would have admitted, but a minor Alexandrian one, on the Corniche, ~~in front of the spot where the Pharos had been Across the bay the Pharos had once~~ **across from where the Pharos had once stood.**

They bowed their heads. Stepho was wearing a squashy Homburg, Aliki a black cloche.

The Papapandelides did not come to their daughter's wedding. Nor did Magda, perhaps out of discretion; she knew her place in Smyrna-Greek society.

Alex, at the time of her marriage, was a vision of camellia flesh asking to be bruised. ~~Her eyelids already had been~~ Identical to Hilary's, her eyelids already **showed signs of spoiling**. Her pale, ~~tremulous~~ natural lips were ~~tremulous, half open,~~ tremulous with the emotion waiting to spill ~~open~~ out ~~of them~~. Knowing Hilary, I could not believe she was still a virgin; it was the ~~approach to a~~ approaching sacrament which made her tremble ~~& see her~~ and visualise a future breaking open in front of her.

The ceremony was performed by a Protestant padre. Some of Hilary's fellow officers and a batman were present. Myself the best man, on leave from my Air Force Wing ~~near Mariut~~ in the W.D. As we came out from the church, two little Greek girls whose father kept a grocery on the corner flung handfuls of rice. It cut. I know because I experienced ~~some of it~~ **particles** myself. It let loose some of the emotion Alex had bottled up. Her beautiful, pale, moist lips were overflowing with joy or grief. Hilary ~~looked rather annoyed~~ **was trying to restrain his annoyance**.

After a short honeymoon at Luxor Hilary returned to his regiment. When the Australians embarked for home and other theatres of war, ~~Hilary~~ he remained behind, attached to a **British** headquarters in the Western Desert. Alex returned to her the parents' house at Schutz. There her to help us?' She was looking at me hopefully, but without expectation.

'How can I alter the course of history?' It was what they knew.

'Exactly,' she said, and her husband echoed, 'Exactly.'

These decent people, in their dark clothes of another period, another fashion – I remember his anonymous tie, her carefully blacked lace-up shoes – were enacting a tragedy, nothing major, they themselves would have admitted, but a minor Alexandrian one, on the Corniche, across from the believed site of the Pharos.

They bowed their heads. Stepho was wearing a squashy Homburg, Aliki a black cloche.

The Papapandelides did not come to their daughter's wedding. Nor did Magda, perhaps out of discretion; she knew her place in Smyrna-Greek society.

Alex, at the time of her marriage, was a vision of camellia flesh asking to be bruised. Identical to Hilary's, her eyelids already showed signs of spoiling. Her pale, natural lips were parted, tremulous with the emotion waiting to spill out of them. Knowing Hilary, I could not believe she was still a virgin; it was the approaching sacrament which made her tremble and visualise a future breaking open in front of her.

The ceremony was performed by a Protestant padre. Some of Hilary's fellow officers and a batman were present. Myself the best man, on leave from my Air Force Wing at Sidi Haneish. As we came out of the church, two little Greek girls whose father kept a grocery on the corner flung handfuls of rice. It cut. I know because I experienced a few grains myself. It let loose some of the emotion Alex had bottled up. Her beautiful, pale, moist lips were overflowing with joy or grief. Hilary was trying to restrain his annoyance.

After a short honeymoon at Luxor Hilary returned to his regiment. When the Australians embarked for home and other theatres of war, he remained behind, attached to a British headquarters in the Western Desert. Alex returned to the parents' house at Schutz. There her

children were born, first Hal, then towards the end of the war, Hilda.
Several times when on leave I was entertained to formal lunches by the Papapandelides. I found that Aliki's acquaintance addressed her as Madame Xenophon and that ~~Stepho loved the telephone~~ *Madame X's husband* was wedded to the telephone. He was always waiting to be called to it. He would jump up, dropping his napkin and his cutlery—to accept an invitation to ~~bridge~~ le thé and to bridge. ~~and~~ In fact most of this Smyrna gentleman's life had been spent at bridge and tea, or in writing complimentary verses to *the* ladies *with whom he associated*. When he died of a stroke /in the garden at Schutz/ towards near the end of the war, the ladies sighed, ~~Ce pauvre~~ as they wiped the porto from their lips. 'Ce pauvre Stepho Pa-papan, il était si gentil...' ~~he wasn't long remembered~~ and soon forgot.
Once in the garden at Schutz after lunch, the pretty dolls of children tumbling round our ankles, their mother in a flowing tussore dress, I asked Alex, 'Do they see much of their other granny?' (for Magda was still around, between Alexandria and Cairo *Cairo and Alexandria*). Alex raised her upper ~~lip on which~~ lip ~~with its~~ with steely pinpricks of afternoon perspiration, and said, replied, 'I'll leave Mamma to answer that one.'
Aliki pursed her ~~lips slightly~~ mouth and faintly smiled (she had complained earlier that she was suffering from /a/ migraine). 'In Smyrna we met I think once or twice. We didn't know them.' The faint smile dissolved in a silvery mist of painful recollection. Aliki could dare anyone to disagree with her ~~opinions~~ standards. In appearance she was to Magda what an etching is to a painting. Aliki's lines had been scratched remorselessly into the (?) copper. Magda was a series of flat, splattered planes ~~influenced by~~ reflecting whichever continent or island she happened to inhabit at the moment it was done. Aliki ~~had suffered~~ was a Greek: she had suffered wars, invasions, revolutions; Magda *the Levantine* had battened on these, along with the black marketeers and the lovers an occupation throws up.

[inserted on a separate page, paper-clipped into the notebook:]
~~Aliki had visited~~ *Later on* Aliki visited her grandchil-

children were born, first Hal, then towards the end of the war, Hilda.

Several times when on leave I was entertained to formal lunches by the Papapandelides. I found that Aliki's acquaintance addressed her as Madame Xenophon and that Madame X's husband was wedded to the telephone. He was always waiting to be called to it. He would jump up, dropping his napkin and his cutlery to accept an invitation to *le bridge* and *le thé*. In fact most of this Smyrna gentleman's life had been spent at bridge and tea, or in writing complimentary verses to the ladies of his circle. When he died of a stroke in the garden at Schutz near the end of the war, the ladies sighed, as they wiped the porto from their lips before the next rubber. '*Ce pauvre Stepho Papa-pan, il était si gentil . . .*' and soon forgot.

Once in the garden at Schutz after lunch the pretty dolls of children tumbling round our ankles, their mother in a flowing tussore dress, I asked Alex, 'Do they see much of their other granny?' (for Magda was still around, between Cairo and Alexandria). Alex raised her upper lip with its steely pinpricks of afternoon perspiration and replied, 'I'll leave Mamma to answer that one.'

When asked, Aliki pursed her mouth and faintly smiled; she had complained earlier that she was starting a migraine. 'In Smyrna we met, I think once or twice. We didn't know them.' The faint smile dissolved in a silvery mist of painful recollection.

Aliki could dare anyone to disagree with her standards. In appearance she was to Magda what an etching is to a painting. Aliki's lines had been scratched remorselessly into the copper. Magda was a series of flat, splattered planes reflecting whichever continent or island she happened to inhabit at the moment it was done. Aliki was Greek: she had suffered wars, invasions, revolutions; Magda the Levantine had battened on these, along with the black marketeers and the lovers an occupation throws up.

In later life Aliki visited her grandchil-

Making Stories

dren in Australia, but could not be persuaded by their mother to stay. ~~She could not because, she said, in that such a vast empty country She missed the scents of thyme and stocks~~ (stet), and the smell of burnt-out candles. 'Though I am not a believer,' Aliki ~~re~~-assured us, 'the smell of an orthodox church is consoling.'
The last time I saw Magda she was down on her luck. It was on a balcony in the Delta town of Mansoura. I had been sent to Egypt by Alex to order the Government to surrender property they had confiscated when foreigners were expelled. Of course they refused, but I had my meeting with Magda. The ~~sunset~~ henna of her hair and the orange powder with which her cheeks were plastered ingrained outdid the /Nile/ sunset. 'Keeping old age at bay,' she explained when she caught me looking at her too closely. Her laughter smelled of **Egyptian** cigarettes. From somewhere inside **the block** came the smell of burning cottonseed and someone was cooking a pot of beans. 'No,' she said, 'you won't see me again. Oh, no, no! What should I do in Australia but die?' Nor did we see her. Not long after my visit, the building in which she was living collapsed, as buildings in provincial Egypt will.
[insert ends.]

Aliki Xenophon settled in mainland Greece when World War II was over. I met her there, in Athens, & on her island. The old cardigans she wore, in black or sepia wool, were as ravelled as post-war Greece (itself).
~~But~~ In her ~~person~~ character she remained as ~~rigorous~~ severe as ever—an αρχοντισσα. She was writing something on Bouboulina, the pirate queen who led the ~~sea war in the Aegean against the Turk.~~ war in the Aegean against the Turk which ended in her country's independence.

dren in Australia, but could not be persuaded by their mother to stay. She missed the scents of thyme and stocks, and the smell of burnt-out candles. 'Though I am not a believer,' Aliki assured us, 'the smell of an Orthodox church is consoling.'

The last time I saw Magda she was down on her luck. It was on a balcony in the Delta town of Mansoura. I had been sent to Egypt by Alex to order the Government to surrender property they had confiscated when foreigners were expelled. Of course they refused, but I had my meeting with Magda. The henna of her hair and the orange powder with which her cheeks were ingrained outdid the Nile sunset. 'Keeping old age at bay,' she explained when she caught me looking too closely at her. Her laughter reeked of cheap Egyptian cigarettes. From inside the block came the smell of burning cottonseed and someone was cooking a pot of beans. 'No,' she said, 'you won't see me again. Oh, no, no! What should I do in Australia but die?' Nor did we see her. Not long after my visit, the building in which she was living collapsed, as buildings in provincial Egypt will.

Aliki Xenophon settled in mainland Greece when the Second World War was over. I met her there in Athens, and on the island of Nisos. The old cardigans she wore, in black or sepia wool, were as ravelled as post-war Greece. In her character she remained as severe as ever. As an old woman the *archontissa* was writing something on Bouboulina, the pirate queen who led the war in the Aegean against the Turk which resulted in her country's independence.

insert Aliki visited etc.

~~Independence: the war cry of all the women in this disparate family—Aliki, Magda, Alex, Hilda, her mother's slave, she may have had it whether she wanted it or not. Independence: the theme song of a quartet of women in this disparate family—Aliki, Magda, & Alex, Hilda a fourth?—the spirit of being a slave to / her mother's slave. She probably was, without knowing.~~

Down to buildings in provincial Egypt will.

independence ~~the theme song of a trio of women in this disparate family—Aliki, Magda & Alex~~ *the grand illusion to which a trio of incongruously related women—Aliki, Magda, & Alex—were all* ~~enslaved~~ *unswervingly dedicated.* ~~To what category Hilda belonged, I sometimes wondered.~~ *From which of these women Hilda's character derived, I sometimes wondered.*

At first appearance, her mother's slave, she was *also* her mother's keeper: she kept the archives, as opposed to Alex's ~~locked~~ ? arcane memoirs.

Whether archives or memoirs contained the truth it might be difficult to decide. The thought of fossicking through the memoirs was not a job ~~I looked forward~~ to which I looked forward, but ~~I agreed out of~~ had a sense of duty to this family whose lives were intertwined with mine, ~~and particularly Hilda. Hilda's~~ The expression on Hilda's face when she made the proposition ~~told showed me I could not reject it~~ dared me to reject it. Although an Anglo-Saxon on both sides, I am a sybarite and masochist: some of the dramatis personae of this Levantine script could be the offspring of my own psyche.

So, I ~~bowed my head.~~ submitted, with misgivings.

(Manuscript pages reproduced courtesy Mitchell Library, State Library of New South Wales.)

Independence: the grand illusion to which a trio of incongruously related women – Aliki, Magda, and Alex – were unswervingly dedicated. From which of these women Hilda's character derived, I sometimes wondered.

At first appearance, her mother's slave, she was also her mother's keeper: she kept the archives, as opposed to Alex's arcane memoirs. Whether archives or memoirs contained the truth it might be difficult to decide. Fossicking through the memoirs was not a job I looked forward to, but I had a sense of duty to this family whose lives were intertwined with mine. The expression of Hilda's face when she made the proposition dared me to reject it. Although an Anglo-Saxon Australian on both sides, I am a sybarite and masochist; some of the dramatis personae of this Levantine script could be the offspring of my own psyche.

So, I submitted, with misgivings.

Notes
p. 14   Schutz: suburb of Alexandria
p. 16   *archontissa*: Greek noblewoman

Sue Woolfe
Painted Woman

I was hoping it might come to something. After all, I had a few hundred pages by then, written in the same chaotic way. It's a process of enormous optimism, to keep pushing on, writing, believing that ideas and bits of story will eventually meet, that precisely because there's so much chaos to it, eventually things will collide and form a pattern.

Sue Woolfe

(1)

Establish her adoration of him. His painting. He guides her hand. To her, they are him & her, alone on wall. Why he is painting a wall. Enter mother, critical. Francis thinks she causes the row. She watches as he rips mother's dress off.

Established — Francis' adoration.
    Father being loving, benign.
    Francis copying her father's stance.
    He's pleased. Takes on his knee.
    Establish Francis' fear of her mother.
        Think mother is going to punish her. Then several
    Francis feels father rips mother's dress off for her.
Francis gets very close to Father.
Feels Mother may kill her.
But Father saves her, by ripping off Mother's dress.

~~~~~~

It's the moment I fall in love. His arm is thick, woolly, full of fluff sticking out most whisker around the wrist that hold the stopping brush. I sit behind, my knees knocking my chin, waiting for him to see say smile painting the wall and turn to see my smile. He dips the brush into the paint tin, eases the dripped bristles against the pot against the tin's side, lifts his arm high over his head, brings it down against then he's sweeping bending the soft hair of the brush, this way, that way, this way, his arm stroking flowing down the wall, a convex curve, a concave curve, a convex curve. He breaks takes the brush away from the wall, begins high up another a concave curve, a convex curve, a concave curve.

Making Stories

Painted Woman, Sue Woolfe's first novel, was originally published in 1989. Four years before, Sue Woolfe had started and abandoned a comic spy-thriller called 'Wigs'. For *Making Stories*, Woolfe contributed a few pages from 'Wigs', although she warned me that it had nothing to do with *Painted Woman*. She also selected what seemed to be a newspaper article about the trial of a man who murdered his wife, early notes, and the original ending of *Painted Woman*.

The connections between the extracts puzzled me. But in our interview, it became clear how these very different fragments were, for Woolfe, paths into writing a first novel.

My interview with Sue Woolfe took place in Sydney in March 1992.

K.G.

INT: The first thing you gave me is a section from an unpublished work called 'Wigs'. I was interested to see how many parallels there are with *Painted Woman*—the same dynamics—an alienated 'I', a *ménage à trois*, Frances with a rather flighty woman and a man.

SW: You may be right, although I've never noticed that before.

INT: Why did you include it, if you didn't think it had any connection?

SW: For that reason. I had the impression as I wrote 'Wigs' that I was doing a comic thriller—well, it amused *me*, and *Painted Woman* definitely isn't a comic thriller. 'Wigs' is a story about a woman who washes down to the bottom of the laundry basket and discovers in it something that changes her life—I wrote and wrote and wrote, without having the vaguest idea where I was heading, but always hoping, until I got to about a hundred closely typed foolscap pages and it fell into a black hole.

INT: Then, you told me, you came across what we have as Extract 2, which is a paraphrase, I think, of a judgment in a trial.

SW: It plummeted into my life, although it had nothing to do with what I'd been writing, or what I wanted to write. I was standing in a sunny street in Paddington, and a friend said: 'Did you read this in the newspaper?' and told me about a man who'd been on trial. He'd murdered his wife in bed—and he'd been acquitted. The judge, my friend told me, had said: 'Any man could do this to his wife in a moment of passion'.

There on the footpath, I was shaken so profoundly, I went home like a blind person. I shook for days and days. I kept on imagining the man's family—the pathos of the wife's life, what must have been disintegrating in her before his 'moment of passion'—I kept on imagining the daughter, I was sure they'd had a daughter although I knew nothing about them, I'd never heard of them before, nothing, I only knew what I'd been told on the footpath.

At that time, I was making another attempt to get back to 'Wigs', but my heart wasn't in it anymore. And deep down, without my willing it at all, I was obsessed about this family from the news story. I kept thinking that the judge must have made his judgment because of his concepts about what a man may be permitted in our culture.

INT: Is the layout of Extract 2 significant—it's a long thin strip of words?

SW: I hadn't seen the newspaper article, but I was so obsessed, I was imagining it.

INT: Oh—you were copying the look of a newspaper article—of course!

SW: Doesn't it look like a clipping from the newspaper?

INT: You were paraphrasing it—you didn't go and find the article?

SW: I felt I knew. That sounds so presumptuous—but I felt full of knowledge about it—I was like an overflowing bucket, too full of that knowledge already—it was as if it explained something I'd always known.

INT: But you wanted it to look as if it was the article.

SW: I was constructing my own explanation—at this stage, I still had no concept of writing about it, none at all. But I was trying to get inside that judge's mind.

INT: So in your musings about the possible background of that murder you'd heard about, is that where you had the idea of the father in *Painted Woman*, and Frances?

SW: The actual beginnings of *Painted Woman* were different. The trial by then was a long way from my mind. I'd heard about it six months before. I was thinking that I would write about a girl who is overwhelmed by a parent, particularly by a father, and who gradually emerges from it. As I tried to think about the mind of

Making Stories

that girl, my fury about the trial kept crowding in. Of its own accord.

INT: Did you have a plan for this new story?

SW: My plan for a new novel was really a new plan to fix up 'Wigs'. A friend of mine, Susan Hampton, had read it and said: Why is this woman like this—she's so self-negating! It was one of those comments that's pivotal, and straight to the heart.

So I thought, OK, what I'll do is I'll write the *early* life of my 'Wigs' heroine, up to the point where 'Wigs' starts (the 'Wigs' heroine was in her thirties), and then I'll join the two half novels together. I'll write about a young girl, Frances, overwhelmed by her father, and by the time 'Wigs' comes in, it'll be perfectly clear to anyone why she's self-negating in adult life.

INT: This brings us to the next extract [Extract 3], which is obviously where you were struggling with *Painted Woman*, which for the first time was emerging in some shape.

Were these notes still at the point where you were simply going to explain Frances for the purpose of 'Wigs'?

SW: Yes, yes. And I was going to write up to where 'Wigs' started. You can see how Painting One [Extract 3] is about *Painted Woman*, and then notes on the old 'Wigs' plot take over. See — Frances in 'Wigs' isn't an artist, or an artist's daughter at all—she's a cook in a snack bar of a dilapidated city pub.

INT: The notes are very plot-oriented.

SW: It was the only way I could get to know the characters—I needed to make them do things, I needed to see what they did in order to find out who they were.

INT: The notes never seem to get very far into the book—it's as if you keep starting and starting again.

SW: Every day they'd be out of date, they had to catch up with the latest shift in my understanding.

Writing fiction was very scary, and plot notes were something to hold onto, to jump into the day's work. I'd go back through the manuscript every working day, and I'd make plot notes on it, and at some stage the notes would break into a bit of Frances' voice and only when they did, would it feel safe to say: Oh, all right, I'll start writing. You can see that in Extract 4.

INT: So you used the making of notes as a way of getting a run-up?

SW: Yes—and then I'd do the big jump.

It took a lot of plot notes for me to discover the simplest things about a character. Till about the last third of the novel, when I didn't need a rope over the chasm any more, by that stage the story was telling itself.

INT: There's a very different tone, even about these notes, from the tone of 'Wigs'. Was that one of the things that eventually made you realise that your plan was not going to work? Where did that plan go?

SW: The notes—and the first draft of *Painted Woman*—were written in Greece, and that's significant because you see I'd left 'Wigs' tucked under a friend's mattress in Australia, for safe keeping. I had no recourse to it at all. That was a bit of an oversight. Also, the story and the characters in *Painted Woman* seemed to dictate the tone. 'Wigs' was written from the outside, which is probably why it didn't work for me. Whereas *Painted Woman* was much more internal—the sensation was that I was writing from a particular part of my body, down below my stomach, it felt somatic. Also, I had no idea how to control tone. Or even that tone *was* controllable.

And there were many things I was learning about writing a first novel, things I'll never have to learn again—I think. I had, for example, no sense that it was legitimate for *me* to write a novel. I came from a large, hierarchical family—the youngest member, and the only girl. I was taught to be silent and to listen. I'd never really felt, deep down, that I had the right to speak. So critics have commented on Frances' tone—she's got a whispered, close-to-the-mike tone, there's a whispered urgency about her as she confides in you, and that's what I was feeling, that any moment the skies could open and I'd get zapped for talking, so I'd better tell the story fast.

INT: Did you work straight from those notes made in Greece to the narrative?

SW: I did enormous, copious amounts of notes, I think my notes were larger than the text of the novel itself, which in its early draft was hundreds of pencil-written pages long. I would write a few pages of text and it'd come to a dead stop and I'd panic and make as many pages again of notes.

INT: So was there a sense of stopping the flow, so you could digest what had emerged from the narrative?

Making Stories

SW: I was always thinking about the way a painter works. Someone has said that every brush stroke not only changes the meaning of what's ahead, but changes the meaning of what's already past. And that was the nature of my notes.

INT: When did you see it wasn't going to work out that way?

SW: I became obsessed with Frances, and I really didn't want to know about the other characters in 'Wigs'. I wanted to know what was going to happen between Frances and her father; I could see that it was a relationship that I could keep on and on exploring, and I didn't want to stop. 'Wigs' would've brought it to a dead halt.

By that stage I was working out Frances' limitations, her distortions of the way she sees the world. I found I couldn't give her an ordinary world view. The obvious thing to do was to give her the judge's simplified world view—as I imagined it. It took a very long time to get her simplifications right, I was still fixing them up in the last draft. And to pace her emergence from them.

INT: The narrative fragment in Extract 4 ['it's the moment I fall in love...'] bears a very good family resemblance to the finished version.

SW: It was one of the few parts that scarcely changed.

INT: And yet it's the beginning of the novel. Many of the writers we've talked to revised their beginnings a lot.

SW: I wrote it on my first working day. It was the only bit I felt sure of—perhaps I shouldn't have.

INT: Did you use the present tense from the start, or was that a matter of trial and error?

SW: It was always in the present tense. Only because I could imagine more clearly—in the present tense I could actually think as if I *was* the character—as the character, I could go into a room, and if I described it in present tense, I could see the surroundings better and I could see the objects that I, as the character, was going to use, the face of the person I as the character was going to talk to. In present tense, I could act the character. Be her. So much so, that if I really had to answer the phone, I'd have an identity crisis.

INT: Where did the older woman's voice in *Painted Woman* come from [Extract 5]?

SW: The shower.

INT: The shower?

SW: I wrote through to what seemed to be the end of *Painted Woman*, about two-thirds of the way through the eventual novel. I was heavily pregnant at that stage. I stopped, and had my baby. Six weeks later, a century later, when I had thought about nothing but babies and how on earth to be a mother, suddenly in the shower a voice started talking. It was not the voice of Frances at all. I didn't know whose voice it was—it was an old woman's voice, coming out of the shower rose. We were living in the Blue Mountains, and it was snowing, and when it's snowing you don't leave a hot shower incautiously, so I shouted to Gordon, my partner, and he brought a pencil and a bit of card, and scribbled down in the steam what I was dictating—which was what the old woman was dictating.

I looked at it afterwards and clearly, it had nothing to do with the novel. The wrong voice, the wrong tone. It was a voice of such experience, and freedom, and self-assurance. So I forgot it until she spoke the next time: again she seemed to erupt out of the air, and again I had to race and get something, a nappy wash receipt probably, to write it down. Gradually, as she kept on doing this, I realised that it was Frances when she was much older. The voice was so rich with wisdom, slightly world-weary, but happy, that I began to realise that something wonderful had indeed happened to Frances, that she had been transformed.

INT: How did you come to the notion of introducing that voice not sequentially but throughout the book, as a periodic interruption?

SW: It never occurred to me not to let her do it. She was always interrupting me!

It was also about that stage that I was doing a new draft of the novel, and I was absolutely impatient with the young Frances. As I wrote I would glance at a page of the earlier draft, without really reading it, and think: I can't stand this! There was a lot about the tone that grated on me; it seemed awkward and clumsy and cloying —I couldn't bear to refer to it most of the time. It was almost at random, what I retrieved and what I threw away.

So I was pleased to have the older Frances interrupt.

But I can't imagine writing without the intimacy I had with Frances. But I don't know—you can't know, after a first novel, what you're going to do in future.

INT: What do you think that virgin experience of a first novel is?

SW: Well, I think when you finally get to an end, that somehow resolves a long long process that's been going on—for me—for two years—at last there's an end of all your fabrications, all your fantasies, all your dilemmas, all your crises, they're resolved. And you think: Well, I've done it once in my life, so I just might be able to do it again.

INT: Even though, as you describe your process, it's a very anxious, uncertain, unconscious one.

SW: It wasn't anxious in a way because I had no concept of a publishable book at the end, I was writing for myself, I never thought I was going to show it to anybody.

There was actually a lot of fun in it, especially in the later drafts, when I knew she'd emerge from her prison, that I was enabling that to happen...making her, and making it happen. And when I got a little more confident that it was alright to do it, to write— I hadn't got zapped. And later, when the story seemed less joined to my fog, it existed on its own, and I was just tinkering—that was exhilarating.

It was like making a bird, and then teaching it to fly.

What was necessary was to find out what happened to this woman, who, in some way, I was pretending to be. I'm intrigued at what must be the cross-over between the writer and the character. The events of the novel had never happened to me; in that sense it's not an autobiographical novel, but Frances must have been a very strong metaphor for me, to compel me through her story.

I was surprised when you suggested parallels between 'Wigs' and *Painted Woman*—but if you're right, I must have unconsciously transformed whatever had been moving me through 'Wigs' into my fury about that trial.

INT: Towards the ending of *Painted Woman*, that's where the reader and the narrator finally discover the thing that sparked the entire book off for the author—which is, the piece from the newspaper. But after that, you toyed with a lot of different endings.

SW: I had no *idea* what to do with her once she'd discovered the newspaper.

INT: In Extract 6, the writing is rather explanatory, which it isn't in the final version. How did you make that shift?

SW: I think that's a reflection of how tentative I was about the ending, and how I had to come slowly to it. When I was stuck and told a friend, she said: 'Patricide is a good idea!' So Frances committed patricide—for a while. I suppose, looking back, I didn't really believe it myself, but I was hoping that it might come to something. After all, I had a few hundred pages behind me by then, written in the same chaotic way. It's a process of enormous optimism, to keep pushing on, writing, believing that eventually ideas and bits of story will meet, that precisely because there's so much chaos to it, eventually things will collide and form a pattern.

INT: So how did you know when it was right?

SW: I did another draft, or two, and started to explore another idea that had been recently obsessing me—the conjunction of violence and art—is art a violent act because while it unifies, it also splinters wholeness? I could never find anyone to discuss it with— so I had to talk about it in the novel. That idea helped me to find the ending. I could see that it was a metaphor for Frances, that she, in becoming an artist, had to deal with her own violence, and she does so by *painting* the death of her father. It resolved her dilemma, and it resolved mine.

INT: All this sounds like a lot of re-writing, a lot of drafts.

SW: There were a lot. The old drafts are knee high. I kept re-writing to get further on into the story. Again, as if I needed a run-up. Every draft, I felt that maybe this time, I'd get to know these people properly.

INT: In the course of revision, did any useful accidents occur?

SW: Lots. Every circumstance of life seemed to belong to my novel. I hoovered in things people said on buses, to me or to someone else —again, not deliberately, I'd just find them protruding next day in what I was writing.

INT: You didn't take notes, as Helen Garner would do?

SW: Oh no, but everything seemed to be about what I was writing. Although I knew that they weren't really talking about my novel on the bus.

INT: In the plot notes, you've described the sections as Painting One, Painting Two and so on, so it looks as if very early you had the notion of organising the book around paintings.

SW: Yes. I was watching the desiccated landscape of a Greek island, all in terraces built long ago. It was so strange to me, that ancient country, it was often surreal, like a painted backdrop, and I thought —the story is going to be a series of paintings. I didn't know at that stage that Frances was going to do the paintings, that thought came later.

INT: Did you do research on painting?

SW: I was brought up with painters; I'd listened to a million conversations about painting; I had that awful feeling that people have when they're very close to something, they feel as if they have no proper knowledge about it. All I had was a kitchen knowledge of art. And all painting from Monet onwards was despised at home. So I had a journey of my own to go through. I'd got to London by then and I dared to go to the Tate Gallery every day for six weeks and stare at twentieth century works—it felt like blasphemy, it was thrilling. And later, much later, I realised I could give that journey to Frances.

For a long while I worried about the genre that the father was painting in, it seemed crucial. But you know, no one has ever asked me about it—they never ask about the school of the painting, all they ask about is the butcher Frances goes to.

INT: The way you've talked about the book, it's a series of steps into the unknown. Is that how it feels, or did you feel there was something there that you were working towards?

SW: When I'm writing, it's easy to think that deep down in something, whether it's my unconscious, the earth, nature, that there's something there—so actual, it takes up its own space, it has its own weight, and I'm trying to grope towards it. And that's part of the reason to keep going. A metaphysical treasure hunt.

Of course I don't believe a word of that when I'm not writing.

INT: Did you ever sit down and say: Well, I need X to happen, so I'll write a scene in which X happens?

SW: Yes, I did try that. It didn't work. I've thrown away stacks of stuff attempting to do that.

It's a funny mixture of being deliberate and being led. Almost as if you're inventing to achieve a few bits but really to prepare for the time when the real discoveries start of their own accord.

There's something else I learned in a first novel, that I'll never have to learn again. You see, I was ashamed of how much I was fabricating.

INT: Why?

SW: I thought I was the only person in the universe who didn't know how to write a novel. I don't mean that other people had actually learned how to do it from somewhere, I thought that it was self-evident, that they *saw* it somehow in the way the world fits together. Like the way maths teachers made you feel that if only you had concentrated hard enough in the bath, you'd have realised like Archimedes that a body in water displaces its own mass. At university we'd always talked about an author's intentions. Any writer with an ounce of sense, I believed, knew the way any particular scene should end. They'd see its inevitable design. There weren't billions of chaotic possibilities for them. Only for me. I had no clear intention. I couldn't see a design. I felt a terrible *sham* all the way through writing the novel, because I alone had to make it all up, nothing was self-evident to me, I alone had to fabricate excessively.

INT: At what point did you discover that it wasn't so?

SW: Long after publication.

INT: So what you're describing is what you gave to Frances as she paints the insides of the kitchen cupboards—she does something secret, and only in her own terms.

SW: It's a strange thing about writing, it can even make use of your misapprehensions and fears.

INT: Given that you worked with that degree of doubt about your whole endeavour, what was it that made you keep going?

SW: I wanted to see the next conversation between Frances and her father, and when Molly bowled in and made a triangle glittering with potential disaster—and she did bowl in, straight out of the blue, I didn't have to make notes about her—I wanted to see where that would lead. I love a story, even when I have to do the telling.

INT: You spoke of feeling very close to Frances—does that mean that finishing this book resulted in a certain sense of loss?

SW: I couldn't let it go. Hudsons agreed to publish it while I was still re-writing, and to my horror they started typing it up on their wordprocessors immediately, and I kept on changing it—I was in Sydney and they were in Melbourne, and I kept sending them down new versions of the whole novel—they were very patient and I couldn't stop myself. Eventually shame did. I had to make a ritual for myself. I got on the train with the manuscript all sealed up, and took it to them, and parted with it like that. It wasn't that I was worried about the novel itself—that's not true, I was frantic —but I still had some business with Frances.

Making Stories

One of the things that freed me was that I realised that she could be born again in a new novel. I've even kept her name—which, a real Frances told me, means freedom.

Extract 1 from the earliest manuscript

This is the beginning of the abandoned novel 'Wigs', referred to in the interview.

I could see he'd been telling her a joke because she was laughing as they came out the front door. She has a pink gold laugh, the colour of her skin, so she always laughed at his jokes, making her eyes sparkle in the way she'd demonstrated once when we were two girls together giggling over icecreams and men in the Al Fino cafe. ~~But even if I'd told Tim how she achieved that glitter, he'd still want to splash in it as if he were in a woodland stream of a Coca Cola commercial.~~ Then I saw his hand move to the back of her blouse, a caress of her zipper, and that must have made her feel good because she threw her laugh right across Cleveland Street, up the windows of the Cedar of Lebanon Dry Cleaning and Pressing Service, and round and round the triangular hips of the body-building man on the neon sign above the Ero Gymnasium. She tottered on her spiky heels and clutched Tim's arm for support, and an old woman holding a supermarket shopping bag with five /odd/ shoes sticking out of it turned in the gutter to watch Tracey whooping and shining and buckling under the weight of Tim's humour.

I called out to them but my voice slid under her laughter, and then the traffic roared past, an ambulance and a squalling police car and four school buses. She glanced around, her hair in loops like molasses, but I was grey in a grey street, a figure in a bulky jumper and sandshoes, carrying too many apples and afraid they'd fall out of the bag and smash on the footpath.

Tim and Tracey had driven off but the ~~keyhole in the~~ front door /knob/ was still warm from Tim's hand. I went inside and sat in the window seat and ate an apple, watching the

traffic and Tim's parking spot, hoping he'd come back
soon, alone, tender. The apple roared in my head like a
semi trailer, and the juice ran down my wrist into the
sleeve of my jumper. Then I threw the core away, and
that's when everything started.

I have replayed that throw a hundred times in slow
motion. A passable overarm, shoulders and nose a
straight line with the garbage tin, tight right buttock
conceding weight to tight left buttock, the left fist
punching the air down, the right arm following through.

But my hand grazed the window, /deflecting my aim,/ and
the apple core landed in the laundry basket.

I hadn't got down to the bottom of the laundry basket for
a long time. There are dark corners in laundry baskets
where clothes lie which are too awful to ~~wear~~ acknowledge. But to retrieve the apple core, I had to tip the
whole thing on its head and when I did, seven wigs fell
out.

I'd thought many times of leaving Tim. Believe me. I'd
secretly scanned the 'To Rent' column of the Saturday
Herald, turning the page fast if he came into the room
unexpectedly, and once I'd phoned up about a flat while he
was out of the country. I'd packed my suitcase several
times and I'd even got as far as the front door, but as I
stood on the doorstop looking out at the street yawning
in front of me, I knew I'd only do one lap of the block and
be back. It was as if I was an actor in a play, and I
couldn't go, because the only real thing ~~in~~ was my life
was Tim. I said, go on, step out onto the pavement, it's
only a few inches, ~~but I shut the door and went upstairs
and~~ but I knew if I did a big part of me would feel bitten
off, a semicircle from the armpit down to the kneecap,
and how can someone as insubstantial as that brave a real
estate agent asking who are you and how do I know you're
respectable? They don't hand out bedsits, own facs,
sunny aspct, handy trnspt to a breath of wind. So I went
back inside and lay on the bed we'd shared for fifteen
years and ~~said~~ thought I was wise not to leave a man who
knew that gravity makes the water go down the plughole in

Making Stories

different directions in the north and south hemisphere, who knew, he said, how to survive a nuclear holocaust and ~~survive~~ live till a hundred and still ride a bicycle. That /escape attempt/ was a while ago. I haven't tried to change anything since. I read ~~about it~~ the phrase: a life of quiet desperation. With only myself to blame. There's a photograph taken on Tracey's last birthday, her twentieth, and I cooked for it so they'd include me in the celebration, and there I'm sitting, amongst the half-eaten food, my face like the shadows in a cathedral because of the birthday candles around me. My eyes are shut.

Extract 2 from an early manuscript

This is Sue Woolfe's paraphrase of the story of the trial, which she mentions in her interview. In the manuscript it is laid out as it is here.

said that it is
all very well to
condemn such an in
jury to woman or
even her death if
this should unfort
unately occur, but
there are more fund
amental issues to
be considered. A
man has a duty to
impose his stamp
upon the world,
he is by birthr
ight the inherit
or and maker of
a glorious firm
ament of greatn
ess and his inst
inct to dominate
is for this end.
If the circumst
ances of an oth
erwise loving m

arriage obstruct
the fulfilment of
his birthright, the
man may have no
other choice but
to use physical
force. It should
not be seen as nec
essarily an evil
thing. Such viol
ence has the most
worthy motives. It
deserves not soc
iety's condemnation
but compassion. War
teaches us that men
may have to be vio
lent in order to
love. They may even
have to kill in ord
er to love.
The judge in his sum
ming up said in the
case we have before
us I think it can be
reasonably said that
any man could have
done the same.

The coroner reported that there was substantial bruising all around the throat, consistent with extreme manual pressure having been applied. Further examination found that two small bones in the throat had been fractured in several places, the larynx crushed, and the oesophagus showed signs of severe contusions. These symptoms combined indicated that massive and prolonged force had been exerted during the act of strangulation.

Extract 3 from an early manuscript

'Painting two' in this extract is based on the already-established 'Wigs'. 'Painting one' is an attempt to work backwards to explain

Making Stories

Frances' character. 'Painting one' finally became the basis for *Painted Woman*.

Painting one?

[Part 1]

Frances is 5. She's in love with Father as he paints. Her mother interrupts them. /Remembers/ terrible row. Frances on her father's lap—he teaches her the alphabet—she is afraid of mother—she wishes Mother dead. Shortly after, mother is. /She imagines for a while her father has arranged it./ Father goes away for a while. When he returns, they are always close. /Frances not allowed to ask about mother./ He makes her paint. Has destructive fits when he calls her nothing. She copes by being extremely docile—then the fit leaves him, and they are close again. She doesn't go to school much—feels set apart, with her father. /He says they're set apart./ On her first period, he gives sad speech. She feels at fault. Has learnt to cope with his mad moodiness by becoming very compulsive.

She is twelve. He has invited his sister over to teach her about puberty. /First time Frances has seen her./ Sister mad also. Tells her that ~~Father~~ she was the only person who knew Father not guilty. She's always right about him. Claims to talk woman to woman to Frances, but reticent on sexual matters, although that's what she's there for. Talks too freely about Father in her desire to show Frances she knows him better than Frances does. Scorns Frances for being only a child. Mentions it was in all the newspapers.

Frances takes another 6 months before she works out she can go to a library and read the newspapers for herself. She reads about the year she was 5. Nothing. Finds it after another 6 months by some accident. All we know is her reaction—she becomes extremely compulsive.

Part 2 Painting two?

Frances trying to keep chaos out—but Tim is leaving her, with Tracey. She resents Jilda at pub, hates Tracey. If men are placated, they will be benign, will keep the chaos out. Father lives upstairs—he's not keen on Tim. Frances likes this hostility—means her father loves

her, despite the fact she's rejected him in three ways
—in refusing to paint, in working in a menial job,
in living with Tim instead of with him. But she is also
terrified of Father—uses Tim's presence, and no paints,
to keep him at arm's length. But still adores him. <u>She
can't leave him, can't stay with him.</u>

Extract 4 from an early manuscript

This extract is from the handwritten notes, where the notes 'break
into Frances's voice', as mentioned in the interview.

Establish her adoration of him. His painting. He guides
her hand. To her, they are him & her, alone on wall. Why
he is painting a wall. Enter mother, critical. Frances
thinks she causes the row. She watches as he rips at
mother's dress.
Established—Frances' adoration.
                Father being loving, benign.
                Frances copying her Father's stance.
                He is pleased—takes /her/ on his knee.
                Establish Frances' fear of her mother.
                / Thinks mother is going to punish her.
                  Then reversal./
                Frances gets very close to Father.
Feels Mother may kill her.

it's the moment I fall in love. His arm ~~is curved, in~~
thick, woolly, ~~balls~~ hills of fluff /sticking out/ on wool
whiskers around the wrist that hold the ~~dripping~~ brush.
I sit behind, my knees knocking my chin, waiting for him
to ~~see my smile~~ paint~~ing~~ the wall and turn to see my
smile. He dips the brush into the paint ~~pot~~ tin, eases ~~the
engorged bristles against the pot's against on the tin's
side~~ the drips, lifts his arm high over his head, ~~but
brings it down against~~ then he's ~~curving~~ bending the
soft hair of the brush, this way, that way, this way, his
arm ~~snaking~~ flowing down the wall, a convex curve, a concave curve, a convex curve. He ~~breaks~~ takes the brush
away from the wall, begins high up, ~~at another~~ a concave curve, a convex curve, a concave curve.

Making Stories

Extract 5 from a later manuscript

This is the 'voice speaking out of the shower rose' mentioned in the interview (page 258). It was scrawled on a card.

Always the gap, right from the start. From when I broke the first doll's head and found only a brand name inside. From when I saw the Christmas paper wrappings emptied of hope. From when I knew that the arm ~~could fall by a holding me could fall by a~~ holding me could fall by a will that was not mine. That there was a distance between the breast and me. I didn't need philosophers to tell me it existed. That it made sense of things, or nonsense. It was there, the chasm.

/Dad should hint that mother knew./

Extract 6 from a later manuscript

This extract is one of the versions of the end of the book (the manuscript is marked 'from Draft 4') and is referred to in the interview. There are four different layers of alterations on this manuscript, written in different pens, suggesting the changes were made at different times.

I stare at the ~~her~~ strand of hair that falls wilfully back.
There's no signature on it, she says. He didn't sign it.
The ordinary kitchen. The ordinary steam rising white from teacups.
The woman frowsy in a dressing down, with tumbling hair.
The question that becomes extraordinary.
/Why wouldn't he sign this one painting./
I've never known him not to put his name on a painting, she's saying. and my answer is cutting under her words. My mother, I'm whispering. I think it was painted by my mother.

<u>You spoke, sir? Was it a masterpiece, you ask? I get your drift. A masterpiece stashed under a wardrobe for forty years, the only extant work of an artist young, unknown and the victim of a cruel murder.</u>

<u>It's over here. The only painting on an easel. Judge for yourself. To me its beauty is its poignancy. And the thing that comes trembling out of it, look, look, before it's too late, it's ephemeral, it's dying. Something, I think, like truth.</u>

I'm very cunning. I ask Molly to peg out clothes, her face is rounded and rosy with pleasure /to be asked, to be part of the ritual at last/. She goes, lifting her feet like a child, the washing basket curving into her. ~~I chuckle at her pleasure.~~

He's at his window, the windows that command /the cliff/, he's there. A god, a sentinel, a ruse. /And suddenly, I am free. Because I'm no longer wanting to be a god with him. I'm prepared to be the little we are./
/It's/ Just simple movements.
/And as he stands there against the fragile glass tottering on the cliff's edge./ And I was bred to violence and it was sweet, for with that breath there was life and with that breath there was death.
/the only answer to violence is violence, and I was bred to it./

And the rest you probably know, ladies and gentlemen, or can at least guess. Some people /in court/ wanted to give me life because I'd intended my father's death. I pleaded for death, I had died in a way. But all I'd done /in pushing him through the window/ was break his hands, some say his heart. I don't think it was his heart, the parabolas of glass fell gently /over the cliff into the valley, they, like a mirror, told him nothing. /Bushes broke his fall. His hands broke his fall./ But without his hands there was no further point to his life and he died, / some time later/, though of natural causes, not at my hands. They told me in the superintendent's office. They brought me there to tell me, they brought me through the rain /through all the prison buildings/. I remember looking out the window, a small one. The storm was blurred by its own rain. The hem of my dress was soaking into their good silk chair. The words leapt across the room but had nothing to teach me that I hadn't already learned. He was, after all, finite.

Making Stories

Oh I cried in my cell afterwards, but after a while I knew I was crying because I was alone with the gap. Though I'd been alone with the gap all my life, and hadn't acknowledged.

So I asked for paints.

There was a wild joy in me I couldn't repress and it became pictures that spilled all over my cell, walls, ceiling, floor, down the corridor and off into the recreation room and the dining hall and the sick bay and the exercise yard but when I aspired to the main administration block, they freed me. /Some said my time was up. Some said my time was only beginning./ Molly sent me the taxi fare. On the way I began to paint the inside of the taxi.

Steady on, said the driver. The boss will have a fit. He'll think I did it. So I stopped. But I started again the moment I put down my bag. Molly offered a cup of tea but that wasn't how I wanted to herald my new life, my new life, my second go. I squeezed tubes of colours in the ritual order I'd heard all my life though now I knew it cast no spell: cadmium yellow cerulean blue alizarine crimson veridian green vermilion. So I nodded to Molly, gave her a hug and got going. One day there would be time for love. There was a life to be told that I'd lived as if I was only living for the telling—as Sartre says—so what was there to do but tell? And so, give myself life.

The paintings I'd done in the past were miserable things, blurred by guilt, clumsy with despair. But I put a bit of my new life into them. It takes a while to redeem a past. The planets kept rotating round each other. Spinning, spinning. But with every stroke, /I knew/ I was painting: with all of me, not just what my mind had learned, not my hands, but everything I'd been, my mother had been, Auntie, Tim, even Dad, everything criss crossed with everything, the memories, /the/ hopes the past the present—Oh, I believe in the present now, now that I'm freed from the past and can carry it with equanimity in my soul.

Sue Woolfe—Painted Woman

I painted every inch of the lower part of the house as you can see and step by step up the stairs I came and at last I gained his studio, it was mine. Molly had mended the windows that commanded, it once seemed, the world. But I would run out into the street just before dusk and see those windows, ~~from the~~ I'd look from the outside ~~looking~~ in, /I'd/ see my painting blazing there, in the house tiny under the first evening stars.
Molly moved out.
I love Art, she'd said. But I can't stand the smell of it. Though sometimes I'd forget where I was, I'd forget I possessed his studio at last and alone with the brushes I'd start to think I was painting on the walls, ceiling, floor, the ~~secret~~ crypts and vaulted heights of /secret/ labyrinths, labyrinths within labyrinths, not just my own, /but/ everyone ~~'s~~ /who's painting secretly,/ I'd hear the swishing of their brushes, millions of them, an orchestra of brushes, and my brush would catch the melody of swishing and sing with it too until I couldn't hear myself think and I'd have to stop and say: I'm in a house which is ~~after all a smallish house~~ now my own, in a studio which is, ~~after all, a room~~ now, my own, and ~~all I am doing~~ I'm painting. /That's all I'm doing. The littleness of it. the wonder./ ~~But the labyrinths kept singing, in spite of what I said.~~

<u>And the gap? the lady on the end wants to ask.
What about the gap?</u>

BUT THAT'S NOT WHAT SHE ASKS. NOT WHAT SHE ASKS AT ALL. AND WHEN THEY CAME, THAT'S NOT WHAT I TOLD THEM. NOT WHAT I SAID AT ALL.
WHAT I TOLD THEM
WHY,
THAT'S ANOTHER STORY.

Extract 7 from the published version

This ending explores Frances' reaction when she discovers the truth about her mother's death.

Painted Woman, pp 164–75.

Making Stories

I stand at night in front of the opened cupboard doors in the kitchen. The whispers in Dad's house, the flurries, they tell me what I love, what's part of me, what's not. I stand at night with the treasure of stolen paints, and on my brush they swirl together like whispers. There are many cupboard doors, the insides of doors, the outsides, these are my canvases, the main kitchen, the main bathroom, the laundry, the hall, my bedroom, my parents' bedroom.

I know at last my life's purpose. To paint the absorbed history of my waiting. My imagination, my body knows it all, its intricate and precise machinations. Every night I listen to voices inside me, I let them paint, I'm full of voices. I find my hands painting girls at school, women in shops, delivery boys, a child who smiled, boys in a dark garden shed, a minister framed by rain and roses, a wedding dress trailing on a blue carpet, a coffin gold with flames, rumours of distant revolutions, the hubbub of years, of my waiting.

My purpose is the rooms of Dad's house. To put patterns of paint everywhere. And one day, all over his studio.

* * *

I don't baulk at ceilings. Though the creak in my neck gets worse, I make ladders from tables, chairs, chairs on chairs. Once, a pyramid topples but my fall is light. Bouncing on the balls of my feet, I laugh at my lightness and the rush of air.

Strange, that when you reach into the mystery at last, it no longer seems like God. Later, people insist: Your limbs, body, mind – you must've been transparent with wonder; surely you looked around, surely you can tell me. But I can't. I was there, but too busy to see. I only looked at my painting.

So it also remains an undiscovered country and no traveller returns with tales.

I thought I heard something crash last night.

Molly, I can see, insists on knowing. Her cheeks are hollows.

Nothing happened, I say. I'm like a balloon in my private joy but tethered by fear.

Probably it was the neighbours, I think to add. They've built those townhouses so close.

I baulk at my parents' bedroom. The door has been shut since Auntie shut it. I double back, find other spaces for pictures. I paint pictures within pictures. On the backs and underneaths of the china cabinet, the kitchen table, the kitchen chairs, their legs. On the hall-stand. The grandfather clock. On china, on vases. On my bedhead, bedbase. I find I've overlooked the inside of drawers. And the sections of floor where I don't often walk. But everything finally leads back to the door of my parents' bedroom.

I'm painting, I know, in a frenzy. The paint argues with me. I work against its argument. It says: you have no right. I argue back, timid, determined. I say: I am painting to save my life.

One day Dad will hear us argue, the paint and I. Certain things are inevitable.

* * *

I open the door of my parents' bedroom.

Everything protects against the imagination. It's difficult to pass through certain door frames. I stand at the threshold, stare at the wood. It's pitted, worn, like the wood of old wharves.

I carry in a jangle of mop, mop bucket, broom, dustpan. The noise rears against the air, dusty through yellowed slats of venetian blinds that won't open. I peer at the dirt in the dustpan, on the broom bristles, on the mop, in the swill of mop water. It's only dirt.

But the room has its own time which cannot be reduced by a swill of mop water. Its own imperative.

Newspaper crackles under the wardrobe, cocooned in shadows. Is Mum's skin like this, forty odd years later? Or has it shrivelled off the bones? The mysterious smile on the skeleton. Things happen so quickly in the grave. Whereas living is very long. Just a few events to pierce holes in the darkness. Menstruation. Almost a wedding. A death that no one noticed. Perhaps it was before the wedding. Making love. Painting with my father. Here's a ball-dress, tattered by moths, unravelling, falling light as ashes.

I feel under the wardrobe for the obstruction that's always been there, that I've never pulled out into the light. A sharp-edged board, I turn it over and find I'm looking at a painting in oils on masonite. It's a portrait of a man, surely it's Dad, this is the way his eyes fit into their sockets, the way his eyebrows rise into the forehead, his lips flare like these, and that's his squared jaw. But something's amiss, it's as if he's been looking at himself in the reflections on rippling water that tell lies, or truths. His eyes, which have always seemed to hold such secrets, the brush has made them slide away, calculating who's watching, and his jaw, arched in determination, no, the brush discovers, no, that's not it at all, that jaw is arched in blind arrogance and those cheeks, they balloon like a clown's, and the mouth sneers.

I stay where I am on my knees in the long silence of my parents' bedroom, I turn the masonite over as if the hatching on the back could offer clues, I turn it round again, wipe the cobwebs from the corners, trace with my fingers the paths of the brush, once so exploratory, now with time solidified, oracular. It's a mean, dishonest, ignorant face. A face that knows nothing.

And I think of Dad, I think of his face, I've examined every bone, muscle, pore of it, I've watched it all my life and now I admit that this is the face I've known, but never seen. And he's always seen it, he must have, to paint a self-portrait like this.

A long, long while after, I put the painting down. The eyes stare at the ceiling, calculating. I turn the portrait face down on the carpet. And remember the newspaper clippings.

The newsprint is thick and black and cryptic with authority. The words on its soft creases become powder on my fingers but fragments reveal totalities.

Violence for Art's sake

Sydney. Thurs. After several weeks of court hearings a man was acquitted of a charge of murder of his wife. The man, an established artist, had been held in custody pending Police investigations of said that it is all very well to condemn such behaviour, but allowance must be made for the by the magnificence of his talent and by birthright an inheritor and maker of a firmament of greatness. Our civilization depends on his like. It has been rightly said that while man might be sacred, his condition isn't. If the circumstances demand that terrible means. It deserves not society's condemnation but its compassion. War teaches us that we may have to use violence to bring peace. The defendant may have had to apply this reasoning

Such an accident could happen to any man at the moment of passion, said Justice Sorenson, in a summing up which lasted

The coroner reported that there was substantial bruising around the throat. The oesophagus showed signs of severe contusions and the larynx had been crushed. Massive and prolonged force had been exerted on the woman by the application of extreme manual pressure consistent with the act of strangulation.

Here are the walls I've moved between most of my life, the bedroom of my parents, my bedroom, the hall, the kitchen, the bathroom, the laundry. Out there the stairs, up there his studio. All I need to do is dissolve into them. Here's my bed, the acquiescent sheets, my chest moving of its own accord up and down, the heart continuing to beat. All I need to do is dissolve. The Gap, the blessed Gap, nothing.

But every now and then a thought intrudes, trembles in The Gap, palpitates. I think: that's the swish of a broom. I think: I'm holding the broom, I'm sweeping. I think: I'll destroy him and all his paintings. I think: I can't do that to my father, whoever he is. I think: there are eggs boiling in an effervescence of steam. I think: I'm boiling eggs. I think: that painting, he painted this terrible truth, it's not a ruse, he knows what he is.

Molly's face looms, connected to the ceiling.

You've taken to your bed a lot. Are you sick?

I turn to the wall, dissolve into The Gap.

I find myself in the pantry, cleaning shelves, in the laundry, water slopping round my elbows, at the washing line, pegging clothes. I watch myself clean shelves, wash, peg clothes. These are the rhythms that comfort. That postpone.

But one morning, I go into the backyard. It's that blur of dawn when the air holds immobility like stones do. Not enough light for shadows under the peelings of bark, not enough life for veined leaves to burrow into earth, no sudden spurting of colour as the bottle brush fights against the grey garden. I think: my mind is clear.

A bird calls, a cry like a mournful child. I think: something must be done. Done by me.

I walk to where the old chook house was, past the bare patch in the lawn where Dad burnt his pictures. After all these years the grass still knows, it hasn't forgotten. There was a gate here, swinging with yellow dandelions where I vowed never to be like Mum, as easily as crossing my heart and hoping to die. Grit was, I remember, noisy against my teeth.

I'm looking back to my father's house. It is, after all, quite small. And top heavy with his studio. Almost the lower bricks stagger to carry the weight. There's a jagged line along the length of each brick and rising to the brick above. As if the house might yawn open. There was a time when it reeled on itself and twisted towards a vanishing point, roof top, guttering, windows, doors, the stone foundations, everything in a grand and precise procession. In this light the mountains slump. There are no craggy secret places, no places to hide. There never were. The dirt between my fingers glints only with the slow grinding of rocks. Leaves are strewn only in random on the ground. The path leads to the gate leads to the road leads to a suburban shopping centre, to other suburbs, cities, to the sea, to other countries, back to here. Only to here. The dull sky, the clumps of weeds, the straggling trees, nothing, nothing is arranged to the glory of my father.

And I have been waiting all my life. The cold ground presses scornfully against my heels. And now I can hate.

I'm running inside, banging doors, finding matches, scooping the newspaper clippings from my parents' room, finding more newspaper, finding twigs. The bare patch will be good for another fire. No, the bare patch is too far from the house. My hands shaking, dropping matches on the frosty grass. Kerosene. I remember the slop of kerosene. There's kerosene in the laundry. Running, throwing open doors, another slop of kerosene. I look up at his detestable window. And realise at last that I've never understood infinity. Oh, I heard his explanation, but I saw his paintings. And his paintings said that everything, the whole world visible and invisible, magnificent and tawdry, everything, the path gleaming with new sunrise, the touch of a finger, the grating of a voice, even the reedy mockery of kookaburras now bursting out of a sleeping tree, everything converged ultimately in the eyes of my father. He was here, yet at that distant vanishing point. At infinity. All things met in him.

Only one painting disputed.

Molly's here in the swoosh of kerosene.

No, she's shouting, arms struggling, her hands and mine fight for a tiny box of matches which the grass claims, dampens. Bruised by her eyes, her hands, I find one of the newspaper clippings. Screwed up into a ball. I rip it apart and the word's here on my fingers.

Strangulation.

Here, I shout. See. Acknowledge.

Dimly I hear a window slam. In the studio. In him. In me.

She will not look. When I shove the newspaper in the new direction of her eyes, she turns her face the other way. She grabs the matches, the kerosene, the hem of her dressing-gown and runs into the house. She locks the door, stands at the window.

I'm on the lawn and though the day slants with sunshine, I'm very cold. My feet are grey. I can't touch, rescue my mother. All I can do is twitch grey feet on frosty grass. I signal to Molly through the window. She unlocks the door, lets me in, hands me a blanket, makes a pot of tea. We sit in the kitchen with all my paintings around us. They dance, these fragments, erratic in the morning light.

The fire, I say, was for my mother. And for me. Not that it would've solved anything.

I'm glad of the warmth of the blanket. I wrap it around my toes.

There is, I say, only one truthful painting by my father.

I go into my parents' bedroom, trailing the blanket. My feet patter on the kitchen lino. I've carried back his one moment. We breathe over it, Molly and I. I hear her heart still thumping. She pushes back a strand of hair.

Who did it? she asks.

I stare at her strand of hair that falls wilfully back.

There's no signature on it, she says. It's funny that he didn't sign it. I wonder why.

The ordinary kitchen. The ordinary steam rising white from teacups. The woman frowsy in a dressing-gown, with tumbling hair. The question that becomes extraordinary.

I've never known him not to put his name on a painting, she's saying.

And my answer is cutting under her words.

My mother, I'm whispering. I think it was painted by my mother.

It's over here, the only painting on an easel, the only painting by my mother.

You spoke sir? Is it a masterpiece? I heard you ask your wife.

I get your drift. What a story that would be. A masterpiece stashed under a wardrobe for forty years, the only extant work of a young, unknown but brilliant artist, the victim of a cruel murder.

To me its beauty is its poignancy. And the thing that comes trembling out of it — look, look, before it's too late, it's ephemeral, it's dying. Something, I think, like truth.

I don't go back up to his studio again, and he doesn't walk down the stairs and through the door. Molly brings me paints, brushes, charcoal, linseed oil, turps, pencils, clothes, palette knives, food, she stands and watches with arms folded, and goes quietly away. It takes a long time to paint pictures on the ceiling, walls, floor, the wardrobe in my parents' bedroom, shadows lengthen and shorten, the air is chilly, warm, chilly, warm, light moves across the window panes and darkness too, planets rotate, seasons pass. But I keep painting. I paint the death of my father.

   I paint him at his windows, the windows that teeter on those giant cliffs, he stands, a god, a sentinel, a ruse. I paint his face a hundred times, the face that knows only itself. I paint his muscles clenched, the lips silent, I paint the way he throws back his head to watch the canvas, the way he walks, his trenchancy. The way his eyes searched for only himself beyond my shoulder. Most of all, I paint his hands, that can hold a brush or a neck, but his grip on the brush is gentle. I paint the landscape that he sees, shapes and distances grotesque with power, I paint the landscape that I see, and shiver. It may be that the room is cold. I paint the landscape through the days and nights, if the colours aren't true, they have their own truth. And then I come back to the wall where I've painted him at his windows, the windows that command.

   I paint movements, simple movements, the creak on the floorboards behind him, his neck taut, the bones lifting the skin, he knows my step, the pressure of my hands, he doesn't look around, he has no need to. I'm pushing, pushing, the parabolas of glass fall so gently, he falls with them, they fall together slowly but they, like a mirror, tell him nothing.

   Do you think you ought? asks Molly, breaking a silence of weeks. You might put a hex on him.

   I don't think people can, I say. And anyway, I have no wish to affect him. This isn't for him. It's for me.

   I paint my violence into patterns, and contain it. But there's more violence than mine in the world.

   There's something wrong with his hands, Molly tells me one day. They're paralysed.

   So I paint his hands falling down the cliff, emerald green in the whorls of skin, cerulean blue in the knots of knuckles, vermilion under the nails as they grasp at sandstone, which falls with him in a drift of gold.

And when he dies, and they carry him down the stairs, I open the stairs door to look, and his face is neither knowledgeable nor ignorant. He was just another person, but used by violence more than most.

Sue Woolfe—Painted Woman

I paint the story of my longing, my waiting, on the stairs and the stairwell wall and the stairwell ceiling and, step by step, at last I gain his studio. Molly moves out, against my persuasion.

I love art, she says. But I can't stand the smell of it.

There's no time for sadness. In another lifetime, if there's one, I'll love well, Mum, Auntie, Molly and Tim. But now I must paint.

Though sometimes I forget where I am, forget that I possess his studio and I start to think I'm painting on the wall, ceilings, floors, the secret crypts and vaulted heights of labyrinths, labyrinths within labyrinths, not just my own, everyone who's spent their lives waiting, I hear them joining in, I hear the swishing of their brushes, millions of them, an orchestra of brushes, and my brush catches the melody of swishing and singing and sings with it too until I can't hear myself think and I have to stop and say: I'm in a house which is, after all, a smallish house, in a studio which is only a room and all I'm doing is painting.

Ladies and gentlemen, I'll leave you alone with the exhibition.

Appendix: Teachers' notes

When we read a finished book, we say: 'But how could it have developed in any other way?' If we approach a novel as a critic does, analysing its themes, imagery and so on, it is easy to slide into the idea that writers are always in conscious control of their works—they intended this effect, they shaped that theme, they deliberately employed these devices. A finished work of art gives an impression of inevitability.

In fact, at the beginning of a work, a writer is faced with infinite possibilities. The process of writing is the process of making choices, consciously and unconsciously, which over a few drafts progressively sharpen the focus.

Making Stories tries to show that what looks like an inevitable development was a complex combination of many things, including technical expertise, thought, great leaps of the imagination, accident, the shiftings of the unconscious and the circumstances of the writer's life and psyche at the time.

Some of the extracts in this book show a novel in its very earliest moments, others show the novel at some later stage in its development. All, we think, give a sense of the enormous amount of invisible work and astonishing creativity which goes into fiction.

The value of seeing this, for a student of literature, is to be reminded again of a fact that becomes obscured in the course of critical study: while we can talk about the effect of a book, we cannot talk properly about intention. A novel is shaped by the author's will acting on a series of contingencies.

Once the contingent nature of a book is recognised, whole new areas of study open up. Study can start to examine not *what* a book means, but *how* it means. What choices did the writer have in shaping the book? What is the effect of those choices? How would the book be different if a different set of choices had been made?

We are not wishing to imply in this book that any jottings or early drafts relating to fiction could inevitably become publishable novels. Nor are we sure that anyone, given the right techniques, skills, mentors and so on could necessarily write a novel. For one reason or another, people become writers because the circumstances of their lives make writing possible, or necessary for them.

What we're examining in *Making Stories* is the *process* of the imaginative leap from early jottings or drafts to final novels, not why the process happens for some people and not for others. We have chosen particular authors not to highlight them but to reveal some of the remarkable shifts that happen within the process of writing.

The following are some suggestions for ways to introduce a class to writing by making use of *Making Stories*. The context could be a literature class, or a creative writing class: these suggestions could create a bridge between the two which many students would enjoy. Most questions are quite extensive in their implications, and could become a lesson in themselves.

Jessica Anderson, *The Commandant*

1. What is the most interesting feature of the research material (Extract 1) to you? Logan's murder? The predicament of Mrs Logan? The suspicion of an official whitewash? The sense of nineteenth-century history? The language of the letters and the newspaper article? What thoughts does it prompt?

2. Anderson used Edwards's letter as a basis for beginning to think about the novel. Find a newspaper article that interests you, and consider how it might be fleshed out into a story. What elements would you add?

What makes reading a novel a different experience from reading a newspaper article?

3. Anderson chose Frances as the person to give a perspective on the events in Moreton Bay. Would you tell your newspaper story from an objective point of view, or from the point of view of one of the people in the story?

4. Anderson, speaking about tone in her interview, suggests that different books have immediately apparent differences in tone. How do her various beginnings differ in their use of tone?

5. Extract 4 is quite close to the published beginning, but its differences suggest that, if Anderson had continued in this style, another novel would have resulted. What differences are there between the various beginnings, apart from plot differences? You might consider language, character, or other elements.

6. What echoes in the published version are there of the girl of Extract 2?
7. In Anderson's interview, what did you find unexpected in what she says about writing a novel? Did anything in her approach or attitude to writing overturn your assumptions about how *The Commandant* was created?

Peter Carey, *Oscar and Lucinda*

1. How does Peter Carey make the nineteenth-century world credible, in Extracts 2, 3, 4?
2. In his interview Carey says that when writing about a character, there's some point when the writing does an 'osteopath's click' for him.

   In Extract 2, at what moment does the writing do an 'osteopath's click' for you?
3. Carey describes the process of Extract 1 as 'following the river of the idea'.

   One of the main images flowing through *Oscar and Lucinda* is of a glass church. Find all the references in Extract 1 that have something to do with a glass church.
4. Carey says that 'the whole business of writing is to live with doubt. . .to place yourself in a position of ignorance and inelegance'.

   What other writers in *Making Stories* have echoed this thought in some way?
5. In Extract 1, Carey makes a note to himself: 'Begin here'.

   Write a page or so in a stream of consciousness way: start with the words 'At this moment, I. . .' and continue by writing whatever comes into your mind. It can be as ungrammatical and rambling as you like.

   Now, go through what you've written. See if you can find a place, or several places, where you could write 'Begin here'—places that suggest an entry point into a story.
6. In Extract 3, Carey developed the Wardley Fish segment which eventually became Extract 4. In an interview, Carey called this process 'cantilevering'.

   Write a two or three sentence account of something that happened to you yesterday. Then do what Carey has done: go back over the material, elaborating and extending it over several attempts.
7. In his interview, Carey says he wanted his characters 'to do some unusual things'.

Making Stories

Why might a writer want to make up fantastical things, rather than use a slice of life as the basis for a novel?

8. In Carey's interview, what did you find unexpected in what he says about writing a novel? Did anything in his attitude or approach to writing overturn your assumptions about how *Oscar and Lucinda* was created?

Helen Garner, *The Children's Bach*

1. In Extract 2, what is the atmosphere of the house in Bunker Street? What elements in the writing contribute to this atmosphere?
2. In Extract 2, what details about the major characters—Athena, Vicki, Dexter, Philip, Elizabeth—reveal their relationships to each other?
3. Trace as many connections as you can between the segments in Extract 1, and the extract from the published novel.

Choose three or four of these connections and consider how Garner has adapted them to her story.

4. Consider the possibilities for storytelling these segments from Extract 1 hold for you:
(a) 'He commandeers other people's experiences, remembers their dreams, tells the story always in the same words.' (Dexter).
(b) 'He was the sort of person who'd put on Ravel's *Bolero* first thing in the morning.' (Dexter).
(c) 'She walks along beside him, gasbagging about her life.' (Dexter).
(d) 'When I'm miserable I feel like wearing tight clothes.' (Vicki).
(e) 'They drag their mattresses out and sleep on the grass.' (Vicki).
5. Keep a notebook of your own for a month. Carry it everywhere and write down appealing words and phrases that people use or that you read, scraps of dialogue you hear, details of mannerisms, clothes, landscape, or events (not necessarily momentous ones).

Each week, pick out one segment of the notes you've kept, and consider how this might be fleshed out to tell a story.

6. Garner talks in her interview about her impression that artists 'know' what they are doing. A phrase from literary criticism like 'the author's deft control' can suggest this. Can you think of any other such phrases? Have you shared her misapprehension? Could you suggest a remedy?
7. In Garner's interview, what did you find unexpected about her way of writing a novel? Did anything in her approach or attitude

overturn your assumptions about how *The Children's Bach* was written?

Kate Grenville, *Lilian's Story*

1. In Grenville's interview, she says that she prefers to begin writing without a plot, because that way 'I discover things I wouldn't otherwise'. What kinds of things do you think a writer might discover in this way? What disadvantages might arise from this approach?

2. Grenville says in her interview that 'the tone was wrong' in the Laura parts.

Compare the two versions, (in Extract 1, page 115, and Extract 2, pages 122-3). Why do you think she felt the tone was wrong? What words and phrases create the tone of the two versions?

3. Again in the interview, Grenville says that, 'I was sure that if I found out too much about the real Bea Miles, I would be locked in then, to her. My own imagination would be blinkered'.

What does this suggest to you about the way writing reflects the real world, but also creates its own?

4. The fragments that make up Extract 1 could be arranged in many different ways. Grenville, in the published book, chose a straight chronological arrangement of all the fragments. Could you rearrange the fragments of Extract 1 in some different way—perhaps as a flashback? See if you can arrange them so that they form a miniature story.

5. Much of the first draft of *Lilian's Story* seems to have been written by free-associating from sentences suggested by other writers (see interview, page 96.)

Find a sentence you like from any book. Don't think about why you like it, just start writing, using the sentence as a springboard for your own associations. If you dry up too quickly, go back to your sentence and try writing in another direction.

6. Grenville says she knew the beginning and the end of the book, but not what happened in the middle.

Get someone to tell you the beginning of a joke, and the punchline. Try to work forwards from the beginning, and backwards from the punchline, to fill in a possible story.

7. In Grenville's interview, what did you find unexpected about her way of writing a novel? Did anything in her approach or attitude overturn your assumptions about how *Lilian's Story* was written?

Making Stories

David Ireland, *A Woman of the Future*

1. In his interview, David Ireland says he has 'a private quarrel with the old style of narrative', and the way it 'wrenches' the reader from one thing to another.
   What do you think he might mean? Do you agree?
2. (a) The whole of *A Woman of the Future* is a kind of collage: hundreds of short pieces, each with a heading.
   If Extract 2 was written out as one long conventional chapter, rather than broken into short sections, many linking sections would have to be created. How would this alter the feel of the story?
   (b) David Ireland talks in his interview about his enjoyment of juxtapositions—and therefore, of Alethea's enjoyment of them. Were there surprising juxtapositions in Extract 2? Together, what picture do they help to build of Alethea?
3. The interviewer says that the voice and the point of view of the final version of *A Woman of the Future* are already present in the early notes (page 133). Do you agree? When you are very familiar with Extract 2, go back through the early notes and underline phrases and sentences that have echoes (of atmosphere or substance) in the final version.
4. What do you think David Ireland means by 'first person has its disadvantages, but it's often more immediate'? What are its disadvantages? What are its strengths? You could refer to other extracts from published novels in this book in reaching your conclusions.
5. What do you deduce about the craft of establishing a fictional character from the following interchange in the interview?

'INT: Did you feel ill-at-ease with a female character?

DI: No, because Alethea was as I made her.'

Often critics consider that a character is well-written if it sounds like a person lifted from life. How does the interchange quoted above suggest other ways to think about the depiction and creation of character?
6. (a) Over a week, make notes randomly on anything you hear or witness—notes from your life, news broadcasts, bits of dialogue real and imagined. Now apply what David Ireland thinks of as the 'magnet' (page 128) to these notes. Your magnet could be anything: you might select all the notes that are memories, those that are sense-impressions, those that are memories, those that are funny, notes that might form a plot.

(b) David Ireland said in his interview 'Don't forget any apparently unrelated ideas can go together'. Using the notes from 6(a), try cutting them up, so that you have a number of unrelated fragments—unrelated words, phrases or sentences. Rearrange them in any random way, and keep rearranging to try to find links that weren't apparent previously. Do these suggest a story?

7. Look through David Ireland's notes on pages 136–46. Choose one that interests you and use it as a starting point for a page of your own writing, interpreting it in whatever way you find interesting.

8. In David Ireland's interview, what did you find unexpected in what he says about writing a novel? Did anything in his approach or attitudes overturn your assumptions about how *A Woman of the Future* was created?

Elizabeth Jolley, *Mr Scobie's Riddle*

1. In what way is the early draft a 'lament'? (interview, page 156).
2. What are the effects of Elizabeth Jolley's use of the first person in the lament (Extract 2)? (To see the difference, try rewriting some of it in the third person.) Examine the effects of the shift to third person in Extract 3.
3. Jolley, in her interview, talks about how she began to see irony as a necessary element in classroom situations. Find in Extract 3, the published version, an example of irony. Is there any trace of irony in Extract 2?
4. How has Scobie altered between Extracts 2 and 3?
5. Which characters in the published version can you trace to their beginnings in Extract 2?
6. For a week, write down the daily events of your life—a paragraph a day. Use the first person, and try to keep the emotions as naked as possible. Then rewrite all the material in the third person. Try giving this third person, who is not quite you, an ironic or distant viewpoint.
7. In Jolley's interview, what did you find unexpected in what she says about writing a novel? Did anything in her approach or attitudes overturn your assumptions about how *Mr Scobie's Riddle* was created?

Thomas Keneally, *The Chant of Jimmie Blacksmith*

1. Compare the first paragraph of Extract 1 with the first three paragraphs of Extract 2. There is a very different feel to the writing. Can you identify some of the differences?

2. In both Extract 1 and Extract 2 we are aware of Jimmie Blacksmith's relationship with Mr Neville, but we are less conscious of it as crucial to Jimmie in the early draft. What rearrangements in the final version highlight it?

3. On page 197 of Extract 1, Keneally gives to Jimmie the thought that if he marries a white girl, his children will be 'hardly noticeable at all'. A little further on, he decides to give this thought to Mrs Neville. Why do you think he might have made this shift? What difference does it make to our perception of Jimmie and of Mrs Neville?

4. Keneally says in his interview that in a novel 'the whole is greater than the sum of its parts'. What do you think he means? Do you agree?

5. In his interview, Keneally says that he starts his books with something that has befallen him. The progression in his way of working seems to be from real experience to a generalised idea about the experience, and then to fiction that is only slightly connected to the original experience.

Think of an experience you have had and distil it into an idea or theme that could be the basis for a story.

6. Keneally describes the way he wrote *The Chant of Jimmie Blacksmith* as 'writing from within', and thinks of it now as 'arrogant'. Why do you think he calls it 'arrogant'? Do you think it is? Is arrogance a necessary quality for a fiction writer?

7. In Keneally's interview, what did you find unexpected in what he says about writing a novel? Did anything in his approach or attitudes overturn your assumptions about how *The Chant of Jimmie Blacksmith* was written?

Finola Moorhead, *Remember the Tarantella*

1. In her interview, Moorhead says that too many novels are 'I' books. What do you think she means? Do you think a distinction is implied between 'I' books, and books written in the first person? Do you think 'I' books have built-in limitations either for the reader or the writer? Could there be some advantages?

2. What differences in style can you detect between the first paragraphs in the earlier version (Extract 1) and the later version (Extract 2)?

3. The mood of the beach scene stays very consistent through the three extracts, even though different things happen on the beach. Underline words and phrases which help to create this mood.

Teachers' notes

4. Moorhead's starting point was unconventional but it resulted in a richly textured novel. She used several diagrams that ultimately helped to create a story, although in the beginning it must have been hard to see what narratives they might suggest.

Try using warm and cold colours in the way Moorhead has used the contrasting elements of the Tarot. In a few lines each, describe four characters for four different colours. Then put them together: what happens when a red character meets a blue character, for example, or a mauve character meets a black one?

5. Moorhead wrote her book 'in the plural of women', incorporating responses from other people. Try doing the same: take what you wrote for exercise 4, and show it to several other people, then try to incorporate their comments and arguments and the developments they suggest.

6. Moorhead speaks of a 'flow-prose' draft, when she wrote without re-reading and without revising.

Try doing the same: using what you wrote in exercise 5 as a starting point, just keep writing for several minutes without thinking about where it might be leading.

7. In Moorhead's interview, what did you find unexpected about her way of writing a novel? Did anything in her approach or attitude overturn your assumptions about how *Remember the Tarantella* was written?

Sue Woolfe, *Painted Woman*

1. There is a very great difference in tone between 'Wigs' (Extract 1) and *Painted Woman* (Extract 7). Part of the difference is in the way Frances as a character is depicted. How would you sum up the difference in her character between the two extracts?

2. In *Painted Woman* (Extract 7) an old woman speaks—indicated by italics—at an exhibition of her paintings. It's the voice of Frances, the heroine, when she's much older, and she constantly interrupts the younger Frances's story.

What is the effect of these interruptions for you?

In what ways are the voices different?

3. In her interview, Woolfe says that she was thinking about art being 'a violent act because while it unifies, it also splinters wholeness' when she was writing the novel, and the idea helped her to arrive to the final ending, Extract 7.

In what way does Frances's behaviour in this extract connect with this idea?

In what ways is fiction a useful forum to discuss ideas?

4. *Painted Woman* is a very visual book, written from the point of view of a painter. It's full of details you can *see*. Go through Extract 7, noting each time the writing presents one of those tiny pictures. Try removing them all. What is the difference?

5. If you had written the extract from 'Wigs' (Extract 1), where would you go with it? Write two pages continuing it in any way you please.

6. In her interview, Woolfe describes her daily work method as writing notes as a run-up, before she jumped into Frances's dialogue. What methods have you used for beginning a writing session?

Find a newspaper article that interests you. Make notes about it, and extend the notes beyond the article, considering character and incident, until you can use the notes as a run-up, and jump into a scene.

7. In Woolfe's interview, what did you find unexpected in her way of writing a novel? Did anything in her approach or attitude overturn your assumptions about how *Painted Woman* was written?

Bibliography

Jessica Anderson
The Commandant, Penguin, Ringwood, Victoria, 1981

Peter Carey
Oscar and Lucinda, University of Queensland Press, St Lucia, Queensland, 1988

Helen Garner
The Children's Bach, McPhee Gribble, Ringwood, Victoria, 1984

Kate Grenville
Lilian's Story, Allen & Unwin, North Sydney, 1986

David Ireland
A Woman of the Future, Penguin Books, Ringwood, Victoria, 1982

Elizabeth Jolley
Mr Scobie's Riddle, Penguin, Ringwood, Victoria, 1983

Thomas Keneally
The Chant of Jimmie Blacksmith, Penguin, Ringwood, Victoria, 1973

Finola Moorhead
Remember the Tarantella, Primavera Press, Leichhardt, NSW, 1987

Patrick White
Memoirs of Many in One, Jonathan Cape, London, 1986

Sue Woolfe
Painted Woman, Hudson Publishing, Hawthorn, Victoria, 1989, reprinted Allen & Unwin, North Sydney, 1990 (page numbers refer to this reprint)